JOURN

The Journeys series celebrates John Murray's history of publishing exceptional travel writing by rediscovering classic journeys from the past, introduced by some of today's most exciting writers.

From solo journeys through the Sahara to canoeing the length of the Mississippi, from the badlands of Utah's canyons to the black tents of Central Asian nomads, from Calcutta to Samarkand, Afghanistan to Ethiopia, the series has captured the risk and wonder that comes from all good travelling, opening our imaginations to unfamiliar places and cultures. Spanning a period from the 1890s to the 1980s, these Journeys give fresh perspectives not only on the places and times in which they were originally published, but on the place and time we find ourselves in now.

As a traveller who has written about journeys on foot throughout Europe (most recently *Outlandish: Walking Europe's Unlikely Landscapes*), I am thrilled to have had the role of seeking out these books. Hundreds of suggestions have come to me from the travel writing, nature writing and adventure communities, and also – in true travellers' style – through serendipity and chance encounter. In this spirit of discovery, we are always open to suggestions for books to republish in the future. Please get in touch on Twitter @johnmurrays or @underscrutiny. #JMJourneys

Nick Hunt, Series Editor

Also by Barbara Toy

A Fool on Wheels
A Fool in the Desert
A Fool Strikes Oil
Columbus was Right!
The Way of the Chariots
The Highway of the Three Kings
Rendezvous in Cyprus
Travelling the Incense Route

BARBARA TOY

In Search of Sheba

Across the Sahara to Ethiopia

INTRODUCED BY LOIS PRYCE

JOHN MURRAY

First published in 1961 by John Murray (Publishers)

This edition published in 2023

2

A CIP catalogue record for this title is available from the British Library

B format ISBN 9781399811040
ebook ISBN 9781399811057

Typeset in Adobe Garamond by Hewer Text UK Ltd, Edinburgh
Printed and bound in Great Britain by Clays Ltd, Elcograf S.p.A.

John Murray policy is to use papers that are natural, renewable and recyclable products and made from wood grown in sustainable forests. The logging and manufacturing processes are expected to conform to the environmental regulations of the country of origin.

Carmelite House
50 Victoria Embankment
London EC4Y 0DZ

www.johnmurraypress.co.uk

John Murray Press, part of Hodder & Stoughton Limited
An Hachette UK company

To my mother

Contents

Travellers cannot keep their friends with them.

Ethiopian Proverb

Introduction

Barbara Toy captures the perennial conflict of the travel writer as she rolls into the Land Rover dealer in Fort Lamy (then capital of Chad), having driven across the Sahara Desert from Libya. 'The journey is too easy in vehicles like these,' sneers the manager, 'You have no mishaps to write about.' 'It's a good fault,' she retorts, 'At least I *am* here to write whatever there is.'

Any traveller setting out on a long journey with the intention of writing a book will know this dichotomy – the natural human desire for one's plans to go smoothly, but the fear that if they do, there will be 'nothing to write about'. Thankfully for us, Barbara's innate curiosity, gung-ho approach and openness to the people she encounters make her an engaging travelling companion, no matter what the circumstances. And, of course, luckily for the reader, there are just enough mishaps along the way to keep us turning the pages.

It's clear from the first page that Barbara Toy knows what she's doing. The year is 1959 and in the last decade (throughout her forties) she has clocked up three solo desert expeditions in North Africa and the Middle East, as well as her 'boldest feat' – a round-the-world journey through Asia, Australia and the USA, all in her beloved Series 1 Land Rover. Her exploits are unsponsored, unsupported and she has written successful books about each one of these journeys. Now, nudging fifty, we find her setting off once again, this time to Ethiopia, via Tunisia, Libya, Chad, CAR, Congo, Uganda and Sudan.

Writing these words, at exactly the same age, I can't help but utter an Oprah-esque 'You go girl!' in tribute to that rare, under-appreciated species: the middle-aged female explorer. And I'm intrigued to see that many of the challenges she faced were mirrored in my trans-Africa motorcycle ride, nearly fifty years later. As both Barbara and I discovered, plotting a route through Africa is a game of snakes and ladders, requiring constant improvisation to dodge the glorious chaos that is thrown at the overland traveller on a daily basis.

With independence movements rippling across the continent, the late 1950s was a fascinating time to be travelling in Africa and, for a woman alone, it was also an unusual one. The 1930s had seen female explorers including Freya Stark and Theresa Wallach make audacious journeys through what were then still 'the colonies', and women aviators such as Amelia Earhart and Amy Johnson also became household names during this time. But by the 1950s, the female emancipation that had grown out of women's involvement in the war effort had fizzled out, and wives were once again returning to domesticity. Not so for Barbara Toy. Upon entering Ethiopia she tells the immigration official she is a widow, but the truth is that she left her husband in the mid-1930s to carve a career in London's theatre world before embarking on her first solo overland expedition in 1950. But as any savvy, lone female traveller will tell you, manipulating the truth about your personal life to wangle a tricky border crossing is de rigeur.

The newly independent Africa that Barbara encounters is mostly brimming with optimism – but not entirely. The continent is still scattered with Europeans trying to navigate this new world – business owners, military men, aid workers and missionaries – some clinging on in denial, others actively involved in building the continent's future. Each country Barbara visits on the way to Ethiopia is at a different stage of its independence journey, from Libya (1947) to the freshly independent Congo, Chad and CAR (all 1958). In Sudan, which gained independence from Britain in 1956, there are already rumblings of disquiet among the Sudanese, following a recent coup which has resulted in a military dictatorship.

'Democracy is a thing you must grow into, not be given on a plate,' one of the locals tells Barbara, while a Northern Sudanese schoolteacher warns her against photographing members of the Dinka tribe – not because he believes it to be disrespectful but that he is 'ashamed of them' for being 'too primitive'. 'We will change all that,' he assures her. It is particularly sobering to read these conversations knowing that in just three years civil war would break out, and Sudan – now split into two nations – would never enjoy peaceful democracy. Indeed, at the time of writing, the country is experiencing a violent power struggle between two military factions.

Barbara reports what she sees and hears, but she travels with no agenda and avoids foisting a world view on the reader. In 1963 she told an Australian newspaper, 'I never meddle with politics, take people as I find them, and I've never met anything but friendliness.' Her objective reportage suggests she believes in respecting native traditions and is reluctant to impose Western values on the people she meets, but sometimes her impartiality feels strained, especially when describing the tribal practices of female genital mutilation and child marriage, and you can't help wondering what she *really* thinks.

Although she refrains from sweeping judgements, some of her

throwaway comments may be grating to the modern reader, especially when discussing the 'glamour' of big-game hunting, the colonial French approach to 'training' the natives in 'good manners', and particularly her unpleasant depiction of the Pygmies of the Congo. But despite being a product of her time, her genuine enthusiasm and curiosity towards her fellow humans comes over in her encounters, whether she's being asked for medical advice on lip sores and infertility by a group of Falasha people, being forced to wear a hat to attend a stuffy embassy function, or being assisted by a convicted murderer at a French Foreign Legion station. As with all the great explorers, she is open to everything, and everything is interesting.

For any travel writer, there is always a decision about how much of one's inner self to include in the narrative. In Barbara's case, the answer is not very much. There is no tortured past to escape, no burning life-goal to achieve, no anxiety to overcome. Her lip only quivers once – and that is under the strain of Sudanese bureaucracy! Maybe this approach is, again, typical of the era – the stiff upper lip and Blitz spirit being ingrained in the British psyche at this time. But the result of her keeping a lid on her emotions is that on the rare occasions she does confess to feelings of fear or loneliness, it is all the more poignant, and we welcome her vulnerability.

The first half of the book covers her journey through North and Central Africa, including an evocative crossing of the Sahara, demonstrating her love and knowledge of deserts. The second half is dedicated to her travels in Ethiopia of which she is a great admirer for its unique mix of cultures, its independent spirit and, particularly, its leader Emperor Haile Selassie and his vision for the country. As the title of the book suggests, the journey is motivated by the desire to seek out the truth behind the Ethiopian legend of the Queen of Sheba. And while she does make some attempts in this direction, we, the reader, suspect that in reality Barbara has hit the road for the sheer hell of it.

In the end, it doesn't really matter, as her passion for Ethiopia and its people jumps off the page. What is heart-breaking to us today is that she clearly believed she was witnessing the dawn of a great future but, as we now know, her visit coincided with a short and precious period of peace and stability in Ethiopia's history. Unlike the prophetic scenes in Sudan that foreshadow its tragic decline over the following decades, her depiction of Ethiopia as the swinging, cosmopolitan hub of Africa, attracting the great and the good from across the world, gives no hint of the devastation that is to come: the military coup against Selassie, the Communist takeover, border wars with Eritrea, the famines of the 1970s and '80s and, now, the brutal civil war raging in the Tigray region.

In Search of Sheba is a compelling snapshot of its time, and it delivers what every travel book should – a great adventure yarn and a window into another world. Barbara excels when pitted against the odds, and the book reaches its climax with a gripping, high-drama action scene worthy of James Bond. I can't help thinking that in a different life, Barbara, with her theatre background and appetite for adventure, would have made an excellent 007.

But the contemporary reader is also left plaintive: for an Africa that did not fulfil its hopes and dreams and also for Barbara's legacy, which has been largely forgotten. In the pantheon of female adventurers, she is the missing link between Freya Stark and Dervla Murphy, and indeed gave her Ethiopia maps to Dervla for her 1966 expedition and book, *In Ethiopia with a Mule*. Yet, Barbara's books have long been out of print, and she has all but disappeared from exploration history despite the fact that her first solo journey took place five years before the much-celebrated six-man Oxford and Cambridge Far Eastern Expedition, also undertaken in Land Rovers.

I hope this new edition will go some way to righting these wrongs, and a new generation of readers will discover Barbara's charms: tough yet human, intelligent without pretension, cheerful but never trite – everything you could wish for in a travelling companion.

Lois Pryce, 2023

A Note on the Text

In looking back into the past to rediscover, and republish, out-of-print travel books, we have inevitably come across terminology that might not be used today. We made the decision not to change Toy's original words, but rather to acknowledge that language and attitudes have moved on since the time of writing.

In Search of Sheba

Prologue

Snow was beginning to fall; already a thin film lay on the vehicles parked alongside the factory wall. The light from the office building opposite caught the snow and it glistened. Amongst the long line of miscellaneous vehicles my old Land Rover Pollyanna stood. Over the years she has acquired in my mind certain expressions and now, it seemed, she had that silent, patient, dug-in look. Gethin Bradley, a member of the Rover Company, unperturbed by the general last-minute rush, held open the door of the office building for me to pass through. Around us buoyant flakes were caught in the high, cold wind.

'Here it is,' he said, pointing to a brand-new Series II Land Rover which stood in front of the door.

I walked towards it slowly. The vehicle had everything that I could possibly want for my proposed journey across the Sahara and east to Ethiopia. The tropical roof was painted white, and attached to both sides of the body were two lightweight aluminium sand-channels in specially prepared sockets. My mind skipped back to the flattened, jagged pieces of old oil-drums used previously for this purpose which had bumped around in the back of Pollyanna.

Two jerry cans, also in sockets, stood on the front bumper-bar and there was an extra petrol tank under the near-side front seat.

Above the dashboard the air vents had been screened with wire to keep insects out, and in front of them were two petrol pumps, one for each tank, placed there to catch the breeze. They worked very well, for during the entire journey the car never once became over-heated. Behind the front seats there was a 'deck' similar to Pollyanna's which covered the entire back; and the interior 'below deck' was lined with Dunlopillo which made packing easier and ensured the safety of breakable things.

As well as these extras, many refinements had been added to the standard vehicle since I bought Pollyanna ten years previously. Firstly, the engine being 2¼ litre, it had considerably more power; also there were dashboard pockets, well-sprung seats, and the interior, although not the *de luxe* model, had rubber-matting all over the front floor of the car.

'I've had them put your equipment from Pollyanna into the back of the new one.' The young man's manner was slightly brusque; perhaps he knew what I was feeling at this moment.

'Oh, what are you going to do with her now?' There was no doubt of the subject uppermost in our minds and he knew at once what I meant.

'She is going to the school in a day or two, and until then she can stay where she is,' he said.

Pollyanna was being given to a technical college where she would be used by the boys for practical demonstrations while, during the holidays, they would be allowed to take her on odd jaunts. I could think of nothing better that could happen to my old car. But for the moment, I panicked; I couldn't just drive off and leave her standing in the cold and the snow, my companion of ten glorious, adventurous years!

'Oh no, she can't,' I said.

'Can't what?'

'Can't stand out there in the snow.'

'Why not?'

'Well – she hasn't any anti-freeze in her,' I lied.

'She hasn't?' He shot a disbelieving look at me, then at the old Land Rover, and gave it up. Women! his manner clearly implied. 'Well, I'll just have to move one of the office cars out of the building – maybe one of the director's,' he added accusingly.

I did not care if he moved the Managing Director's car out in the snow, and I turned, concentrating hard on the new one.

For the last three days I had been attending a course that the Company provides for Land Rover owners who are going on a journey to places where repairs are not always possible, or for those living in out-of-the-way places. Taking the course with me were two young missionaries, one from the Congo and the other from South America. They gleaned more knowledge from the course than I did. I could only hope that I would become as well acquainted with the new one's engine as I was with Pollyanna's and, after all, during those ten years she had never once completely broken down.

I climbed into the car; it was bigger than Pollyanna, higher. I settled down into the soft seat.

'Sorry to have kept you so late – last-minute rush,' said Gethin Bradley. 'How far are you going tonight?'

'Just to Warwick.'

'Then you had better use your low transfer gears – it's a tricky road – but you'll be going slowly, in any case.'

It was in these gears that I finished the journey 25,000 miles later.

I let in the clutch. 'Thanks for everything,' I called, and moved forward. Past the long line of vehicles, past Pollyanna; I noticed with relief that Gethin was approaching her. I hadn't said goodbye to her, but how could I?

The engine hummed quietly and I felt the extra power. The wind-screen wipers moved in a steady rhythm, two of them. I passed the high gateway and turned left. It was incredibly difficult to see anything! 'The damned snow! The damned road! This damned car!' I said to myself, 'I can't see a damned thing!' and wiped the tears from my eyes.

Part One

The Sahara and Onwards

I

All Roads Lead from London

Telegram received: Bon voyage for
Ethiopia remember to turn left late
Tchad and right at Khartoum R.M.

I was determined to go to Ethiopia to fulfil a wish that had come into being years previously in Southern Arabia. I had been camping on the outskirts of Shabwa, a little village that stands round the ruins of the ancient city like roots shooting from a fallen, half-buried tree. The village is owned by the Yemen and surrounded by the British Aden Protectorate and, as relations between the British and the Yemen were far from cordial, we British were forbidden to enter the oasis.

Ahead stretched a wide shallow valley where the remains of an ancient irrigation scheme were still visible. The ridges, like giant paddy fields, were blurred by the overlay of sand and, near by, a large stone sluice-gate lay on its side.

I stayed for a long time that evening over the ritual of tea-making with an old man from the Wadi Erma. He sat in an Arab chair which he had made by winding a long red scarf round the small of his back and below his knees; one adept bit of manipulation and he was sitting comfortably on the sand. I was cross-legged, and the embers of the fire glowed between us.

He was trying to persuade me to go into Shabwa, liking the drama of the situation, for, now that peace had been established amongst the tribes, life was a little dull.

'Shabwa, it's something like Sheba,' I said into the still, quiet night. 'Saba, Belkis, Makeda – call her what you will. I wonder if *she* was ever here?'

The old man inclined his head and pointed with his chin towards the north indicating Marib where, it is reputed, the Queen of Sheba lived.

'Who knows? Some say she came from Ethiopia,' I said.

The old man looked puzzled.

'Ethiopia. Abyssinia,' I explained, and pointed to the southwest.

'Ah! *Yimpkin! Yimpkin!* (possible),' – and a look of supreme-knowledge spread over his face as he pointed with his chin again to the north and then towards Ethiopia. It was knowledge passed down for centuries from father to son and had the ring of truth that surpasses written records. He nodded again.

The great sky became a silver dome as the moon advanced up the shallow valley. 'Somehow, some day,' I said suddenly, 'I shall go there and have a look for myself.'

'*Yimpkin*,' said the old man, and he noisily sipped his glass of tea.

It was to become one of those goals tucked away, naggingly, at the back of my mind.

The mountainous country of Ethiopia is a Christian stronghold surrounded by Moslems and pagans; famous for its beauty, it is of all the countries of Africa the most remote – and the most challenging. Its Emperor, Haile Selassie I, who rules over more territory today than at any time in the country's history, is bringing his isolated peoples, almost single-handed, into the twentieth century.

But it was a risk and an even bigger gamble to contemplate taking a vehicle to Ethiopia. Outside the few cities the country was wild and, except for the main roads, almost inaccessible. I had been told that because of *chiftas* (bandits) it was necessary to travel by daylight in convoy, and to sleep either at police posts or in villages; travel permits had to be acquired to move around at all. If, as a lone traveller, I was stopped from venturing anywhere off the beaten track, the effort and expense of the long journey east would prove fruitless. But, as it was a risk I should have to take, I decided to arrive at an out-of-the-way border and try to see something of the country before officialdom caught up with me. I should cross the Sahara, go east and enter Ethiopia by the north-west Eritrean border – by the backdoor.

There are easier ways of reaching Ethiopia than via the Sahara, Equatorial Africa, the Congo, Uganda and the Sudan; though few routes cover such exciting parts of the continent. There is the desert of sand, rocks and mountains; the savannah of Central Africa; tropical Congo where people grow and blossom as quickly as the surrounding jungle; the majestic Mountains of the Moon, and the slightly tamed, orderly beauty of Uganda – a touch of suburbia in the wild continent; and, by this time, the White Nile, with its tributaries and waterfalls, is spreading over the earth, in preparation for its four thousand miles' journey north. It is joined at Khartoum – where it miraculously fails for a while to merge – to the Blue Nile whose effervescing waters have made their spectacular journey through the Ethiopian mountains, from Lake Tsana, in the heart of that magic country.

There are two ordinary routes across the Sahara, the Hoggar and the Tanezrouft, both of which start from Algeria. The French organise the routes extremely well and, at one time, a bus made the journey regularly. The number of times the Sahara has been crossed by these routes, and the books written about the journeys, is legion; but people will go on doing so because there is nothing quite so satisfactory as crossing from one side of a great desert to the other, whether it is by car, lorry or on a camel.

I intended to make the crossing further east, going south from Tripoli in Libya, through the southern province of the Fezzan; towards the Tibesti Mountains and on to Lake Tchad in the Republic of Tchad. This route is seldom used and is in no way organised. During the French administration of the Fezzan, lorries belonging to the Tunisian Automobile Transport Company, commonly known as T.A.T., occasionally made the journey, but when the French left here the service dwindled and finally stopped, so that now there is no direct communication between the French in the Tibesti and the Libyans. Even telegraphic communications must go through Tunis and Algeria.

The journey takes one from Tripoli on the coast, 600 miles to Sebha, the capital of the Fezzan, and roughly 200 miles further south in the Libyan Desert to the oasis of Gatrun, the country's Customs Post. From then on, the desert is a complete no-man's-land until you come to Zouar in the Tibesti Mountains, and there are no people, animals or birds. The journey can take a vehicle anything from five days upwards and is about 600 miles from Gatrun, *if* you keep on course. The French control the desert from here, and they insist on all vehicles travelling in convoy and with a guide for the rest of the journey through Largeau to Koro Toro where the Sahara officially ends.

The men in the visa department of the French Consulate in London have, over the years, come to know me quite well. They are always willing to be helpful, but their preliminary arguments were ones I had expected. *If* I wanted to cross the Sahara – and our acquaintance, by now, was such that they did not question this – why did I not go by one of the ordinary routes? Then there would be wireless communications to advise of my departure and my intended arrival at each police post. Eventually, they listened to my reasoning, for the French have that rare quality, an open mind. Letters were sent off to Paris, Algiers and Dakar, asking for permission to grant me a visa, and the answers, they hoped, would be back in three weeks' time.

'I have always wanted to read your book – what is it? The one where you visited Tunis,' asked the young man who attended me. 'I was born there.'

'I'll send you a copy,' I said, only too willing to be helpful.

'Thank you very much,' he beamed, 'and come back in three weeks' time.'

When I returned the replies had been received.

'I have now read your book,' said the young man, and there was a certain reservation in his manner. 'Very interesting.'

'Oh, I am glad you liked it.'

'Yes. You say: "The English make everything seem easy while the French make the easy seem a mess." '

'Oh, it was a joke.' I always *had* thought the line rather cheap and now I was paying for it.

'And then, when you were in Oudja, you put your age back five years. That was not wise to change the facts.' He had drawn a green tin box from under the counter and was going through a series of cards.

'It also – was a joke,' I repeated lamely. 'The official understood when I explained.'

'Not good.' He was picking up a few cards which had been in a special place. Was he looking me up in the 'wanted' files?

Finally, satisfied, he thrust the green box back under the counter and grabbed my passport. 'Now,' he said quite cheerfully, 'we shall want fifty-five pounds' security and then, your visas.'

The French take this deposit to cover any rescue work they may have to undertake in their territory; it is the only deposit I have ever made that was refunded without the slightest difficulty.

I could find no one who had taken the actual route and, as the Tibesti Mountains were administered by the French Military, any enquiries about the route or facilities to be had were not encouraged. Maps were equally difficult; there were no British ones worth having, but the ordinary Michelin Sahara map had reasonably accurate mileages. The French Ministère du Travail Publique et du Transport map, dated 1944, gave more data, but marked tracks which were merely a direction taken by lorries years ago. Having once realised this enthusiasm for 'filling in the desert' and made allowances, the map was useful. Finally, armed only with a French report of the journey which was years old and the maps, I decided to look for more up-to-date information nearer the starting point.

The main and last problem was petrol. The Paris and Algerian authorities both referred me to the T.A.T. who replied they were no longer functioning, otherwise they would have taken a drum of petrol and left it half-way down in the Sahara for me. The head offices of the various oil companies having no connection or link-up across this part of the desert could not arrange for a petrol supply; and finally, enquiries about obtaining petrol when I should eventually arrive at Zouar drew a blank. The Touring Club of France suggested that I call at their office in Tunis for more on-the-spot information and with this vague piece of advice I had to be content.

On the last day of January, I flew my new Land Rover across the Channel to Le Touquet with nothing but the unsolved problem of petrol supplies on my mind. As I turned south from the airport at Le Touquet on my way to Marseilles to catch the ship for Tunis, the sun, shining in my eyes, made me scramble for sun-glasses; these were to be my constant companions for the next ten months.

Tunisia had become independent since I was last there, and the city of Tunis was untidy with a dusty air of exhaustion. Now that the fight was over, the people looked listless with a slight air of having been cheated. It comes often after the struggle for independence. But the intricate one-way street system had not changed and I spent an hour disorganising the traffic before finding the Touring Club of France's representative. The office was on the first floor of a small building over-looking a crowded, narrow street. Two pretty French girls greeted me. They knew I was coming. Petrol, they said, was *very* difficult and they really did not know. The T.A.T. did not run any more and nobody went across the desert that way; therefore, it was difficult to go at *all*. One must have two vehicles, one could never go alone.

I listened impatiently; I had not come to hear these things.

'About petrol? . . .'

'To drive alone it would not be allowed . . .' they broke in, talking with that lightness and intensity of French women.

'All right.' Somehow, I must make them see the importance of petrol. 'I'll probably go with someone, but about petrol . . .'

'*Ah bon!*' they broke in again. 'It is providential. Another party is going to Zouar and Fort Lamy. It is providential, is it not?'

'But I am leaving for Tripoli today.'

'No matter, we will telephone direct.'

One of them removed the telephone receiver from the little upright machine and asked for a number in Béja, a town many miles away. I had come about petrol and was now being involved with people wishing to take this unusual route across the Sahara!

'*Attention!*' The girl held out the spluttering telephone. '*Le docteur*,' she said, with the air of a conspirator.

'Well, hello! I hear you want to cross the desert to Zouar and Fort Lamy.' The voice had a strong American accent. 'I am going with a friend at the end of the month; we can make a party.'

'Oh, but I shall have left Tripoli by then. I am going on to Ethiopia.'

'That isn't possible. You are not allowed to go alone.' The voice was firm.

'Well, maybe not, but . . . have you arranged for petrol?'

'We can take all we need.'

'Have you done much desert travelling?'

'I know sand well. I'm going to Fort Lamy and then returning via Djanet to Tunisia.' He made it sound like a weekend jaunt. 'It is not permitted for one vehicle to go alone, you know,' he repeated.

'What kind of vehicle are you driving?'

'My car's okay.'

The line became really bad. 'I shall write to you,' I said and put down the receiver. Until I arranged about petrol there was no point in continuing the discussion.

'How much do I owe you for the telephone call?' I asked the girl.

'*Rien!*' She wiped the whole incident out of existence with her expressive little hands. The mission was completed.

'And you have *no* suggestions about petrol?' I asked once again.

'You must take all with you,' she said.

'And at Zouar?'

She shrugged. Might as well ask if there is a petrol pump on the moon.

I felt a little uneasy. The threat in the doctor's voice, the free telephone call, the companions for the journey miraculously found; it all seemed a little laid on. Would they follow it up? Before leaving Tunis I wrote a note to Bèja telling the doctor that I had experience of desert travel and was well equipped, and hoped this would allay their fears as to my capabilities.

The blanket of rumour and uncertainty that lay over Libya during the early days of the country's oil prospecting has lifted. After four years of extensive search by British, American, French and Dutch companies, oil was struck in workable quantities – and in widely separated areas – late in 1959. Now the country knows it has oil, and relaxes.

The French made the first inroads into the Sahara and secured a permanent foothold there when they came to Algeria in 1830, opening up the first main trans-African route and so annexing much of the Sahara for Algeria. The route was a bridge between North and South Africa and it accelerated the search and discovery of oil that is now going on all over the desert.

After the last war, Tripolitania and Cyrenaica were put under British Military Administration and the Fezzan was given to the French Military to administer. Finally in 1951, with the United Nations' blessing, the three provinces were declared independent and were formed into the kingdom of Libya under the Senussi king, Idris. This premature independence started a wave of nationalism throughout North Africa and speeded the independence of both Morocco and Tunisia.

Before the discovery of oil, Libya relied on outside aid which was given, and still is, by European powers and the USA. She also collects rents from both the American and British air bases in her country and from the British Military Mission. The king has strong Egyptian sympathies and the country is a member of the United Arab Republic. However, Libya still has many western influences and she keeps her agreements with the Americans and the British.

There was no new information about my journey here in Tripoli and there was definitely no petrol to be had south of Sebha unless I should run into some of the oil-prospecting camps. The oil company personnel gave me what information they had.

'From Sebha you take a well-defined track to the oasis of Umm-el-Araneb sixty miles south, and a few miles further on you cross the Gatrun Dune. Run due south to the oasis of Gatrun and after that . . .' the tall geologist shrugged.

It was evident that I should have to take enough petrol for the entire journey, so I waited several days while two ten-gallon tanks and a luggage-carrier were made; finally, with four more jerry cans, I had capacity to carry seventy gallons of petrol.

The physical preparations for a long journey no longer bother me, though there had been the extra equipment needed for the new vehicle. In London a lean-to tent was made that clipped on to the side of the Land Rover; it had two poles, four tent plugs, a couple of pieces of rope, and could be put up, alone, in less than five minutes. Two wooden boxes, lined with Formica, held my cooking utensils and perishable food. The rest of the equipment came from my old car, Pollyanna; the old army camp-bed, the RAF sleeping-bag, the wooden box that took the place of the middle seat and held everything of value such as cameras, compass, film and money. My small portable Olivetti typewriter had a home-made cover that was lined with Dunlopillo, and it worked, as usual, right through the journey.

I traded my old Bell and Howell 16-mm camera for a new model of the same make. It became known as the 'little tank', for, no matter how much it was knocked about, left in the heat, had stones thrown at it, rolled around in the Land Rover, it continued to work.

Finally, the extra tanks and equipment were loaded and I set off, driving along Tripoli's waterfront. All I needed now were two *djerbas*, the goatskins that are used for carrying water which I should buy at one of the oases on the way south. Turning off the waterfront I was hailed by two men. They were the gentlemen from Bèja. The doctor, a large, fair Teutonic-looking man with a square face, was the spokesman. The other was younger, and worked in an insurance office in Tunis.

'Where is your car?' I asked.

They pointed to a little grey Renault.

'Are you going to cross the desert in *that*!'

They nodded, amused and pleased at my surprise.

'Can you put all your equipment and petrol in it?' It seemed barely large enough to take the two men.

'We're okay,' said the doctor, 'we're just going to Fort Lamy and back via Djanet. We have a few weeks' leave.'

'That's not long for such a journey.' Experience has taught me that to hurry in the desert courts disaster. 'I think you should find a lorry to go with, so that the men can help you out.'

'We don't know of anyone going and, in any case, *you* can't go alone. It is forbidden.'

I looked at the low undercarriage of the car. 'It's incredible! However, if you know the desert . . .'

'That's okay. I am used to sand,' said the doctor again, with finality.

I suddenly felt rather silly and over-cautious with my big, strong Land Rover. 'I'll meet you this evening at Misurata,' I said.

'Yes. We shall stay two or three days in Sebha, for we have letters to people there.'

I set off along the coast. I had companions – for better or worse.

The road runs along the coast for 120 miles to Misurata through superb avenues of giant date-palms that stretch as far as the eye can see on every side, romantic, ageless. Then there is the sudden contrast of bright petrol stations and busy roadside cafés. There are glimpses of white sands and choppy seas near Homs and the magnificent ruins of Leptis Magna remind one of the past glories of Libya. Occasionally patches of desert creep up to the coastline, and after Misurata the road passes the last of the abandoned houses of the Italian colonisation scheme and the desert takes over.

Seventy miles after leaving Misurata, we turned south into the desert at a spot where, on my previous visit six years ago, the turn-off had been difficult to find, for there was only a hut made of empty kerosene tins and a few tracks trailing off across the stony desert. That other journey had been adventurous and slightly hazardous for I had seen only one lorry the whole way to Sebha. Now, at the turn-off, there were three petrol stations, a large white building – and a general air of expectancy. In place of the straggling tracks, a fine tarmac road ran south into the desert. The road is in process of construction and will eventually be paved right through to Sebha 300 miles away. The project is scheduled to cost three million pounds and to take three years to complete, but already there have been difficulties in coping with the desert's treacherous terrain so that it will cost a great deal more and take longer.

The traffic, swelled by the contractors' vehicles, the oil companies' equipment and ordinary commercial vehicles supplying the steadily growing Fezzanese capital of Sebha, has turned the unfinished track into one of the worst and most unpleasant I have ever experienced. The heavy traffic has ridged the ground into giant corrugations and in the softer places the soil was churned up, and vehicles moved from one great pot-hole to the next, in an enveloping cloud of dust.

I saw the oasis of Bu Djem for the first time, for the contractors had already run a tarmac strip through its centre. Sand piles up around the palms and buildings of an oasis and, on my previous visits here, it had been necessary to skirt the cluster of huts and make for the deserted Italian fort which stood on the hill to the east. Inhabitants had come across the sand from the oasis, struggling against the perpetual high wind, eager for a chat and news of the outside world. But now, we whisked through and heads barely turned in our direction. Vehicles were only of interest if their occupants stopped to buy, and the Bu Djem of Roman times seemed further away than ever.

The track was strewn with blown-out tyres and great strips of rubber that had been ripped off the treads. The corrugations play havoc with tyres and it is necessary to run at a speed of thirty-five miles an hour or over, otherwise the car skids. If there are pot-holes as well, the choice is between risking crashing into one of these or slowing down to walking pace.

I was remembered at Hon and given the V.I.P.'s guest house, an honour I never acquired in the old days; and the gentlemen from Béja were allowed the same privilege as my friends. Despite the long and tiring day, the doctor and the boy unloaded the entire contents of the little car, swept it and changed the tyres round. Next morning they donned tropical suits, for we were now in the desert.

Hon was the military desert headquarters for the Italians during their occupation. They built a picturesque fort and an administration centre with an avenue of villas that lay between the native village and the palm gardens. When they withdrew, the villas were ransacked and then the oasis went back to its former leisurely life. Now, with the coming of the road, the houses are being repaired, and an hotel will soon be opened.

Socna, twenty miles further on, however, received no such attention from the Italians. It is a golden cluster of mud houses and palm gardens where we used to picnic beside a natural spring that is famous for having the sweetest water in these parts. Now, as we whisked through the oasis, I wondered how many passing travellers knew of this lovely picnic spot.

These oases lie in a depression running along the north face of the Jebel Soda – or Black Mountain – and soon we climbed into the volcanic mountains which are completely covered with black stones. A track had been cleared through the boulders and high in the hills, near a well, the road construction men had their huts. A few palm-trees grew, the only ones in sight, and where the earth had been turned it showed vivid red, making a bizarre picture of dark green palms and the streak of warm red in a black world. Only the men, incongruous in dingy khaki shorts, struck a sad note.

Crossing the great black mountains, a wide flat plain stretched ahead, and previously, a magnificent avenue bordered each side by high sand-dunes had led straight to the horizon. Now, these same dunes had moved right across the plain to the east where, in the distance, they made a far billowing horizon. It would be useless to build a road across this stretch, for the dunes could shift again and, coming back, completely cover it.

At the far end of the plain lie the dreaded Dunes de Kneir which form the eastern end of Wadi Sharit. It is the most northern of three great and shallow *wadis* along which the settled Fezzanese live. As we approached the ground fell away from golden rocks and the great dunes of soft fine sand lay in folds and curves, without even a footprint to mar their surface. They are incredibly beautiful, infinitely treacherous – and best left alone. A causeway has been built skirting them now and there were no rescue crews with their long-handled shovels, waiting to dig us out of the sand. To the left stood the 'head of rock' mentioned by the Romans and the Garamantes, an amusing little top-knot of a hillock, familiar and indestructible over the centuries. But who knows, when I come this way again, perhaps a bill-poster will be perched on its impertinent little face?

The French have left Sebha for some years now and taken with them the Sahara Corps, the Foreign Legionnaires – and most of Sebha's glamour. The high fort, which housed the Legionnaires, is empty and falling into disrepair, as are the Sahara Corps Officers' quarters in the compound below. The fort and its occupants had completely overshadowed the little native oasis of Sebha, three kilometres away, where an aged and charming Emir received me in the only solid building in the place. But native Sebha had changed out of all recognition. There was a traffic policeman, a bank, an hotel, swimming-pool and electricity. Rows of square buildings surrounded by white walls stolidly withstood the desert winds, and the stretch from the old fort to the town was paved and lined with eucalyptus trees which were watered each day by means of a huge mobile water-tank. There were schools for both boys and girls, training establishments, and the various well-known organisations were distributing the world's wealth a little more evenly; while the Tuaregs, the veiled nomads of the desert, have a school that follows them into the sands by means of a camel. I drove through the busy little town, dismayed – the desert was running away from me!

The hotel, with its minute bar, was doing a good trade. Sunburnt oil men in battered Land Rovers whisked in for emergency supplies of beer, their vehicles lined up beside American limousines used by a delegation of the World Bank who, in their turn, were being whisked round at top speed to see the various oases.

There was a continuous passage of pilots and crews of the Silver City freighter planes that are used by the oil companies to transport cargo into the desert. The pilots fly in all kinds of weather, dropping down on makeshift airstrips and in completely unknown, often unmapped, terrain.

By some oversight, my Land Rover's springs had not been reinforced and, by the time I had arrived in Sebha, they were already quite flat. There was no commercial garage in the town, and eventually the Chief of Police, Brigadier-General Bardi, gave me permission to use the government workshop. But for this, I would have had to retrace my steps all the way to Tripoli.

On my way to the workshop the French doctor hailed me. 'We want to move on, there is no point in staying here.'

'I can't go until my springs are reinforced.'

'They're okay,' he said, not looking at them, 'let's start. We haven't much time.'

'I know, but it's better to fix the springs here, than to break down in the desert.'

He gave them a quick look. 'What does it matter if they are flat?'

'There are still seventy gallons of petrol to be loaded, they just wouldn't stand it,' I said. 'I'll be as quick as I can.'

But it was three days before we were able to set off from Sebha. The springs now had a reassuring upward tilt but unfortunately as the oil company's personnel had bought up all the *djerbas*, there was not one to be found.

'We have borrowed two from the French Consul,' said the doctor, when I was making final enquiries, 'so let's go.'

The track took us seventy miles through grey stony desert to Umm-el-Araneb, which was a long straggling oasis of fenced-in gardens, palm groves and mud huts. Beyond, on a series of firm, stony dunes, a rough wooden signpost had the word 'Gatrun' scratched on it and a few tracks led into a hollow where a cluster of untended palms stood in a deserted landscape. In front of us was the Gatrun Dune, a great spreading hill of sand that stretched from east to west and brought the horizon reasonably near. No definite tracks lay ahead, for the top sand changes all the time and vehicles find their own way to hard sand. We had been advised to keep slightly east of south so as not to veer into the heart of the sand mass, and eventually we would run down on to a flat plain beyond.

'Shall I go ahead and find hard sand?' I asked.

'No, we're okay,' said the doctor and set off into the sand.

I watched the small car, impressed; perhaps it was going to skim over the sand while *I* dug myself in! Moving forward, the dune appeared to flatten out and the distance to the top was far greater than I had judged. This matter of distance, with no landmarks to set the perspective, is always difficult in sandy deserts. I concentrated for some time on finding firm sand and, when I glanced towards the other car, found it had stopped. The doctor was revving the engine and the wheels were digging deeper into the sand. By the time I had found sand firm enough to stop and walked back to the other vehicle, the wheels were already half hidden by the sand.

'Where are yonr sand-channels?' I asked.

'We have some sacks.' They produced some ordinary grain bags.

'They won't be of any use.'

'They're okay,' said the doctor.

'But they'll just fly out behind the wheels,' I said.

'I don't think you'll find they will,' said the doctor confidently. 'Let's try them.'

We put the sacks as far under the wheels as possible but, at the first spin of the wheels, they flew far out behind the vehicle which stayed in the same position only a little lower in the sand.

I went back to collect my own sand-channels and, by the time I had returned, a strong wind had blown up and the whirling sand made it difficult to see ahead. We put the channels under the wheels; the car ran along their length and then dug itself into the sand again. The doctor kept on revving the engine.

'Don't do that!' I called out, 'You're digging her in.'

'I can't understand it,' said the doctor, as he started to scoop sand from the wheels again. 'It never stopped on the beach at home.'

I sat back and looked at him. 'Is *beach* sand the only kind you've tackled?'

'Yes. Why, it's sand, isn't it?'

'It's *wet* sand and has absolutely nothing to do with desert sand.'

'It's sand, isn't it?' he repeated.

'Have you never done a desert journey before?'

'Well – I've driven along the sandy beach at home . . .'

'You've driven . . .' I suddenly felt rather sick. 'Then you haven't *any* idea how this little car will stand up to the journey? Come on, let's take everything out of the car and see what we can do.'

But, even with the lightened load, the narrow tyres dug right into the sand each time they left the sand-channels.

'I had better try towing her,' I said at last.

By now the sand-storm was at its height; the sand stung our lips and got into our eyes. We piled the jerry cans into my Land Rover and the rest of the luggage back into the little car, fastened my towing rope and, after an unsteady start, the car moved forward. We churned through the soft sand and I drove blind with my eyes on the compass, for the swirling sand had brought visibility down to nil. To call it a 'dune' was ridiculous for it went on for miles. My engine became hot as we strained with the heavy load in the soft sand, and there were awful moments when we struck a bad patch and the car faltered, making me spurt forward, racing the engine at a terrific speed. After an interminable time, the soft patches became less frequent and the ground began to fall away until, finally, we ran on to flat ground and I pulled up thankfully. It was nearly two o'clock.

'Good!' I said. 'Now we can have some food.'

'Why stop?' asked the doctor, impatient to be off.

'I'm starving, aren't you?'

'We have wasted enough time, let's move on.'

'Sorry, but I must have some food, especially if we are to do more digging.'

They ate with me, but were impatient to be off. Within ten minutes we were moving again, running due south with the Jebel ben Guenema, a low line of hills, to the left, and the great dune to the right. Within a few miles recently made tracks appeared running south-east and we followed them for thirty miles, when curious tiny blobs appeared on the horizon. Nearer, they became sheds, caravans, Land Rovers and lorries, for we had followed tracks to the oil exploration camp of the Darcy Gompany. It is a new hazard in the Sahara today for they could just as easily have led us to an abandoned oil rig miles out of our course.

Our arrival caused a stir as visitors are rare. The boys offered us tea and beer and crowded round for a chat; boredom, it seemed, was the worst hazard for these young men. Their sleeping quarters were a long line of air-conditioned caravans and beyond was an upright little house where a deep bore had been sunk making an extremely effective toilet system, being from time to time merely removed to a new bore.

From the base the men circulate over the concession area which sometimes includes old minefields and completely uncharted ground. The drivers, with their vehicles, perform fantastic feats over the rocks and sand-dunes. Sometimes they find crashed war-time planes and can piece together the sad story and fate of the occupants.

'You came too far east,' said the camp manager when we enquired about Gatrun. 'The top of the Gatrun depression is due west from here. We'll come along and show you.'

Six men piled into a lorry and went ahead until the first palms of the seventy-mile depression in which Gatrun lies came into sight.

'Gatrun Oasis is half-way down,' said the driver, 'there's the police and customs post there.'

'And the actual border?' I asked.

'About 200 miles further on, I think. Keep away from the palms until you come to Gatrun; the sand is very soft and, more important, there are mines. A vehicle was blown up three weeks ago not far from here.' With this cheering piece of information, we parted.

It had been agreed that, as the boy did not drive and the Renault's speedometer was in kilometres, he should keep account of the distances and so save confusion.

'Stop before it gets dark,' I said, and we set off to the south.

The ground was hard and flat, and the doctor, exhilarated by the beer and the good going, sent the little car tearing across the desert. On and on they sped. The sun began to sink and I signalled them to stop. They waved, but drove right on.

Finally, when it was quite dark, they stopped. Setting up camp and cooking in the dark is not my favourite occupation; but this, I supposed, as I tripped round in the dark, is what is known as give and take. My companions had a store of onions, vitamin pills and some oranges, but they enjoyed the warm food immensely and it was quite late before I finally crawled into my sleeping-bag. But if I had thought this day was tiring I had not yet lived the morrow.

We woke at dawn to make an early start for we had wasted so much time on the dune the day before.

'How many kilometres to the entrance to Gatrun?' I asked the boy.

'Forty kilometres.'

'So much?' I was mentally multiplying by five and dividing by eight.

He nodded vigorously.

We set off, skimming the hard flat ground and when, by my reckoning, we had covered the forty kilometres, I caught up and motioned them to stop. They merely waved and drove on. I tooted my horn. They nodded in a placating manner. If I had been annoyed the night before when they ignored me, I was livid now. Also, I was worried. If they were going to do this sort of thing when we were in the real desert, it would be plain suicide.

Finally, when they came to the end of the palms, the car stopped. I pulled up beside them. 'We're miles past the forty-kilometre mark and you're wasting petrol,' I said.

'There weren't any tracks back there; and here are some.' The doctor pointed to some new squared tracks that the oil men used for their preliminary surveys.

'They are new oil tracks,' I said. 'Come on, let's go back to where we had covered forty kilometres and you can wait on firm ground while I go towards the oasis and find the tracks.'

But they had not heard me for they suddenly started to argue with each other. They were pointing in all directions and their French had gone far beyond my comprehension.

'It's all right!' I yelled above the din. 'You just wait . . .'

They took no notice and the desert rang with their high voices until suddenly they climbed into the car and set off – to the south-east!

'Hi!' I called to no one in particular and climbed into the Land Rover. There was nothing for it but to follow them. The ticking of the petrol pump above the dashboard was a steady reminder of the petrol we were wasting. The little car began to weave in and out over the ground. Were they arguing again? If so, to come alongside and expostulate would merely irritate them. My one chance was to set their tracks in a pattern with my own, in case they lost their way. They went on and on, changing course frequently and then, as they began to double back, recrossing their own tracks, I knew they were lost!

What was going on in the car? One thing was certain; I dare not leave my tracks to find out, for by now I also had no idea what direction we were taking. Suddenly the car stopped and the doctor climbed out, looking around him.

'You're lost?' I asked, and he nodded.

'Well, follow me and please don't go ahead.'

They were rather chastened when we were finally back on our original tracks, for they had been able to see how their car had gone round in circles.

'Did you take into account the mileages we did yesterday evening?' I asked and, on making another reckoning, we found that these had been left out. We had camped one mile from the entrance to Gatrun!

This time we found the tracks into the oasis quite easily, but the piled-up sand around the palms ahead meant more trouble.

'It will save time if I take you in tow right away,' I said.

'The sand is quite hard,' replied the doctor.

'I know these oases, it will not be hard when you reach the palms.'

He looked amused at my concern. 'Don't you worry,' he said, 'we shall be okay,' and set off before I could reply.

Once among the palms the ground became chaotic with sand piled up around the trunks and there were deceptively hard-looking stretches that crumbled beneath the wheels. I found the trace of a track, where palm fronds had been thrown across to give a grip, but the doctor scorned such help and cut off across a patch of undisturbed ground which suddenly gave way and the car sank, surrounded by soft sand. I climbed out of my Land Rover to test the sand before venturing off the path to the little vehicle.

'The ground *looked* quite hard,' said the doctor.

I nodded. The sun was already setting before I had the car on firm ground and in tow again. We roared through the still oasis, past the straw-matting Tibu huts that stood beneath the palms like great gold bugs. Camels looked up disdainfully as we rushed by. I crashed the gears into low and rushed the steep hillock of soft sand leading to the Police Fort. We faltered once or twice and, finally, the gears roaring, lurched up on to flat ground in front of the fort. To our right across the sand stood a small white school building; beyond the hillock was a cluster of native huts and a well. I drew up and sat for a while, too exhausted to move.

The police sergeant and customs official consider it lucky if one group of travellers a year pass through, and they found us a welcome diversion. They shook hands warmly and we were given rooms in the fort. I cooked a meal that we all needed and later that night I lay, too tired and worried to sleep. We had wasted a whole day – and a day's petrol – for nothing. If I had to tow the car most of the way across the Sahara, I would be using more petrol than I had budgeted for so, tomorrow, I should have to go back to the Darcy camp and beg some petrol to fill up every container I could lay hands on. This would waste another half-day at least. In any case, would the little car ever get through the rocky sand-dunes that lay ahead? But most worrying thing of all was the behaviour of my companions. They knew nothing about travelling in the desert, in spite of what they had said originally; and if they repeated the performance of today, quarrelled between themselves, panicked and went off without consulting me, we would end up as three piles of bleached bones in the desert somewhere between here and the Tibesti!

'Some day,' I said to myself, 'all this will seem very funny indeed.' It wasn't much consolation, but it sent me to sleep.

Next morning, parked in front of the fort entrance was a large lorry belonging to an American oil company, and a young man with a crew-cut was just climbing down.

'Good heavens!' he said, turning, 'a woman with a face. Haven't seen one for some time.'

'You'd be justified in not recognising the fact,' I said.

'Where are you heading for?'

'Across the Sahara.'

He pointed to the little car. 'Not in that, I hope?'

'It's coming too.'

'Phew!'

'Well, you've given yourself a task there,' he said when I had told him of our exploits of the previous day. 'How about coming and having a glass of tea with the schoolmaster? He's a pal of mine.'

There is nothing like the ritual of Arab tea-making to soothe one's nerves, and we set off across the sand to the school house. The schoolmaster was just getting up; he wound a *kuffiyah* quickly and deftly round his head, wiped the sleep from his eyes – and made us welcome. We sat on rugs in the bare little room and a small boy brought a battered piece of tin with live charcoal embers on it. As the tea boiled we cracked baked seeds and chatted about the gossip of the oasis. By the time I had drunk the customary three glasses of strong, sweet tea I was prepared to tow the two Frenchmen to Timbuktu, if necessary.

Back at the fort, the doctor was having his papers checked. 'Didn't sleep much,' he said, 'I'm worried. Time is running short.'

'Yes, let's hope we do more than a mile today,' I said.

'You had better come to our camp to fill up with petrol,' said the American boy. 'We are nearer than the Darcy camp, by a little.'

We towed the small car to the outskirts of the oasis while the sand was cool and hard. We would be able to start immediately I returned with the petrol.

This American camp was entirely on wheels, with a large bathroom-caravan complete with showers. As we arrived, a Silver City cargo plane was landing and, as soon as it touched down, unloading began. A representative of the Dunlop Rubber Company had thumbed a lift and was looking round.

Tyres are of great importance in desert travel. On my previous journey I had motored round the world on one set of

Dunlop tyres; now I was running on Michelin Desert Track. The air is let out of the tyre to a pressure of eleven and the tyres spread over the sand like a camel's foot, and this saves many a bad stick.

The boys generously filled my tanks with petrol and put me back on the right track. I found the Frenchmen had been having a conference in my absence.

'We have decided there won't be time to do the whole journey,' said the doctor. 'We shall just go to Zouar and come back again – just to say we have crossed the Sahara.'

'But you can't come back alone?'

'We thought you could bring us back.'

'But I'm on my way to Ethiopia.'

The doctor looked surprised. 'You won't come back with us?'

'Of course not.'

'Well, then there's nothing for it, we'll just have to go back to Sebha now.'

'It would have helped if you'd had this idea before I bothered to go all that way for extra petrol.'

'What's the difference? You'll need it to go on alone, as soon as you've taken us across the big dune.'

'So it's quite all right for me to go on alone, now that you don't want an escort?'

The doctor grinned and shrugged. 'Why not? No one will know.'

'Well, that is the last straw!' I turned on him. 'First of all you said it was forbidden to go alone, and then that you know all about sand. You quarrel between yourselves, panic, go off without consulting me and get lost. You ignore my experience in deserts; and now you not only want me to take you across the Sahara *and* back again, but it's become quite all right for me to go on my own. Of all the people I could have crossed the desert with! . . .'

They looked at me aghast.

'Come on, I'll take you back across the dune.'

'Even so,' said the doctor, recovering slightly, 'we want to go via the Darcy camp.'

'Why? It's much quicker to go directly north.'

'The sand is too soft; the boys told us so.'

'Oh, all right. At this rate I'll *never* get to Ethiopia.'

We had difficulty in finding the tracks to the Darcy camp, and it was very hot when we finally drew up alongside the mess building.

'No tea for me,' said the doctor, in answer to their invitation. 'I'd rather have a beer.'

'Why didn't you go directly north?' the boys asked me. 'It is good going and would have saved a lot of mileage.'

'I suggested we come this way,' said the doctor, with a grin, 'I wanted a beer.'

The boys sent a lorry to help us over the dune. 'If you get badly stuck, don't worry,' they said, 'we have another lorry going into Sebha in the morning.'

The little car stuck badly and it was dark before we finally crossed the dune and camped for the night on the track leading to Umm-el-Araneb.

Next morning my companions, though subdued, had a slightly forced, jaunty air.

'Thanks,' said the doctor, 'we are quite safe now; we are on the track.'

'I have to go back to Sebha to find some water-containers. You had better come with me, you may break down.'

'No, you push on. We have lots of time now and in any case the Darcy lorry is coming along this morning.'

I had already collected some more provisions, filled up with petrol again, and was looking for water-containers when the Frenchman arrived back in Sebha. The French Consul gave me an abrupt 'no' when I tried to buy the borrowed *djerbas* from him. He may have realised I was contemplating going on alone and try to stop me, so I decided to leave quickly.

'Good-bye,' said the doctor, 'my family *will* be pleased to see me back, they were never happy about the journey. We should have had a vehicle like yours.'

I nodded. 'Or else, you'd better stick to wet beach sand!' and climbing into the Land Rover turned once more towards the Sahara.

2

The Libyan Desert

Somehow good will be the final goal of ill.

This time I did not go into Gatrun. Things were not exactly rolling for me and to be stopped here would be the last straw. Only the oil boys knew where I was, but that was a risk I should have to take.

Passing the last of the Gatrun palms, complete desolation lay ahead. While palms could be seen the desert looked alive, almost romantic, but the landscape ahead of sand, rocks and a far line of flat, stony hills was forsaken and dead. This kind of country would continue until I came to the other side of the Sahara at least five days' journey away. But the stillness of the uncluttered, uncomplicated world was a pleasant contrast to the stormy days behind me.

Soon, outcrops of rock appeared ahead and old T.A.T. tracks zigzagged between vicious stones that stood upright with razor-edge sharpness and were capable of puncturing a tyre quite easily. The flat-topped Jebel ben Guenema to the left, and the sandy overlay of the Idehan of Murzuck to the right, formed a channel through which I must go. The tracks led past the wreck of a small plane, a relic of the last war, and everything of interest or value had been taken from it; such is the life of the desert that its framework may stay here, a landmark for hundreds of years.

The ground began to break up as though a *wadi* was near at hand. Sixteen miles further on there stood an old oil drum with the word 'Koui' printed on its side and some definite tracks ran off to the south-west. The French P.W.D. map showed Koui south of an oasis called Tedgeri, and deep in the Murzuk sands. Half-way along this track another branched off to the left to Refuse Sarazac, on my route. There was reputed to be a well here, the last this side of the Tibesti.

I took the Koui track, running along a *wadi* that was as white as a salt pan. Pink rocks, eroded in strange, human-looking shapes, stood in the base of the valley; macabre sentinels in this still, empty world. As I ran parallel they glowed in the afternoon sun, reminding me of the balustrades of giant gods and demons of Angkor Wat in Cambodia.

Finally I came to a signpost pointing west to Tedgeri and, six miles further along the original track, I topped a slight rise and saw the Nissen hut of Refuse Sarazac lying in open desert beyond. This hut and another which lies in the very heart of the desert were used by the T.A.T. drivers, and the encircling sand was scarred with myriads of old tracks made by overloaded lorries years before. There were the remains of fires and blown-out tyres; while on the floor of the hut lay a dead starling. A whole saga of endurance, tenacity and courage seemed to be embodied in the tiny still body that had managed somehow to gain the shade, if nothing else, of the Nissen hut.

I could not find the well. I shovelled sand from everything that might disclose it, spreading far out over the sand in my search, but with no success. After two hours I decided to continue with what water I had.

From this point, it was necessary to cut due east towards a flat-topped mountain called Jebel Damose, before heading directly south. The terrain confronting me was chaotic; hills of high, jagged rocks disintegrated into a rocky *wadi* full of pockets of soft sand which led finally to a big basin where dead tamarisk trees spoke of water not too far below the surface. The sand piled up around their trunks forming high mounds and the car lurched from one to the other as I rushed towards them to prevent sinking into the dips between. Sometimes it became too soft and I retraced my steps, looking for a better way through.

I had been doing this for over an hour when, glancing at my speedometer, I realised that it was still registering the Refuse Sarazac mileage. The speedometer was not working! After checking the lead, it still did not work. I was in a quandary. I had no spare speedometer and to navigate without one was beyond me. It might have been possible with my old car for I knew how much petrol she used in most kinds of terrain, but of the new, higher-powered engine I had no experience.

I pulled up on high ground to camp for the night, and later reviewed the situation. I was setting off with barely enough water for the journey, the authorities did not know I had left, and the French in the Tibesti did not know I was coming. It would be impossible to keep check of the time and approximate speed, as well as drive, while, if I had to retrace my steps often, I would have no check on how much ground I was covering.

I *could* take a chance. But wasn't this the sort of foolhardy thing I was often condemning other people for doing? Had I set out on the journey alone in the first place, fresh and not tired, perhaps I would. In fact, *had* I started off alone the speedometer would not have broken until I was almost in the Tibesti. But now it looked as though I had lost the one ingredient I have always had before – luck. There had been the telephone call in Tunis; my two companions with their inadequate vehicle and odd behaviour, the delay over the springs, the failure to buy *djerbas* and also to find the well at Refuse Sarazac; and now, finally, the speedometer.

'To hell with it,' I said to myself, 'it is not my lucky day,' and resolved there and then to return to the coast, go to Benghazi, buy a new speedometer and persuade friends there to help me go through to Kufra and the Wadi Haifa. With my mind made up, I turned over and slept till dawn.

Next morning as I ran towards the cluster of palms on the other side of the Gatrun Dune, my mind a jumble of regrets in time wasted, expense, the possibility of having to procure visas for Egypt with others to be renewed, I saw, drawing up at the base of the dune, two new Series II Land Rovers similar to my own. As we stopped, a man climbed out of the first vehicle. He was wearing bush-jacket, trousers and a khaki topee. The figure was slightly familiar as he came towards me.

'Miss Toy, I believe,' he said, peering at my face wrapped in its *kuffiyah*. 'You are going in the wrong direction.'

It was Colonel le Blanc who, with his party, was making for Fort Lamy. Five minutes later and I would have missed them, passing somewhere out of sight on the dune. In his party was his secretary, Mademoiselle Leila Shammas, who was Turkish; Stanley Johnson, the engineer and driver of the other Land Rover; Habbib Aila, a Sudanese civil servant returning to Khartoum, and Mahommad, the Sudanese cook.

'You would have difficulty going the Kufra way,' said the Colonel when he heard my story, 'you had better come with us.'

'Oh, thanks,' I said. My luck had changed!

The Darcy boys greeted us with very little show of surprise – they were sure by now that I was quite mad, and the Gatrun officials accepted me as part of the landscape, the way such people do if you stay around long enough.

We camped that night just south of the oasis; and the small world of the convoy, that was to make its solitary journey south to the Tibesti, began to fall into place.

The two Land Rovers looked as though they were out for a day's jaunt. Except for two jerry cans on the front bumper-bar and a small winch on the Colonel's vehicle, everything else was stowed inside. The three vehicles were put at right angles, making a cul-de-sac against the cold and wind. A folding table and chairs were set up in this space and, in an incredibly short time, Mahommad had placed a huge blue enamel pot full of strong tea on the table.

'You're not going to cook separate food,' said M'amselle as I pulled out my tucker box.

'I have lots of food,' I said.

'Nonsense,' said the Colonel, 'there is plenty for everyone. If we should run short we'll have some of yours.'

'Cooking for one extra makes absolutely no difference,' said M'amselle.

This was desert travel properly organised and at its most comfortable; it was bliss stopping after a long day and not to have to start building fires and cooking. That evening Mahommad produced a three-course meal and another large pot of tea.

Once the sun goes down desert nights are cold, and by eight o'clock we were preparing for bed. The party set up their camp-beds in the cul-de-sac, putting sheepskins bought in Tripoli on the canvas to keep out the cold. My sleeping-bag, however, is by far the most permanent way of staying warm. We kept a sharp look-out for scorpions as we unrolled things, for they are the colour of the sand in these parts and often crawl into sleeping-bags, shoes or canvas wash-basins.

I lay for some time before I slept, suffering from reaction. The sanity, the good organisation and the comfort around me was such a contrast to the previous days. I would not be doing the first part of the journey alone but now I would have the advantage of being with the Colonel who has travelled in deserts for many years. If I could not get on with these people, then there was no hope for me as a travelling companion!

A tiny alarm clock beside M'amselle's bed let out a tinkling sound that contrasted incongruously with the vast expanse of the desert. I lifted the flap of my sleeping-bag to find we were still in complete darkness.

'*Bonjour*,' came from the Colonel's bed, and odd responses, in different languages, stabbed the surrounding darkness.

'It is still dark,' I said.

'It is five-thirty,' said the Colonel, 'we make an early start.'

The beginning and end of the day, during desert journeys, have an especial quality and they stay clear in the mind for a long time afterwards. There was a concentrated silence as each one tackled his toilet with the least possible contact with the cold outside. Odd remarks came from the silent moving figures; the camp-bed had tipped up; the badly-cured sheepskins had rustled all night and kept one awake; where *was* Mahommad with that tea!

Mahommad, a skinny bird-like little man, had the patient air of a martyr. He was extraordinarily vain, and could be seen at odd times studying himself in a mirror, or rearranging his *kuffiyah* in more becoming folds.

Breaking camp takes longer when travelling in convoy, and the sun had just tipped the horizon when we were ready to move off. The Colonel's Land Rover went first, then Stan's, and I brought up the rear. This was the correct formation for a desert convoy, three sets of tracks, setting a course that would be easily recognisable should the necessity arise to do so.

There are, I soon found out, many things for and against travelling last in a convoy. Some sands and alluvial dust take a long time to settle and it is better to travel far behind, otherwise one moves in a shroud of dust. However, in hilly country this is not always possible as one may lose sight of the cars ahead. Sometimes, on coming to a flat stretch of good country, the leading vehicle puts on a spurt and it is necessary to double speed to keep up. The advantage for me in coming last lay in being able to stop at times without holding up the rest of the convoy.

We made another attempt to find the well at Refuse Sarazac, without success, and set off towards the Jebel Damose. The vehicles ahead looked like little tugs in a choppy sea as they dipped, reared and disappeared in the chaotic terrain. We passed the point where I had camped and finally ran on to hard ground near the jebel; and now a few T.A.T. tracks could just be seen.

Heading south, a line of flat hills, grey and pink, appeared to the south-west. In the distance they seemed to hang from the sky and only, as we drew nearer, settled down on the horizon. Apart from the hills, there was nothing in the landscape until blackened oil-drums began to appear ahead. They marked the general direction of the route, and for long stretches it was possible to drive from one to the other. At other times they disappeared completely, having been covered by sand, and then the Colonel *felt* his way across the landscape, keeping a general direction as much as the soft sand and terrain would allow, until finally another oil-drum appeared. His way of picking a course, despite elaborate detours, of keeping a picture of the whole landscape and general direction in his mind, had the sureness that comes from long desert experience.

The flat jebel slid slowly past us to the right and we climbed a series of sandy hillocks where a jumble of sand-dunes, overlaid with large black rocks, made the going doubly difficult. Old tracks splayed out in a chaotic manner as each type of vehicle had picked the ground best suited to it. Low depressions ran in every direction and these disjointed hills were dreary and ominous. Whilst finding firm ground we were, at times, facing every corner of the earth. Occasionally there were large holes filled with stones and surrounded by old tins and ashes that told of days of sticking by lorries, years ago.

We stopped at noon and ate beef sandwiches and oranges. By now we had removed our heavy coats and sweaters, and it was too hot to stop for long unless we constructed an awning. While we moved the heat was just bearable and it was not necessary to drink much, but if we were to break down, it would mean consuming more than double the amount of water.

An occasional plaque on a pole, set on high ground, appeared. I judged they were originally about ten kilometres apart but some had fallen so that distances were irregular. The discs gleamed an odd opaque-white on the horizon ahead; these, and the tiny black specks which became oil-drums, were of exaggerated interest to us in the wide expanse, for they formed a lifeline across the desert.

We drivers had to concentrate completely, judging the sand, swerving to miss the large boulders and, in this way, we passed from one kind of terrain to another, almost without noticing. Now we were on a high bluff of flat red rocks that were interspersed with deep pockets of sand and rows of jagged rocks that stood up like giant teeth. It could have been a line of coastal rocks where water filled the pools instead of sand, and, who knows, perhaps the sea did seep up over the bluff at one time? In the desert, time has a different value; there was life in these parts thousands of years ago and there may be life once more as a result of the discovery of oil, for the water that lies deep below can be brought to the surface again. We crawled cautiously across the dangerous surface at about eight miles an hour till, towards the end of the flat rocks, we saw a board that had been erected on two posts, marked 'Mouride'.

We stopped in confusion. We were now seventy-seven miles from Refuse Sarazac and the Michelin map marked a place called Mourisidie at 127 miles from the Refuse which should have been 50 miles further on. The French P.W.D. map also marked it at that mileage, but called it – as here – Mouride. Finally, there was reputed to be another Nissen hut at this spot. Had we taken a short cut? Were there two sets of tracks following oil-drums; if so, were the second tracks taking us right out of our way? If not, then where was the Nissen hut? We looked round the empty landscape confused.

Nothing showed that we were on the right track except that our course was roughly south-south-east; but as it was the only track we had seen, we decided to stay on it.

A sandy escarpment led us away from the rocky ledge and soon we were confronted with a great gorge of parched, grey rock. If we had thought the country we had passed through was desolate, it was nothing compared with this. We were surrounded by grey rock and nothing else existed as far as the eye could see, not even a grain of sand. It was the ghost of what the country had been millions of years ago when water rushed down the gorge, cutting deeper into the rock that was now cracked and flaked with the ravages of wind and sun. We bumped over the rocks, following the base of the gorge, although no track could be seen, driving deeper and deeper into the canyon of shattered rock, where not even an echo came back from the parched stone. This was Dante's Inferno; it had the bleak, death-like quality of Gustave Doré's drawings which I had looked at with morbid fascination as a child.

Finally, ahead lay a wall, a jumble of hills and cliff sides but, as we drew quite near, sand showed for the first time beneath the rocks and, rising out of the gorge, old, deep cracks were faintly visible. We took the steep rise at a mad pace, risking crashing the cars on large boulders and finally made the top. Around us was a confusion of high rocks and uneven ground but we stopped, pleased to be out of the bleak valley and tired after the long day.

'It will be very cold tonight,' said the Colonel as we were settling the vehicles to make a shelter from the wind.

There were no flies or birds, not even a scorpion in this world of grey rock, and our voices fell away into the evening air, unchallenged. The wind was rising, and with it came intense cold. Mahommad had trouble with his fire, so we made a windbreak of camp-beds and boxes. Finally, the blue teapot was set upon the table. It was the moment all of us had been thinking about many times during the day.

We drivers sat relaxing for the first time. We had encountered all kinds of rough country. Every inch of ground had needed our constant attention; one slip and a boulder might crash into the sump; or inattention for a second could find us floundering in soft sand and it would have taken hours to unstick the Land Rovers. But there is something exhilarating about driving in this manner, for every bit of the car, and oneself, is used in the battle to cover the ground ahead. There is a unison between the car and the driver as between a man and his horse, and I have accomplished things with my Land Rover at such times that in the ordinary way would seem impossible with any vehicle. It is exciting to realise the full capacity of the vehicle and to tackle the rough country rather than to glide along a smooth, sealed road.

M'amselle, though younger than myself, mothered me as she did the rest of the party. Although she was Turkish, I always thought of her as French. The convoy became her home and she had organised and stocked it so well that, despite the neat appearance of the two vehicles, every necessity and comfort came out of one or the other of them. When she took over in the evening, her personality expanded as she assumed complete control. We all ran at her bidding for, though decidedly feminine, she would stand no nonsense. But her sense of well-being became complete when she finally presided over the dinner-table and lavishly administered to us all.

'You don't eat enough,' she would say, putting huge portions on my plate, adding, if I dared to leave any, 'Don't you like it? Isn't it cooked well?' Despite her enthusiasm and concern that everything should be all right, hers had been a long day; for the passenger on such journeys has to anticipate the bumps, the sudden halts and the swerves. There is no steering-wheel to wedge them in and it is just as tiring as it is for the driver.

The stars excelled themselves that night as though to compensate for the grey desolation of the earth. They shone with fierce brilliance in the cold, clear air, and, not long after dinner, the camp was quiet with everyone rolled either in sleeping-bag or blankets. It was difficult to believe that the torrid day could turn into the icy cold night and, had there been insects or animals, they would have found their way into the warmth of our enclosure. But nothing stirred; we were the only living things for hundreds of miles.

3

The Remaining Wilderness: The Sahara

The Sahara: *Grand Sphinx qui nous attire là-bas.*

Isabelle Eberhardt

Had the tiny tinkling of a small alarm clock disturbed the hush before dawn in these regions before?

'Ugh! I was so cold I couldn't sleep,' said the Colonel.

'*Mon Dieu!*' came from M'amselle's bed. 'You do not commence the day with such a remark. You say, "*Bonjour*". You greet your companions.'

Silence. Then, from the Colonel's bed, '*Bonjour, mes amis.*'

'*Bonjour, Colonel,*' I said.

'*Bonjour*, Bar-bara. Did you sleep well?' M'amselle asked.

'Yes,' I said, 'but it was cold.'

'Yes. You too, Colonel, you were cold?' she asked.

'Yes.' And now, at liberty to expound his grievances, he did so.

As we set off, glad to have the protection of the vehicles, we climbed to ground which fell away in a series of spreading valleys, the sides of which looked deceptively firm but were, in fact, *fech-fech*. This is the most dangerous type of desert ground, for the hard crust on top is made of flat, clay-like stones and myriads of smaller ones. Sometimes the crust holds if one is going fast; but if the crust breaks through, the car flounders in bottomless alluvial dust. There is no firm base at all and the car sinks deeper and deeper. Sand-channels, canvas and everything is placed under the wheels to give a firm grip. Because *fech-fech* stretches over a very large expanse, it is often difficult for another vehicle to come near enough to winch it out.

Suddenly, out of the heat haze ahead, we saw in the centre of a wide and empty plain a Nissen hut and tower similar to Refuse Sarazac. Such a scene is planted indelibly on one's mind; this small man-made hut in the most solitary of positions was like a hand held out from the rest of the peopled world. Now, also, the mystery of Mouride was cleared up. Both maps had marked it here; whereas *Gara* Mouride, which means small hillock, was the post we had passed fifty miles back.

Above the door of the hut was a sign marked Refuse Baudelaire and, inside, people had scratched messages on the corrugated iron. There were three oil-drums, with water, petrol and diesel oil, which had been left by the French for chance travellers and the military who patrol the border from time to time. The Libyan–Tibesti border is somewhere around here, but, owing to treaties made by different people who have administered Libya, the exact line is not clear.

We took some of the water which was old and dirty and a little of the petrol, before setting off across the wide plain. To our right lay a long line of hills, disappearing to the south. A wind had risen and it was no fun driving through the swirling sand into the sun. Our eyes were bloodshot and smarting from the sand. High dunes lay to our left so we climbed into the rocky hills to the west. But the sand had crept up here as well so now we had to contend with both rock and sand.

Sixty miles from the Refuse we came to a board marked 'Bissen' and the tracks disappeared completely. The T.A.T. must have abandoned this route long before the convoys finished, and those who knew this part of the desert during the war kept well away from the hills for they lead to the treacherous Bilma Sands.

My compass was pointing persistently towards the west but, by the direction given on both maps, we should have been going south. Also, according to my written information the 'great massif of the Tibesti can now be seen standing up to the south'. Tracks can disappear but the Tibesti Mountains must still be there, and all we could now see was an unimpressive line of hills and rocks, white and windswept.

The only way through took us more and more into the rocky hills, and finally we stopped to have a conference. *If* we were on the right track, then the mileages showed that we were thirty miles from two posts that stood fifteen kilometres this side of the Koritzo Pass. The pass led from the desert into the outspan of the Tibesti. If we were too far to the west we could spend hours, even days finding the sandy pass which was reputed to be the only way in and very difficult to find.

'Perhaps we'd better do the thirty miles and then see what happens,' I suggested. It was agreed and we set off. We drove along, each mentally working out mileages and our petrol capacity in case we had to turn back.

Habbib's eyes were badly bloodshot. He looked tired and near to panic, and the Colonel was quieter than I had yet seen him. M'amselle, with the concentration of a dedicated person, wrote down mileages and kept a wary eye on her little brood. Mahommad sat in the back of the Colonel's Land Rover, protected by Allah. Stan, who felt the heat badly, was perspiring in every pore, and I had toothache.

Suddenly, out of the swirling sand, on a ridge ahead two plaques could be seen! We drove excitedly towards them and pulled up. The sign read: '185 kilometres Mourisidie, 15 kilometres Koritzo Pass'. We had made it! (On my return journey one of these plaques had fallen. Other travellers should note this for it may still be down and one plaque is not so easy to see.)

The 'high massif of the Tibesti' was still out of sight when we had covered the fifteen kilometres and come to a huge dune running right across our path, but near by there was another signpost which read simply 'Koritzo Pass'. There was no way into the pass except over this great sand mass and no tracks ran across the dune, but a deep scar with rocks, empty oil-drums and broken iron sand-channels told of a desperate stick long ago. We tested the sand on the dune and found it reasonably firm but took the precaution of letting air out of our tyres.

I watched the Colonel's car climb the hill of sand and then Stan's. As they disappeared over the top I prayed that I should be able to do the same. In cases like this, if the previous vehicles have been successful, it is safer to drive as near the preceding tracks as possible, without actually using the same ones, for the broken sand can become soft. My Land Rover climbed steadily and easily, and I could appreciate the extra power of the new vehicle. On reaching the summit, I ran down to join the others on firm ground beyond.

The mountains of the Tibesti are shaped like a 'V' and the pass leads to the outer western arm of this 'V'. We made our way between the jumble of rocks, sand and high, interlocking hills until the path narrowed towards the actual pass, dynamited in 1942 by General le Clerc to allow his army through. Already he had taken three months coming from Fort Lamy and the worst part of the journey – across the desert to Kufra in Cyrenaica – still lay ahead. It became one of the epic marches in the war's history for it not only was successful, but gave hope to every free-thinking Frenchman in those uncertain days.

A definite track of large stones had been built along the narrow defile and, at the end of the pass, a small, dried acacia tree stood alone. On one of its branches a tiny bird perched, the first living thing we had encountered since leaving Gatrun, and it brought the landscape suddenly to life. There still remained hundreds of miles of difficult country ahead of us but the bird showed that no-man's-land had been crossed. We could still lose our way, but, from now on, there would be other living creatures around us. However, the transformation from desert to green vegetation, that we had been led to expect, was not there. Instead, a wide, shallow valley, almost a plain of rock and sand, lay ahead, and the spectacular Tibesti still eluded us to the left. In that direction, there was merely a low, far line of hills and occasionally the ground broke up as a *wadi* petered out from the distant mountains.

We stopped, still in desert terrain, thirty miles from the pass, and now that we were on the right track, relaxed. The uncertainty and danger of the last few days had held us together, each being dependent on the convoy as a whole. Such journeys make for a fraternity that binds you always; years later you meet in a crowded restaurant and the smell of desert sand is immediately with you and there is an especial recognition in your eyes. But now we had become individuals again, even critical, and indulged in the luxury of losing our tempers. Mahommad, being a Moslem, believed all people of different faith from his own, and especially Christians, were inferior. The best of everything, therefore, went to his fellow Moslem, Habbib, and himself. M'amselle, who fought like a tigress for the comfort of her little brood, now let fly.

'That man!' she said, her eyes flashing, for we were sitting sipping the first cup of tea from the great teapot, 'he washes Habbib's and his own plates and cups in clean water, and *anything* does for ours. These cups taste of last night's soup!'

She was right, but I wanted my tea more than I objected to the taste of soup. She took the cups from us and washed them herself while Mahommad stood by with an air of injured dignity. She knew, as we all did, that no amount of scolding or display of temperament would change the stubborn Moslem's ways. For me the luxury of having a cook at all fully compensated for a few greasy cups and plates. Travelling in convoy gave more space for luxuries, the comfort of chairs and tables, the extra tinned things and, if you could afford it, a cook and a mechanic. It was luxury indeed and they were things a lone traveller does without.

We set off next morning to the south, keeping well away from the sandy *wadis* below Tibesti. The high peak of Tousside, grey with distance, looking like a mountain in a Japanese print, could just be seen far to our left. There were no tracks and very few barrels. An inexperienced person could waste much time and petrol here, for the rocks and sand suddenly deteriorated into soft patches, impossible to cross, and people, who have crossed the main part of the desert, have perished in this stretch.

Just when we were despairing of ever seeing the lush vegetation referred to, a long line of trees appeared ahead, and running right across our path was the Wadi Wour. It was quite dry and filled with soft, deep sand, but along the edges trees and bushes grew abundantly. Flat-topped acacias with clusters of yellow blossoms gave the first shade we had seen for many days, and the straggling red-barked variety grew far out into the sand. The spreading acacias grow right across Africa. I saw them in the Sudan, Eritrea,

Ethiopia and Kenya; they link the countries as a race or tribe can do and they became friendly landmarks. None of them, however, stand out so vividly in my mind as this first green line along the Wadi Wour. Many small birds flew among the branches and there was a flash of white and golden brown as two gazelles sprang away from the bushes and sped across the sand. We stood transfixed by their speed and shining cleanliness; I, for one, was thankful we had no gun.

There were signs of an abandoned encampment; footprints of humans, camels, goats and the tiny imprint of the gazelle. The Tibu who inhabit the mountains come down after the rains and stay until the grass dries, and if we were to follow the *wadi* up into the mountains we would eventually come to the Tibu village of Wour forty miles away where there is a small French military post.

The Tibu are found on many fringes of the Sahara, as far north as Gatrun and east to Kufra, though their main stronghold is the Tibesti from where they get their name, Men of Tu or Men of the Rocks. They are a fusion of Berber and Negro and have been identified with the Garamantes, although Leo Africanus placed them in the heart of the Tibesti in the Bardai Oasis. Although the Tibu are black, their thin clear-cut features are not negroid and their slim, almost emaciated bodies belie their strength and endurance. The Tibesti forms a natural fortress and hide-out and it is not known how many Tibu actually live in the mountains. Similar to the Tuaregs, they have become something of a cult, although one notices that the Tuareg enthusiast speaks of the Tibu as dirty and unintelligent, the scum of the desert; while those who try to fathom the Tibu, regard the Tuareg as an exhibitionist who parades his quaint customs to suit the observer and the tourist. But the main fascination that all desert-dwellers have is their capacity not only to demand little, exist on little, but to do so extremely gracefully; and, above all, to enjoy the moment as it is there.

Reluctantly we left the cool shade and ploughed across the wide soft stretch of sand. After many miles of rough going we sighted a gallery of red and purple rocks that rose in curious high sharp peaks. The map marked them as *Aiguilles de Sissa* (Needle Rocks) and they appeared to be the high summits of mountains buried deep in hundreds of feet of sand. We ran past them on to a plain of black volcanic dust where flood waters and wind had made a series of giant ridges across the ground. The vehicles crashed over the ridges and, as they became larger, we were forced to slow down to walking pace.

Finally, we joined a definite track that veered to the south-east which brought us to a large *wadi* intersection – a kind of giant pocket on the south-west corner of the Tibesti. Another tree-lined *wadi* ran off towards the mountains, and there was an old iron sign with the words 'Enneri Tao' justly faintly discernible.

'*Enneri* Tao?' I enquired.

'From now on, *wadis* are called by that name,' said the Colonel.

The intersection was so large that one could get lost trying to cross its rocky, sandy space. Many routes converged here. One hundred miles up the Enneri Tao to the north-east was the oasis of Bardai; the Zourke, a mountainous *wadi* leading to Zouar, was almost due east across the rocky space; to the west was Bilma – while due south a direct route led to Fort Lamy, by-passing Zouar.

During the rains the intersection becomes a whirlpool and all transport stops. Now, we plunged into the soft sand and set off across the expanse to find the rocky entrance to the Zourke.

By our reckoning it was only thirty miles to Zouar, but we had been warned that the entrance was difficult to find and we might take the whole afternoon locating it. The heat increased as we neared a line of jagged red rocks that appeared out of the haze ahead, and somewhere amongst them was the entrance. Trees and bushes became thicker and finally, when we were right under the cliffs, a track suddenly appeared that ran along their base; it cut through dense foliage and was barely wide enough to take one vehicle. Flood waters had formed a series of sharp little *wadis* filled with red dust which, the vehicles having disturbed, hung in the hot, still air and covered the bushes with a red film.

Suddenly, amongst the undergrowth, we saw a Tibu woman. She stood motionless in the dusty haze, draped in black and watching us as we passed. It was the first human being we had seen for many days and our small domain of six people was finally broken. The entire population of the world seemed embodied in that one still person.

By some miracle none of us bashed a sump on the large boulders or stuck in the soft sand as we leap-frogged over one ridge after the other; but for me, eating the dust at the rear, the journey seemed interminable.

Near the track, but very easy to miss in the chaotic terrain, there is a deep rock-pool of water which I visited on my return journey. It is one of many that can be found in the crevices of the hills, though the Tibu guard them jealously. As the Zourke widened we began to climb, for a high fertile plateau has been formed by the silt brought down from the mountains by the rains. The covering of dried grass had turned to golden, and the trees, now free from dust in the open space, stood out startlingly against a canopy of red and gold cliffs.

We stopped near a small Tibu girl who was walking with a bowl on her head. She watched us warily and cautiously lowered to the sand the other things she was carrying in her hands. Her black dress, embroidered with beads of many colours, was faded so that it merged with the sand and the trees. The men asked her the way, but she was apprehensive of them. She smiled, however, when we women spoke to her and nodded when we pointed ahead and said 'Zouar'.

The red cliffs receded more and more, and by the time we reached Zouar we were on a wide plateau with the red cliffs far in the distance each side. A picturesque mud-washed fort with its tricolour flying, had a line of Dodge Power Wagons parked along one side and near by a group of colonnaded buildings housed the men's mess and living-quarters of the French military. South of the fort was a walled garden shaded by acacia and tamarisk trees; it was the kitchen garden belonging to the lieutenant-in-charge. A shallow *enneri* filled with the blue-flowered plant that grows around the fringes of most deserts served to cut off the native quarter. The inhabitants here were mainly Tibu and Gorane ladies of easy virtue and a few Fezzanese merchants.

As we drew up in front of the Frenchmen's mess, they came quickly out to greet us, enthusiastically shaking our hands. They wore shorts and *tiraul* which is little more than a piece of material with a hole for the head and tags under the arms to keep it in place.

The lieutenant-in-charge had recently been transferred from Largeau, the military headquarters of the Tibesti and our next stop, south.

'You will have to wait until I radio to Largeau for permission to lend you petrol,' he said.

'How long will that take?' asked the Colonel.

The lieutenant shrugged. 'Maybe one day, two days. Who knows? I shall have the guest house cleaned up a little. Come to my house until it is ready.'

We followed him across the sand to the last bungalow. On the colonnaded verandah was a large refrigerator from which he extracted tins of ice-cold beer. It was the best beer I have ever tasted.

4

The Living Desert: The Tibesti Mountains

The Great End of life is not knowledge but action.

T. H. Huxley

The Tibesti Mountains are becoming fashionable; archaeologists and geologists arrive to dig and look; naturalists – some highly professional, others just using the tag to get around – are followed by journalists of all kinds. The French take this invasion with extreme good-humour despite the fact that the Tibesti is a military zone. Once Paris, Dakar and Algiers have given permission, the French on the spot, with their traditional open hospitality, entertain these wandering specialists magnificently. People write chattily about the Ouingea Lakes, the volcanic mountains and their hot springs, to say nothing of the squadrons of baboons that invade the villages from time to time, and have, it is rumoured, carried off the women-folk.

The guest house lay between the men's mess and the lieutenant's quarters. M'amselle and I had the bedroom with a shower alcove, and the men slept on the verandah. It was very hot. We were given a prisoner from the fort to look after us; he was a massive, coal-black man who came from south of Fort Lamy and he cheerfully rolled a large oil-drum of water up from the well and heated it so that we could have hot baths. He arrived every morning at dawn but, like Cinderella, disappeared each evening when the bugle blew.

'Yes, he's a good man,' said the lieutenant, 'my best, in fact. He's in for murder. They are always the most reliable servants. Petty thieves give the most trouble.'

A couple of men attached to the French Sahara Camel Corps, who had been patrolling the border north of the Koritzo Pass, were spending a few days' leave in the mess. A fair young man whose hair, skin and freckles were as golden as the surrounding sand, chose to speak German with me.

'You find the life lonely?' I asked, as he described his months of wandering on a camel.

'No, it's peaceful. Two or three days here is enough for me. It's too crowded. I'll be glad to get back to the desert again.'

'But you don't see anyone except your own men?'

'Yes, of course. We sometimes run across a camel caravan. There is always something going on in the desert.'

A group of small boys watched with interest everything that went on round the guest house, and with them was a little girl named Awah. She mothered and protected a younger brother who was fairer than the other children and could have had some European blood; he was timid and often near to tears which is most unusual in native children. Awah was the ringleader and the only girl in the group. Each morning they arrived and stood near the Land Rover, too polite to say what they had come for, until one, suddenly bold, murmured '*Bon bon*'. There was a hush, half in expectancy, half with shock at the audacity, for they had not yet been spoiled by contact with westerners. Then my large tin of boiled sweets was brought from the Land Rover and they all held out their hands. The smartest, having quickly concealed their sweets, held out their hands for more. The excitement increased to a scramble and Awah, knowing that everybody had their share – and enough is as good as enough – called a halt. A tiny hand was held up, first in restraint and then with a gesture of benediction towards me.

They would sit on the sand watching as I cleaned the engine or sorted things out, occasionally picking up a piece of string, an old box, or a piece of paper and asking if it was to be thrown away. If I confirmed that they could keep the article, a look of pleasure would cross the small brown face, though they never took anything without asking.

Sometimes I would go into the village, and there was a rush to climb into the car. Awah was always allowed in first and, if there was room, others could follow. When her brother was missing she pleaded with me to wait for him, while the others piled in the back, sitting on boxes and spare tyres. The seat was undeniably Awah's as I had asserted and she sat in possession as we bumped over the rocky *enneri* towards the village, throwing me an occasional look of intimacy or amused tolerance as our male cargo kept up a ceaseless chatter behind.

Amongst my possessions was a small china cup decorated with red roses, and each morning when the water was delivered outside the guest house, the children clamoured to be allowed to drink out of the beautiful cup. The morning we were leaving I called Awah over and gave it to her. She took it and then looked sharply up at me.

'*Vous départez?*' she asked.

'*Oui.*'

'*Maintenant?*'

I nodded.

She held the cup closer and her small body shook as she tried to control her feelings.

'I will come with you,' she said, almost inaudibly, and held her breath.

I shook my head, although it would have been such fun to have her with me! But I shook my head again, and she saw the regret in my eyes. Giving a slight, quick sigh, as though I had put everything into words, she looked from me to the convoy; and in the glance was all the patience and acceptance of the Tibu womenfolk whose life has always been, from force of circumstance, one of self-sufficiency. She gave me a last intimate smile and stepped back, away from the bustle and clatter of departure, still clutching the china cup.

The track out of Zouar took us into the hills to the south where we mounted a giant staircase of rocks. The vehicles lurched and skidded from one boulder to the next, and on one side a precipice drop fell away into a deep ravine. I climbed precariously over the boulders and dared not look into the ravine below; I was petrified. When, finally, the ground levelled out, we ran across the high plateau of Daski, a dim landscape of black alluvial dust and small black stones. It was a macabre landscape of stunted acacia trees, murky with black dust, and dreary after the purple and gold splendour of the Tibesti proper.

The French insist that all vehicles go in convoy and take a guide to Largeau and on to Koro Toro 240 miles beyond. Our guide was a Gorane. This tribe and the Tibu are half-brothers and live in the lowlands south of the Tibesti. He sat behind the Colonel, his face swathed Tibu-fashion, and led us into all the worst terrain, expecting our vehicles to put up the same performance as a camel. He had presented himself at Zouar with nothing but a walking-stick, and the lieutenant had sent him back for a *djerba* of water. This comprised his entire luggage and, if we did not give him food on the way, he would go without, even though we were not expected to do so.

Thirty miles from Zouar we passed the deserted fort of Sherda which had been built by the French during their advance into the Tibesti. The guide took us far to the west for he wanted to visit his family who were camped beneath a cluster of acacia trees. Their huts were made of straw-matting placed over a frame of sticks and curved to form a dome. When the family moves on in search of better grazing for the camels and goats, the mats are rolled up and taken along but the frames remain and they become a familiar sight as the dry season advances.

The guide disappeared into one of the huts, and several children came running to the vehicles. The smaller boys were naked except for a few bangles, but the girls wore brightly-coloured aprons of leather, studded with beads and shells. Flies clung tenaciously to the rims of their eyes. When the guide reappeared he was concealing some money in the folds of his wrap. It was to buy provisions, slippers and cloth in Largeau, some of which he would resell on his return to Zouar. His wife followed, talking all the time and, although he nodded, he gave a sigh of relief as he climbed into the Land Rover and slammed the door.

From Zouar to Largeau we were skirting the Tibesti massif, coming round to the south and into the province of Bornu. There are two routes or directions to be taken, the eastern one, used mostly by camel caravans because there are wells *en route*, and the other one further west which has no wells although the sand is not quite so soft. We were on the latter.

Many of the dry riverbeds presented a formidable sight, for lorries had made great grooves which the Land Rovers, with their narrower wheel-base, could not straddle. The choice was to drive with one side in the groove and the other up on the mound at an angle of forty-five degrees, or risk a completely untouched stretch of sand and hope that the extra speed and the lightness of the vehicle would get it through. Crossing one of these, I stuck badly trying to climb the steep sandy bank on the other side, and had to be ignominiously winched out. The operation took no more than ten minutes but, had I been on my own, it would have taken as many hours.

The wind had risen and the guide climbed out of the car several times to look around. He had led us into stretches of vivid white sand that was as hard as rock and deeply ridged where we were forced to skim quickly across as on a corrugated road. Suddenly the car would crash into a deep unseen ravine and all loose equipment landed on one's head. After a couple of these bad crashes we stopped for the night and climbed out dispiritedly, struggling against the stinging wind. The guide added to our general irritation, for it had been absolutely unnecessary to take us over the ridged plain.

'Have you a cold, Bar-bara?' asked M'amselle, as I blew my nose.

I shook my head. 'It's this blasted wind, it's . . .' I shrugged.

She, however, was more articulate, for Mahommad had mislaid the tin-opener. '*Why* am I here?' she asked, throwing up her expressive little hands as she looked round the vast windswept desert. 'I could be at home, comfortable in my apartment; my own dear *domestique*; but no! I must look to this!' The gesture of scorn towards Mahommad was worthy of Bernhardt and would have quelled a less conceited man than he.

The Colonel let the small irritations of the camp pass over his head; from the moment the vehicles were set in place for the night, he passed the whole thing over to M'amselle. All he asked was that, as soon as possible, the large blue enamel teapot would be put, filled, on the table. And, despite rising tempers and rising winds, this always seemed to happen.

*

Next morning I loitered behind the others; it was hot and the wind was still blowing. This part of the journey was an anti-climax, we had all the discomfort but none of the fun for, being forced to take a guide, we had to follow him no matter how bad he might be.

Suddenly, I realised I had been loitering too long and that the other vehicles were out of sight ahead. I put on a spurt to catch up with them and rushed across the uneven ground. The wind, coming in sudden gusts, completely obliterated the ground ahead and it was in one of these gusts that I dived into a steep sharp ravine, crashing on to a branch of a tree that had helped some vehicle out of a bad stick. The branch caught in the front axle and wedged its other end against the back near-side wheel. As I revved the engine to climb out of the ravine, the full force sent the tree trunk right through the tyre so that when I landed on the top it was sticking out both sides. It was more than a puncture, it was a complete wreckage of the tyre.

The other vehicles had entirely disappeared. They might stop soon to check that I was still with them, or they *could* drive on for many miles; in which case, in this wind, they would have difficulty in retracing their own tracks. Also, now that I had to stop and change my wheel, I might have difficulty in finding *their* tracks. How simple it is to get lost if one dares to day-dream and so turn an orderly convoy into a story of tragedy! As the navigating was in the hands of those in the front vehicle I had only a rough idea of our general direction. I could set off, thinking I was on the right track, and they, retracing their steps, would have little idea where I had turned off. It is better, if in any doubt at all, just to stop and wait.

The heat blazed and pounded around me and the wind was so strong that the Land Rover shuddered on the jack. The swirling sand stung my eyes and dried my lips as I worked. The vehicle rose slowly on the jack and the changing of the wheel, usually a simple operation, was aggravated by the heat and the wind. Getting the damaged wheel back on to the bonnet is always very difficult for it is heavy and ungainly for a person who is not much more than five feet tall. It slipped from my grasp a couple of times and my language was far from Christian.

'What a route to take to get to Ethiopia!' I was muttering angrily to myself as, at last, I was standing on the bumper-bar and had edged the wheel on to the bonnet. At this moment, the other two Land Rovers appeared, pulling up with a rush, one each side of me. The occupants looked rather strained, they had driven many miles before realising I was not with the convoy and it had not been easy to follow their own tracks back again.

'Are you all right?' asked the Colonel.

'Just finished,' I said.

'We thought you might have followed some other tracks.'

I nodded. 'I am sorry to have broken our record,' for it was the first mishap of the whole journey.

Just before midday we ran alongside the haunted oasis of Galaka where no one lives. The people of Largeau still tend the gardens and water their stock in the oasis by daylight, but they leave at sunset and at night the oasis is completely deserted. Galaka was the scene of a fierce and final battle in 1914, in which the French defeated the natives, many of its inhabitants were killed and those remaining moved to Faya near by, which was renamed Largeau after the French colonel who defeated them. Today, they will tell you that it is their dead companions who haunt the oasis, and camping near at hand, as I did on my return, I found the desert night made eerie by the howling of wild dogs.

Finally we passed the oasis and out of the swirling grey sand ahead the wireless masts and dingy sheds told us that we had come to the airstrip of Largeau. There was a bleakness about the site that the ugliest of deserts does not have and it personified the westerners' vain attempt to come to terms with a land that the desert nomads have called their home for thousands of years. The track from the airstrip became a long, straight road lined with incredibly tall, swaying palms that led directly into the main square of the oasis.

Largeau is reputed to have 330 windy days a year and a film of sand lay over everything. At the far end of the square was a market where women in black sat under the palms. Each had improvised some sort of shade with matting or umbrellas that came just above their heads as they sat cross-legged behind piles of peppers, eggs, onions, tomatoes and several types of millet-like grain. They watched us, their expressions inscrutable, except for a slight touch of arrogance. The beautiful, finely drawn features were framed by hair braided into dozens of tiny plaits, and the silver rings they wore in their noses suited their aquiline features.

Beyond the women, in an enclosed part of the market, there were bundles of sticks, crudely-cured pelts and charcoal. Many of the pitches were deserted for it was mid-afternoon and their owners slept under the colonnades that surrounded the square. Opening on to these colonnades were tiny dark shops where the shopkeepers, mostly Arabs and Fezzanese, sold anything from beer to hula-hoops. The activity of the market, even in early afternoon siesta-time, looked frenzied to our unaccustomed eyes.

We were too early to present ourselves to the authorities and sat beneath the colonnades in a café owned by an old Frenchman who had spent twenty-seven years in this hot windy outpost. He was a great mountain of a man with kind, wise eyes and, if the wind and dust had ever stirred emotions of irritation or hate, those days had long passed. He sat surveying the scene, pleased to have new faces around him and talking slowly as such people do.

A crowd of women and children gathered round us. The women had eggs and chickens to sell, and M'amselle began the absorbing business of bargaining. She had the concentration and bargaining power they liked, and knowing the exact value of things she would insist on a fair price. Occasionally she broke off to expound to me.

'Do you hear, Bar-bar-a? *200* francs for that old chicken. Phsst! What do they think . . .?'

But before I could reply she was back in the absorbing game again. Finally the transaction was completed, and friends, it seemed, had been made for life.

The Commander-in-Chief, Colonel Chapelle, was away in the desert. We were disappointed but not surprised, for this amazing person has spent most of his career in the desert, refusing many higher appointments because they would mean leaving it. He is a great authority on the Tibu tribe and has recently published a book about them. A young captain inspected our passports.

'Is there a guest house here?' the Colonel asked.

'The guest house,' said the captain, 'is for military personnel and guest of the military.'

'Then, where do we stay?'

'The military is no longer responsible for travellers. You must speak to the local administration.'

We were directed to the other side of the room where a young man in civilian clothes sat. He also inspected our passports.

'As there is no accommodation for us, where do we stay?'

'M. Coussa has a small hotel.'

'Where do we pay for the petrol we took at Zouar?'

'M. Coussa will replace the petrol. You must pay him.'

'And we need more petrol.'

'M. Coussa.'

'Where can we find some tinned food.'

'M. Coussa's store is the best.'

'And how do we find this M. Coussa?'

'He is the agent for Air France. You will see the sign in the street the other side of the square.'

We dived into a narrow alleyway, scattering children and chickens and adding a little more chaos to the activity in the swirling sand. Over a door set in a mud wall was an Air France sign. We climbed the high steps leading into a wide courtyard and were welcomed ecstatically by a large black dog. The arch behind us was immediately filled with the interested and expectant faces of several small boys, caught up, as it were, in our wake. There was a concreted platform raised a foot above the level of the ground with rows of up-ended beer bottles sunk in the earth to make an edging. To the left was a smaller piece of concrete with a ping-pong table and, on the far side, a low wall with large blue and white *jardinières*, one each side of an opening, led to M. Coussa's office and cluttered general store. A huge dusty acacia tree shaded most of the court. There was a feeling of resignation in the air; the heat and flies, and the perpetual wind had slowly killed whatever initiative and enthusiasm there had been to make the place attractive.

M. Coussa was a kind, tightly-drawn little man from Egypt. He gave the small community of Largeau all they needed and made them pay for it; which was understandable, considering the distance and difficult country over which everything had to be brought.

A continuous stream of people passed through the archway on their way to the store or to M. Coussa's office; French soldiers and officers, civilians, chic young French wives of the military, and any local people who would brave an attack by Baron the dog. He was a long-haired black hound who had a deliriously happy time as watch-dog. Europeans were allowed to enter – in fact welcomed, as we had been – but a native had no sooner put his foot through the archway than Baron was at him with a series of blood-curdling barks and growls. He could make a split-second decision on his reception of whomever crossed the threshold and the natives added to his pleasure by reacting with a startling display of fear, the whites of their eyes showing as they leapt back in terror.

We penetrated deeper into the oasis to find M. Coussa's hotel. Along the narrow alleyways which were lined with high walls, people were forced into doorways to let us pass, and chickens flew excitedly ahead. The hotel was a native house built, *purdah* fashion, around a court. There were some crude beds and a few tables, but the room, fitted up with a shower, was the only advantage this accommodation had over the peace of the desert camp.

Later, I went in search of an old friend, M. Utz, who had been in charge of the T.A.T. workshop in Sebha years ago and had later been transferrred to Largeau. Everyone in this part of the Sahara knew this kindly, quiet man with his beautiful collection of desert roses. However, he had retired and his place was taken by a young man who would have looked more at home in a boulevard café in Paris. He was business-like and efficient and took my extra tyre away to have it placed on the spare wheel-rim. When I returned for it later, and asked how much I owed, he shook his head.

'Nothing,' he said, 'it is a pleasure.'

A small boy helped me find and mount a camel, and he walked ahead as I made a leisurely inspection of the oasis. He came from the Ana Kazza tribe, the original inhabitants and overlords of this part of the desert who were famous as hunters and fighters. They are tall and very lean but physically much stronger than the Arab. We ambled off towards the outskirts of the oasis. 'Tibu,' said my young companion, nodding rather condescendingly towards some little rounded huts, and later, as we neared a great dune that was creeping towards the oasis, he pointed to a long line of camels coming slowly towards us, 'Arabs,' he said, as though showing a tourist attraction.

An air of dissension hung over Largeau; slowly the administration is moving from military to civil, and already at Largeau the reins were being handed over. It is a difficult situation, for the Tibesti is still a military zone and the army has been administering the area from the beginning of French rule here. The more complicated system of local government must necessarily cause trouble at first and the local authorities have no experience in dealing with visitors in such a remote place. But the military were still very much in evidence, and in the evening two jeep-loads of soldiers roared noisily through the oasis in search of the '*M'amselles Inglese*'.

All night tom-toms kept up a steady beating, for a wedding was in progress not far from the hotel. It was the first beat of Africa, penetrating, insidious. From now on, for months ahead, I heard it wherever I went; it broke into our sleep, and we longed for the quiet of the desert.

The Land Rovers leap-frogged down the ridged avenue of palms out of the oasis. We had another guide to take us to Koro Toro 240 miles away, and ahead of us stretched the dreaded Djourab, a region that is reputed to be the most difficult of the whole journey. Going south it was now possible to see that Largeau lay on the north side of a long rocky valley and we ran into a jumble of sandy, rocky ditches and high soft banks, for the guide favoured the camel track. Finally, exhausted, we ran down on to flat ground that was completely covered by a uniform rash of sharp little hillocks of sand. The convoy wove in and out, while I, bringing up the rear, found it difficult to keep the other vehicles in sight.

We stopped to camp on the edge of the main part of the Djourab, so that we could start across it in the early morning when the sand would be cool and firmer.

The Djourab is not a series of sand-dunes but a vast dried-up lake where the wind blows perpetually. The landscape is decaying and has flat pools of fine sand, alluvium dust and deceptively firm-looking hills that crumble beneath the wheels. We skirted flat depressions that were treacherous *fech-fech*, only to stick badly on the sandy surrounds. In the chaotic disorder of a great lake long since dried up, the ordinary rules of desert travel did not apply, and for this reason we ran into trouble time and again. Each time we stuck, everybody lent a hand. If the Land Rover with the winch could come near enough on firm ground, the job was soon over; otherwise, we all got down and scooped the sand from the wheels before the Colonel's heavy iron sand-channels were put into position. It was so hot that the perspiration dried in the pores and only our colossal thirst made us realise how dehydrated we had become. The relentless wind made our lips crack and, after a particularly bad stick, I stopped to cover mine with lipstick, more for comfort than vanity.

'My! You're getting a little lovelier every day,' said Stan, mistaking my motive, 'you must be using "fabulous Camay"!'

'Necessary – "in a man's world",' I said, spitting out another mouthful of sand. M'amselle, listening, but not being a T.V. fan, eyed us dubiously.

Finally, the ground improved, for all such trials must come to an end, and we picked up a track running over a series of low, firm sand-hills of the 'Beau Geste' fort of Koro Toro standing in a sea of sand. Behind the high white walls a tricolour flew from a tower and the only entrance was a huge green door. This romantic-looking fort was a big milestone, for the rest of Africa, completely new to me, lay ahead and we had finally left the real Sahara behind us.

I stood looking back across the sand, the way we had come. I had failed to cross the desert alone, and to try and return that way would be doubly difficult, for the French generally refuse to allow one vehicle to proceed alone. The sand north, with the single track curving off towards the horizon, looked innocent enough, even inviting, but I had a sense of failure that was to dog me for the rest of the journey until, in spite of accidents, floods and opposition, I was to stand once again on this spot facing the long trek north.

We passed through the high green doors and up enormous steps to a parapet where a baby cheetah lay shivering from the startling effects of capture and a bath. The French lieutenant was alone except for a small contingent of native troops. He had an intense face with quick, darting eyes and smiled enthusiastically as he led us into the living-quarters. The walls were three feet thick and we entered a small vault-like room where a large table and refrigerator took up most of the space. He offered us everything in his refrigerator which held beer, light wine and lemon juice, but ice-cold water was the only luxury we needed.

'It is like living in a great basin of sand,' I said to the lieutenant. 'There is absolutely nothing *but* sand.'

He smiled. 'M'amselle must return after the rains. First we are surrounded by water and then it becomes a magic carpet of wild flowers.'

Forty miles from here, still deeper in the desert, is an elephants' burial ground, used eons ago when this part of the desert was fertile and when these animals, that can now only be found further south, roamed the countryside.

We parted with the guide, paying him the set fee which was the equivalent of six shillings a day and set off in the fierce mid-day sun for Fort Lamy 460 miles away. From now on, we were running along the Bahr-el-Ghazel which extends from Lake Tchad to the lower section of the Djourab. It is sometimes confused with an area in the Sudan of the same name. Here in the north, as it spreads towards the Djourab, it is wide and almost a plain. For the first 170 miles we ran through a Game Reserve where animals living on the fringe of the desert are protected. Clusters of bushes appeared more and more frequently until the whole landscape was covered with the dusty green. With the foliage came the animals, first the gazelle, the ariel and oryx; then the ostrich, many more females than males, the crested crane, the greater buzzard, the odd hyena – the dreariest of animals – little clusters of sand-grouse and large flocks of brightly-plumed and irridescent guinea-fowl. A grey squirrel-like creature crossed my path. He was the first of hundreds I was to see all the way to Ethiopia and became as familiar as the dung-beetle is in the Middle East or Australia.

The trees and the grass were drying fast and the leisurely migration of family, cattle and goats going south towards Lake Tchad had begun. These moving communities, uncluttered by many personal possessions, had the same air of freedom as the wild animals around them.

We were still in the Game Reserve when we stopped for the night and the surrounding bushes gave us a sense of claustrophobia after the openness of the desert. The ground was flat like a riverbed and people came out of the undergrowth to tell us where the wells were, for water was still of primary importance. A lorry, the first we had seen, stopped and the driver informed us that the tracks were well defined and '*facile*' all the way to Fort Lamy.

The valley narrowed and became deeper as we went further south; camels were giving place to cattle and goats, and men rode bullocks as they tended their flocks. Now, as well as the Tibu and Gorane there were signs of other races; the fairer-skinned northern invaders, the Negro, the tall Nuba from the east, the Fulani and Haussa from the west. Odd characteristics from all of them could be seen in the faces that pressed towards us each time we stopped.

By the time we had left the Game Reserve and come to the village of Moussoro, where we woke the petrol attendant from his afternoon nap, we were in African civilisation; for although it was not much more than a native village, with a tiny military fort on the hill above, the petrol pump linked us with the rest of the civilised world.

During the rains all transport stops from here to Fort Lamy and, from now on, great stretches of dried and cracked mud lay each side of the track. We had forgotten the bustle of traffic and humanity, and when we stopped near the market in the little town of Massakori, we stood bemused. Jeeps buzzed around us, they were driven by Frenchmen whose wives managed to look incredibly chic in safari clothes, despite the heat and wind. Even the nuns, in white habit and topee, mounted on scooters, looked highly decorative. Lorries, with the usual overflow of human cargo, stood near the market square, and hundreds of voices mingled with the barking of dogs and braying of donkeys.

'What a lot of people,' said Stan, wide-eyed, 'and the *noise*!'

We began to adjust ourselves as the traffic increased and, finally, the track led us through an opening in a high barbed-wire fence to Fort Lamy's airport; from here a sealed road took us to the heart of the capital.

5

Heart of Africa: Republic of Central Africa

A bee slumbers
Amongst the briars of my heart.

André Gide

Fort Lamy is the Piccadilly Circus of Central Africa. Many routes converge here; from Nigeria in the west, the Sudan in the east and several routes from the south. The main trans-Saharian route passes through the city, and its airport is used by many trans-African flights. Its history, as a staging place, goes back for centuries though the modern European section of the town is all that most travellers see. In this part of the town all buildings must be made of stone or concrete and this makes the division between the French and the older quarter very pronounced. The French have laid out wide streets with roundabouts; and long, white colonnaded buildings have been erected in the main shopping streets. There are petrol stations, shops, a super-market, modern blocks of flats, and the roads leading away from the main shopping centre are lined with low modern bungalows standing in small gardens. Buildings are going up at a great pace, and a fine bridge, the first to span the Chari here, is just being completed. Despite the buildings, the tree-lined streets and the air of French café society so carefully fostered, the relentless sun and the stinging sandy wind remind one always of the desert beyond.

Old Fort Lamy is centuries away; the mud buildings and its *indigènes* have never tried to keep the sand out, for the desert and the town are one to them. In the crowded noisy streets, the vitality is overwhelming; the heat and the sand has no effect on them.

French Equatorial Africa no longer exists. It consisted of Gabon, the Middle Congo, Ubangi Chari and the Tchad area. The French have given these territories their independence within the Republic of France, and the take-over has been quiet and without incident.

The Republic of Tchad, though of some strategical importance, is too remote, desolate and lacking in enough natural resources to make it a territory worth developing to any great extent. The south territory, Ubangi Chari, now called the Republic of Central Africa, has several forests, coffee plantations, gold and other minerals, but its remoteness also makes any large-scale development impracticable.

The hotel situation in Fort Lamy is acute. There are two small hotels in the main square near the Mairie that are always full and do not encourage enquiries. The older Air Hotel on the way to the airport overlooks the river; it has two low buildings, one for the restaurant and the other with a few bedrooms opening on to a long narrow verandah. Beyond, the muddy Chari River makes its sluggish way towards Lake Tchad fifty miles to the north-west; and fishermen, moving in groups, wade out with great circular fishing-nets which they throw with a pleasant rhythmic motion on to the opal-coloured surface. They catch a large, coarse-fleshed fish called *Capitane* which is both eaten locally and exported south to the Congo.

The Frenchwoman who managed the hotel shook her head; there were no rooms vacant.

'Let us have lunch,' said the Colonel, 'and then we shall see.' He knew the French.

We went into the restaurant, out of the glaring sunlight, and stood in darkness until our eyes became accustomed to the gloom. The shutters were all up and dim table-lamps gave the only light. The place was decorated with red-checked curtains and cloths, and a long high bar made of dark mahogany ran along one side. The food was excellent and very French but much more expensive than it would have been in Paris. The beer worked out at ten shillings a bottle.

Madame had been in Fort Lamy for many years and had weathered the heat and isolation remarkably well. 'We are going to make all the money we can, fast, and then get out. Now there is independence here, things will change quickly,' she said, pocketing our large sheaf of notes. They were ordinary French francs and she was very pleased to have them.

As the Colonel had surmised, a couple of rooms were finally found for us. Stan slept on the verandah, and Habbib and Mahommad lay out under the garabia trees in the garden. It was very hot.

A large organisation known as S.C.K.N., an off-shoot of Unilever, was the dealer for Land Rover cars. They had garages, general stores and were responsible for a great amount of produce-buying. M. Fourestier, the general manager, a lively and busy man, handed us over to the works' manager, M. Pallard, who took the Land Rovers away to have them serviced. Our vehicles had made the desert crossing without any trouble except for three punctures, but they needed an overhaul and the desert sand removed.

'The journey is too easy in vehicles like these,' said M. Pallard to me. 'You have no mishaps to write about.'

'It's a good fault,' I said, 'at least I *am* here to write whatever there is.'

The convoy was going south immediately to Bangui, the capital of the Republic of Central Africa, but I intended staying in Fort Lamy to see something of the town. That morning M. Pallard drove me to the post office in his small Renault. The sun was shimmering on the flat, open streets and the white buildings; ahead of us was a wide roundabout and near it lay a bicycle in the centre of the road at an ungainly angle. There was no one in sight although a flat, round hat lay near the bicycle.

'An accident,' said M. Pallard.

The hat was covered with insects. 'Is it blood on the hat?' I asked.

'Bees! Close the window! Close the window!' M. Pallard yelled as they came swarming through the window into the car. As I struggled with the unfamiliar catch, for the windows open out and up, the bees attacked us. The car made a zigzag course along the deserted street. 'Open the door, to let them out!' he yelled.

When we were past the main swarm, my companion stopped the car and we leapt out, trying to brush the bees away from our faces and hair.

'Come,' said M. Pallard, 'we must go to the hospital and have the stings removed.'

As we drove into the hospital court another car rushed in after us tooting its horn. As it stopped, a young man jumped out and ran round to the other side of the car to help his young wife. She was a beautiful girl, bronzed and wearing a strapless dress of deep browns and reds. She had received the full force of the swarm and there was not one square inch of skin on her face and shoulders that did not have a bee-sting sticking out of it. She looked directly ahead, dazed, unseeing as her husband led her towards the entrance of the hospital. Some of the bees still struggled in her hair and, as she passed, she gave a deep, shattering sigh. We watched them disappear into the building.

'She'll surely die,' said a man standing beside us, 'from shock if nothing else.'

'Come,' said M. Pallard, 'they have more important things to worry about in there than our dozen or so bee-stings.'

The convoy had left during the bee incident. Alone, I found it impossible to erase the picture of the poor girl from my mind. Already my own neck was swelling and the pain was continuing down my back. Fort Lamy had already taken on a nightmare quality and I wanted to get away from it as soon as possible and be with friends. So, paying my hotel bill, I set off in the convoy's wake.

A good road of red earth ran through flood-washed country that was already giving promise of the jungles that lay ahead. This part of Africa becomes a huge swamp in the rainy season and the whole area, stretching for 500 miles south to Fort Achambault, is closed to road-traffic during the rains. The waters are so strong that many of the bridges are removed to prevent their being washed away. The rise and fall of the waters of Lake Tchad near by has puzzled geologists for a long time and many questions still remain unanswered. Although the lake was known to the Ptolemys and is believed to be Lake Kura of the Middle Ages, it was not seen by any European until Clapperton made his journey across the desert in 1833 when he followed a route similar to the one we had taken.

I had been advised to try and reach a rest house 170 miles from Fort Lamy before nightfall as it was wild-animal country and there was nowhere else to stay. The Colonel's convoy, having left some hours before me, would, I thought, be many miles ahead, but towards sunset, as I reached a bridge crossing a deep narrow river, I saw the two Land Rovers pulling up in front of a red bungalow. It was the rest house.

M'amselle was delighted. 'Bar-bara! Stan, he said to me, "Do you see what I see?" and I said to him, "It cannot be!" But it is. Welcome, once again!'

'I decided that if I was going to die from these bee-stings, then I would die with friends!' I said.

'Of course!' and she enveloped me in her expansive grasp. Then, thrusting me from her, she burst into action. 'Come! I shall massage your neck with oil. Mahommad! Where is that lazy – oh! here you are! Where is the big bottle of oil? Quick!' and we all jumped to her bidding.

The rest house had a wide verandah running along both sides and a huge garabia tree with low-hanging seed-pods made extra shade. Wide doors either side of the building opened, to turn the one room into an airy covered way. But it was too hot to sleep indoors and we drew the vehicles up in front of the bungalow, putting our beds in a row.

'We must stay together tonight,' said the Colonel, 'in case there is game about.'

The slight breeze made very little difference to the oppressive air, and M'amselle fanned herself in the bed next to mine.

'I hope we don't get an elephant's foot in the small of the back,' I whispered, peering into the gloom of the jungle.

'Even a snake wouldn't be very welcome,' she whispered back.

It had been a long day and the incident of the bees was very much in our minds. It was not easy for me to forget the horrifying picture of that poor girl. The stings had affected the glands on my neck and it was stiff and painful. With the help of two Vegenin tablets I was almost asleep when suddenly I started. Something had woken me. There it was again! A sharp, decisive sound.

Suddenly, M'amselle sat bolt upright. I rose, more slowly because of my neck.

'What is it?' I asked in a whisper.

'I do not know. Oh!' She gave a suppressed squeak. 'There! Did you not hear?'

'It's coming from under the car at our heads,' and I slid down on to my pillow again and looked under the car. There was the noise again and my companion gave another muffled squeak. In the clear light reflected on the white ground I could see what it was and, stifling a giggle, sat up again.

'What is it?' she asked.

'It's one of the seed-pods being blown about by the breeze!' and we spluttered together.

'What's all that whispering and giggling about?' came from the Colonel's bed. 'Eh?'

'Just a seed-pod,' we explained lamely, sliding down simultaneously on to our beds again and trying, like schoolgirls, to suppress our laughter.

The natives like to settle along the main road and the authorities encourage them in this, so that they can keep an eye on their activities. The jungle is pushed back, and a bare, flat space is covered with huts, some made of mud, others of straw or leaves. There is always a fire and a small shed set on sticks to keep it safe from prowlers and termites. The life of the little settlement goes on before one's eyes; the women pound the millet or durra in high, wooden containers, using rhythmic movements as they swing the pestle up and down. The older men sit around under awnings made from leaves, and the old women hold their grandchildren on their laps. There is a feeling of extreme youth and age, as most of the younger men are away hunting, tending crops, or fishing. Naked children play in groups, and most of the villages have dogs, small, light-brown hounds that look well fed and happy. Fowls take to the air before the vehicles, flying in the most surprising fashion.

Between the villages, the jungle crowded on to the road, and one could have been driving between walls, except where occasionally there were gaps made by elephants who had bulldozed their way through the undergrowth, pushing trees over as they went and leaving behind droppings that looked like great baskets of straw.

We were in the world of black people and already I liked their bland, open faces, for here they had not yet acquired the expressions of greed and hate. The Negro was predominant but there were some of the Fara, tall, black creatures similar to the Nigretian Sudanese. The women covered the lower part of their bodies with loin-cloths or skirts, and their long pendulous breasts were considered a sign of beauty. Further south the Pagan women wore nothing but a bunch of leaves – fore and aft – which were picked each morning, and they looked fresh and enchanting.

Despite the amount of game reputed to be in these parts, we actually saw very little, and even the monkeys kept out of sight. Once, two colobus monkeys leapt from the undergrowth, crossed the road in front of me and disappeared the other side. Their long, black coats billowing as they swung from the bushes, and their alert, white-rimmed faces seemed more amused than frightened. They were beautiful and so free that I felt like an intruder.

Fort Achambault is famous as a rendezvous for big-game hunters and the French give it their own particular brand of glamour.

The small modern Chasse Hotel overlooked the river and served excellent meals on the terrace. Big-game hunters arrived in their large lorries, piled high with expensive equipment. They swopped tales of their massacres, for the surrounding country is a hunter's paradise, with a great variety of antelope, hippopotami, lions, cheetahs, herds of buffalo, and the elephants in the southern region are the biggest in the world.

'It is not more than a few years ago,' said the Colonel, 'that one could sit here and watch the elephants on the banks opposite. Now they have become more cautious.'

Now, in the hot, sultry undergrowth there was reason at last for the various health precautions I had taken before starting the journey. The desert is healthy and the air so dry that any sign of rheumatism lifts from the body like a heavy cloak; there is no malaria, no tsetse fly and very little chance of getting dysentery.

Here, life teemed around us; there were swamps, bad breeding-grounds and all kinds of diseases. I had been taking Novacrine, as it protects against *every* kind of malaria; had been vaccinated against smallpox and injected against yellow fever, typhus and para-typhoid. My first-aid kit had several additions to the usual pack; there were pills for fever, a large bottle of Sulpho-mysatone for amoebic dysentery, a snake-bite outfit, and sleeping pills for the times when a good night's rest would be difficult, but essential. I also had a large supply of Horlicks Malted Milk tablets to be given to natives suffering from sleeplessness or nerves; and prescribed to be taken in hot milk at bedtime. Finally, there was a huge supply of aspirins for general distribution for, although it is still believed that most white people know a lot about medicine, there are the perfectly healthy ones who just like to join the medical queue.

We drove through country cleared of all livestock because of tsetse fly and it was not always easy to tell when we had left the infected areas; this, and the thick jungle, made it difficult to find camping ground. Very few of the small villages had rest houses and to camp on the village market square turned us into a continuous peepshow.

Late in the afternoon we arrived at Batangafo, the seat of local administration. The village clung to the main road for a long time and there was no sign of any Europeans amongst the crowds of cheerful Africans. We found a rest house set near the main market square; it was a dirty hut which had been taken over by a local family and, as we heard rumours of typhus in the area, we beat a hasty retreat. But M'amselle, suddenly tired of the nomad life, wanted a roof over her head and went off with Stan in search of the District Commissioner. We sat in our vehicles on the red-earth road and after ten minutes they returned, triumphant, with permission for us to stay at the Governor's rest house.

'The District Commissioner is very *sympathique*,' M'amselle said as she led the way.

The rest house stood back from the road and was not so grand as one might have expected, though the view over the River Chari below was magnificent. The thatched circular building had a wide verandah, and in the rooms were a few pieces of furniture, including a large four-poster bed with soiled linen on it. But there was a room with a shower which was always a luxury to us women. Below, the river made a wide curve before disappearing into the forest, and, on a crescent of sand, fishermen with long dug-out canoes pottered around with their craft, while women and children, diminutive figures from this distance, washed and splashed in the water.

After our meal, the District Commissioner paid us a visit. He was a well-mannered young African who spoke perfect French and had none of the servility of manner or bravado that is found so often in such people in other countries. The French train natives without giving them a sense of inferiority, for they are teaching them, firstly, to become Frenchmen and this gives their pupils the feeling that they can become equals. They teach them also the French good manners.

Nearing Bangui, the capital of the Republic of Central Africa, we joined a sealed road and were amongst traffic. The houses now were more substantially built and the walls beautifully decorated with traditional designs painted in bright colours; one, more up to date, had a realistic head-on crash between two aeroplanes. Large bushes of poinsettia and flamboyant trees made a bright background to these picturesque dwellings. Africans dressed in shorts and shirts were riding bicycles and some of the women were dressed in European-style cotton frocks while beside them walked others, infinitely more attractive in their native clothes. Nearer the centre we passed the huge shaft of a modern hospital, each room with its own balcony painted a bright colour, and opposite was an African housing estate of blue and white bungalows.

The town has a beautiful setting along the north bank of the Oubangui River, which divides the country from the Belgian Congo, now known as the Independent Republic of the Congo. Bangui is thousands of miles from any coastline and the roads are governed by the dry seasons so that much of the traffic in and out of the city is by air. It is a busy little capital with a mixture of modern shops, super-markets, banks and business houses, run mostly by the French. The native market is right in the centre and there is no sharp division between the communities. Many luxuries are flown into the capital and living is expensive for the Europeans, except for meat and local fruits. The air-conditioned

Rock Hotel overlooks the river, and is always full, despite the high prices; it is surrounded by a beautiful tropical garden and, in the dry season, there is a sandy beach beyond that disappears when the river rises. Adjoining the hotel is the Rock Club with a large swimming-pool and a good restaurant. Some day Bangui will make a first-class tourist centre. It has the ordinary attractions of swimming, dancing, fishing and good French food; and it offers safaris that are not just a photographer's jaunt.

The convoy was finally breaking up here. The Colonel and his party were going due east to the Sudan while I was crossing the river into the Congo and going east to Uganda. They came into my bedroom to say 'good-bye'. It was not yet six o'clock, but the day was already hot. I was going to miss them; they had taken me up in the desert when I needed help so much, and brought me along; they had never made me feel an intruder or that their plans had been upset in any way. They had insisted I eat their food and it was only to make me feel better that they took any of mine. But it was their companionship, their humanity and good common sense that I was so grateful for, and would miss so much. It had come just at the right time and put me back on my feet again. I watched them go with a great sense of loss.

M'amselle put her head back, round the door post. 'Don't forget, Bar-bara, to eat!' she said, and was gone.

6

The Congo: Alone Again

I am involved in all mankind.

John Donne

I came out of the hotel and looked at the solitary Land Rover. This time I was definitely on my own. As a lone traveller I was an oddity and in the spotlight again. Gone was the anonymity of the larger convoy and with it a certain relaxation for, from now on, I must think of everything; be on my guard the whole time. I checked the door-locks and equipment thoroughly, for to lose things now would be disastrous. It would be easier to find accommodation for one person rather than five and I would be helped more individually; but any break-down, hold-up, or trouble would have to be coped with entirely alone. A drive through any jungle road would become just that much more risky, and to stop and camp for the night was not going to be easy. All this had been part of my many lone journeys, but the recent sense of security that I had with the convoy made me now very conscious of the difference. I thought with a pang of regret of my cheerful companions, driving towards the heat of southern Sudan.

I wanted to photograph some of the decorated houses on the outskirts of the city but the local authorities were not happy to have me wandering amongst the tribes as there was a local election coming and tempers were running high. No one, it seemed, went into the bush alone or without a guard. However, Frenchmen may be a political target but a foreign woman would have no such significance, I thought.

The road ran for some while along the river and the surrounding country was surprisingly flat. On the river an African family was punting its way up-stream in a long dug-out canoe; a few bundles, blackened pots and a large bunch of bananas were interspersed with three small boys. They slid past me leisurely, looking immensely happy and secure in a little world of their own. Near by on the bank two trees, similar to those from which the canoe had been made, reached to the vivid blue sky, and the base of their trunks spread like great claws, clutching the ground. The road left the river bank and turned into the jungle. Finally I stopped near a long, low hut that had some bright decorations on its walls. A woman was pounding meal on a flat stone; she wore a sarong and her breasts hung down to her waist. Three boys stood near by and there was a small group of men at the rear of the hut. They were sullen and silent as I approached and raised my camera, asking with a gesture for permission to take photographs. A small boy shook his head and this was the only movement except for the woman who went on pounding.

At this moment, a stone whizzed past barely missing the camera. I stood uncertain not knowing who had thrown the stone and then another larger one struck my leg. It did not hurt but the contact could be a cue for further demonstrations and I quickly indicated that it was the *house*, not the people, that I wished to photograph. But a very good shot caught the side of the camera and pulled me up short and, mustering more nonchalance than I felt, I turned and went back towards the car. No more stones followed; they had achieved their purpose and stood silent, watching me climb into the Land Rover.

On the narrow jungle road a small boy hailed me; he had been catching butterflies and held up a bundle of triangular pieces of paper, each containing a butterfly. I paid some francs and took the packets. Nearer the town was a small Christian Travellers' Church; its altar was a half-circular, thatched building completely open to a cleared piece of ground where the congregation sat. Children played on the levelled ground and they welcomed me enthusiastically, showing the altar with great pride and crowding round to have their photographs taken. On getting back into the Land Rover, I heard a strange rustling sound and realised with horror that the butterflies were still alive. The children were delighted to watch me open each piece of paper one by one and let the brilliant creatures fly away . . .

The route which goes from Algiers to Cape Town diagonally across the continent passes through Fort Lamy and, although it is often no more than a track indicated by oil barrels, it is known by the grand title of Trans-African Highway. It bypasses Bangui and runs east to Bangassau where it crosses the Oubangui River by ferry to the Congo opposite, continuing south. Now, just before the rains, the river was too low for the ferry to cross at Bangassau and I would have to use the ferry from Bangui to Zongo opposite, although it meant entering the Congo in the isolated western area.

For the next seven months, my movements were governed by the rains. The times of the rainy seasons which hold one up so badly are confusing. The dry season is often in the winter in these parts, and the rainy seasons are between April and June, and from early September to early October. The exact *opposite* applies to the corresponding latitude south of the equator, even though the distance between them is comparatively small.

It was nearing the end of March and I had my first taste of the strength of the rains as I left Bangui, for they had started the previous night. The water came down in a steady curtain, falling into the deep foliage and, wherever there was clear ground, making miniature lakes. The street was deserted as I made my way to the river's edge, for even the traffic cops had gone in out of the rain. The three-ton ferry ran when there were vehicles or enough foot-passengers to make it financially practicable, and the charge for the Land Rover was 1,000 Republic francs. As I drove on to the ferry a young man with a bicycle was leaving it but, on seeing me, he turned round and made the journey back again.

The view from the river was magnificent despite the rain. To the east the low rocky rapids sent water rushing past small islands bristling with vivid green foliage, while to the west the river, already widening, made its course through the jungle towards the sea, on a journey that takes some weeks by steamer. The high, narrow Rock Hotel, its balconies painted in various colours, was backed by the near green hills where attractive modern houses could be seen between the trees.

As we neared the Congo side everything appeared greener. The reds and ochre-browns of Tchad and Central Africa had gone, and the undergrowth here was more voluptuous. The stone Customs House of Zongo, standing in a sea of mud, and the couple of low bungalows, dripping and sodden beneath huge banyan trees, were in great contrast to the busy city the other side of the river. A bungalow hotel run by a garrulous Russian woman had the deserted air often found in seasonal hotels, for it was used as head-quarters by big-game hunters.

My fellow passenger with the bicycle left the ferry ahead of me and disappeared into the Customs House to reappear in the uniform of the customs' official. I had been warned there might be trouble about my cameras and large stock of film, but he was not very interested.

'Have you any fire-arms?' he asked.

I shook my head. From an official point of view this was all to the good but it would have been more 'prudent', he suggested, had I been armed. Also, as the route was seldom used, there were no facilities for changing money.

'It would have been more prudent to change your money in Bangui,' said the official.

'Where is the nearest bank?' I asked.

'If you are going east, it is at Buta.'

'That's quite a distance, I think.'

'It is just about 1,000 kilometres.'

'A thousand kilometres!' I could not return to Bangui, for my passport had been stamped there, automatically cancelling my visa. 'Is there no one here who can change money?'

'I can change 2,000 Republic francs for you,' he said, 'but that is all.'

I accepted gratefully. They were worth roughly three pounds seven shillings and, as I had already filled up with petrol, was well equipped with food and could camp out, the money could be kept for extra petrol, if it was necessary.

At first glance, there seemed no outlet from Zongo except by the river, but finally I found a track leading into the undergrowth where high trees met overhead. I turned towards it with a feeling of excitement, I was about to plunge into the heart of the Congo; my lone journey had begun at last!

The track was completely waterlogged in places and the car skidded badly on the clay surface but, being hemmed in on both sides by the jungle, the skidding was confined to the track. Sliding down a watery hill, bumping from one side to the other, I came to rest broadside on at the edge of a wide stretch of water that covered a dip in the road. Beyond, the track ran out of it but it was difficult to judge the depth of the water in between. The rain and general dampness gave a feeling of chill and I was bracing myself against the thought of having to wade ahead and test the depth when the bushes near me stirred and out of them stepped a tall Congolese. He looked at the car and towards the sheet of water ahead. He was wearing a battered old topee and carried a pair of leather shoes under his arm; he wore nothing else at all. As he moved towards me, he raised his hat politely. I smiled and indicated the road ahead. He gave a slight bow, put up a hand of reassurance and went ahead of the vehicle into the water. I watched the dark figure as the water came up to his calves and, when it was just below his knees, he had reached the deepest part for, as he continued, the water receded. He turned when he was on firm ground and beckoned me towards him. I let in the clutch and moved towards the dark figure, finally drawing up beside him.

'Thank you very much,' I said, leaning out of the car.

He looked surprised, unsure.

'*Merci, merci, je suis Anglaise.*'

'Ah!'

It was obvious that he spoke no French and had very little idea of what, or who, the English were but he studied my face, looking for a clue, and as if to fix it in his memory. Then, standing back, he raised his hat again, bowed and disappeared into the jungle as silently and quietly as he had come. Were there many such people in the jungle around me, who had heard the noisy clatter of my vehicle?

The track ran out of the wet, steamy jungle on to clear ground and, with tropical suddenness, the rain stopped and the sun came out. Finally, we ran head on to a better track where a signpost pointed west to Libenge, and I swung sharp left to follow the east-bound track. Now there were cone-shaped huts, and people wearing tiny aprons made of bark called a *negwe*. Most of the men wore hats which they raised to me and bowed, though some moved quickly into the long grass so that they need not bow.

We had passed a few isolated missions in Central Africa but, from now on, they spread all over the country. There are thirty-one different Roman Catholic orders which have several hundred missions and eight denominations of teaching and nursing nuns, as well as Protestant missions from England, the USA and Canada. Under the Belgian regime, missions received their land free and were given legal status which made the administration of their large estates much easier. In many instances they were the first white people to penetrate into the more remote parts of the Congo and to establish schools and hospitals there. They trained the native secular clergy and, in 1953, the Congo had its first native bishop.

The vast majority of the native population received its education at the mission schools and attended their technical and agricultural colleges as well, and in many parts the mission hospitals were the only ones in existence. Many denominations have become very wealthy. The Sudan Interior Mission, which works as far afield as Nigeria and Ethiopia, has become a large business concern owning bookshops that sell many kinds of literature and often have a general store attached. It has been said that the missionaries go in first and the geologists follow; that the natives will embrace any god so long as they are given three meals a day; but, despite scepticism and criticism, no local authority could have opened up the country nor made such an early start on education as the missions and the convents have done. It would have been possible for me to wander through the whole of the country and be sure of a welcome, a bed and meals, at any of the missions, regardless of my religion.

It was getting late when I arrived at the little town of Bosobolo which was set in the jungle with wide tree-lined streets and orderly villas surrounded by well-kept gardens. There was a Catholic mission of the Capuchin Fathers on the outskirts, and a native market near by. Beyond, in the trees, was a group of native huts. But there was no sign of a *gite* or rest house along the main road and I drove up to a bungalow set in a garden of crimson poinsettias. A young Belgian couple, both tanned a golden brown, came to the door.

'The *gite*? It is the house there,' said the man pointing diagonally opposite. 'It is for Government officials, but you can stay.'

Outside the *gite* was a large American limousine, similar to many I had seen tearing over the earth roads, and a stocky man was climbing out of it.

'Surely, you can stay,' he said. 'There are two bedrooms and you may use the lounge.'

He led me into a bare bedroom which had a large bed, a lumpy mattress and a table.

'Not luxurious,' he said with a grin, 'but it's better than the jungle.'

I agreed. He let out a yell which brought an old man and a boy running. He spoke to them in Lingala.

'They'll help you cook anything you have,' he said.

'That's all right, I can do it.'

'Let them – if you want anything else, just say,' and he was gone.

On the back verandah there was a long bench and a large stone oven with an open fire. The men were quiet and withdrawn, and had none of the curiosity or vivacity of the Africans north of the border. But it was, as my companion said, better than the jungle.

We sat drinking beer in the sparsely furnished lounge. My companion seemed taut and edgy.

'It is a long way to go for a bank,' I was saying, '1,000 kilometres.'

He smiled. 'Well, if you *must* come into the country in this unox . . .?'

'Unorthodox?'

He nodded. 'Yes, unorthodox manner, and at such a border. You must remember, not so long ago no European came here and this is a country eighty times as big as Belgium.'

'But I'm safe wandering round?'

'Er – yes. But you must never stop – or argue with anyone who has been drinking. They go mad when they have a drink.'

'What is to happen now that they are becoming independent?'

He shrugged. 'They're not ready, of course, but what can you do? There's no privacy any more – internationally, I mean.'

'Europe was a little surprised that you agreed to independence so quickly.'

'It was those in Europe who agreed – not us.'

'Do you spend much time up here in the north?'

'Yes, I like it. There are some interesting races; the Sudanese and the Nilotics, just a small group of these – fine people. Tall, handsome creatures and really free, mentally, I mean.'

'They're not Negroes, I think?'

'No, but they are in the minority, most of the people are Negro and nearly ten million of them are Bantu. They inhabit two-thirds of the country.'

'I suppose they will take control when the country is free?'

He shrugged, the same hopeless gesture. 'There are *so* many races and tribes, it's a continent not a country.' Then he smiled suddenly. 'Have another beer; it's not bad, local brew,' and he poured another tin. 'We have the largest number of pygmies in the world,' he said. 'You must go and see them in the rain forests, on your route.'

'You like them?'

He laughed outright this time. 'Yes, they are funny little b . . . buggers.'

'"Beggars" is a better word,' I said.

'Oh? It's a pity you can't spend more time around here with the river folk. The Sango tribe can do anything with those *pirogue* of theirs. They seldom leave the river.'

'They speak Lingala?'

He nodded. 'In the bigger communities they learn French; that's like getting a work-card for a job.'

At this moment the lights began to fade.

'Gosh,' I said.

'That's just the warning light. They go out completely in a few minutes. Better finish up your beer,' but as he spoke the lights faded finally and we groped our way to our respective bedrooms.

In the morning, I signed the visitors' book and was charged the equivalent of two shillings for my lodgings.

Now, occasionally, there were cotton fields, trim and orderly and in great contrast to the voluptuous jungle they had reclaimed. Wherever there was a cotton ginnery, a small community had grown up and the inhabitants were better dressed and looked more alert and diligent. They waved cheerfully, the men bowed and the children curtseyed. Just as suddenly, it was jungle again.

I drove into the pretty little town of Banzyville which was the territorial headquarters of the district. The town stands on the left bank of the Oubangui River which becomes little more than a couple of lakes in the dry season. Many Congolese soldiers wandered round and near the river a market was in full swing. The European sector was strictly divided from the native quarter, a segregation that sprang not only from fear but dislike. There was no civilian petrol pump in the town and I was directed to the Military Headquarters that were set high on the hill, overlooking the town. It was a solidly built bungalow and the main office opened on to the wide verandah. Three Belgian officers sat at desks and a number of N.C.O.s stood around. The officer in charge gave me a permit to buy petrol at the military garage and directed an N.C.O. to take me there.

'It's a beautiful little town,' I said, 'may I stay here for a while?'

The officer looked startled. 'Oh no,' he said, 'it is military and there is nowhere, nowhere, for you to stay.'

'I could camp.'

'No,' he said firmly, 'you could not camp!'

I wandered round the market and the N.C.O. trailed behind me. At last, he plucked my arm and smiled.

'*Vous départez?*' he asked imploringly.

'All right, I'll go,' I said and was led away to the military garage.

The landscape changed with exciting suddenness; in a moment I was driving through a wilderness of bamboos that grew to a great height and so thickly that nothing else lived; they leant magnificently over the track, forming a huge arch. Just as suddenly I was in a wide savannah plain of triangular anthills covered with golden grass that rippled in the breeze and set the whole bizarre landscape waving. Then there was a plain called *Kota Koli* (Big Man) that had been an inland sea, where great blocks of granite stood like sentinels in the sparse landscape and suddenly it was jungle again with fast-moving, hemmed-in streams and exuberant waterfalls. Occasionally, and quite incongruously, in the isolation a woman would appear wandering through the undergrowth, her vivid sarong striking a startling note against the green. It was a kaleidoscope of lush, vibrant growth.

They were brave men who first tried to explore this wild country. Everywhere there is either a dangerous river or jungle and between them they produce nearly every hazard imaginable. The mouth of the Congo River was discovered in 1482 by the Portuguese, but 230 years elapsed before anyone was able to penetrate the barrier of the Crystal Mountains, and the Englishman, Tuckey, who finally succeeded, died in the attempt. Just to look into the tangled mass of the jungle makes one marvel at the explorations of Livingstone and the journeys of Stanley who crossed the country from east to west to discover the Congo. Not long after Leopold II of Belgium, in 1878, had sent Stanley to explore the lower regions of the Congo, Belgian officers followed and established posts along the river. After them came the missions, whose journeys were almost as difficult, as they settled amongst people who, until this time, had never seen a white person. In little more than eighty years, they are trying today to make the Congolese do what it has taken much of the rest of the world eons to achieve.

Under the Belgian administration, there were six provinces each with its own Governor and in the provinces there were many races whose loyalties lay first with their own tribal chief should a big dispute arise, so that without overall authority they naturally revert to their old tribal customs.

Information was difficult to obtain; the Belgians were the same here as in their own country; they were not interested in outsiders.

The Frenchman in Africa is expansive and enjoys the task he is set; he hopes to make good Frenchmen of the Africans and he believes that everything he does is for the country's good. The Englishman tries to instil in you some of his enthusiasm or wishful thinking and he is often touchingly dedicated. But the Belgians, though kind and helpful, were just not interested. This was accentuated by their being on the defensive, apprehensive and surprised at their Home Government's decision to give the country independence at this time; had one arrived from the moon the Belgians would merely have said: 'Well, in that case, your vehicles will need a good oil and grease' and left it at that. It was only the Congolese who asked questions and showed any interest.

The road led to the water's edge at Yakoma, which is a town with one of the oldest Capuchin Missions as well as having a ginnery and locals who make enchanting pottery. The river splits into two, the Mbomu continues east forming the border with the Republic of Central Africa, and the Uele runs parallel, but south of it. There was no sign of a ferry, and as I waited several boys came up and indicated that I sound my horn which not only summoned the ferry but the rest of the boys of the village as well. They ate my sweets, were delighted to use the horn and showed me how to manipulate a tiny *pirogue* which was afloat at the water's edge.

Finally, the ferry, which had disentangled itself from the reeds and bushes on the far bank, sidled alongside below us. It was made of six dug-out canoes with planks across to hold them together. Twelve oarsmen greeted me cheerfully, delighted and a little surprised that I managed to drive the Land Rover across the connecting planks from the shore to the ferry. The men sat, one at each end of the canoes, and dipped their flat bat-like paddles into the water. As we moved into mid-stream they began to chant, a lilting rhythmic sound that floated out across the river; it was idyllic and peaceful, but at the same time I realised how dependent one was on these oarsmen in such a country, where roads led to crocodile-infested rivers.

Suddenly, there was a jolt, for we had struck a sand-bank and the ferry was firmly stuck on the sand. The men looked vaguely into the shallow water and some started to paddle again so that the craft became even more deeply embedded. Then the leader, a tall, thin young man with a round European-style hat and a sweater with 'Staner', the name of the local beer, printed in broad letters across the front, ordered everyone but me into the water to push. With a concerted effort of men and boys, and much chattering, we were afloat again. For a moment I was alone and afloat on the raft, but they all made a dash and climbed laughing into the canoes.

There was no charge for the ferry and the entire company shook hands with me; they declined, amused, the offer of money, but the men accepted a cigarette each.

It was quite late when I arrived at Bongo on the north side of the Uele River, for I had lost my way and had to cross three rivers by ferries which were smaller and more precarious than the one at Yakoma. There was an immigration office near the ferry, even though the actual border lies 120 miles north at Bangassau, for a check is kept on all people passing through the Isolated Northern Province.

The European part of the town followed the now familiar pattern of tree-lined streets and a mission not far from the centre. This universal similarity was like a great trade mark stamped all over the country, alien and superimposed. There was an air of desertion about the town, the hotel no longer served meals, and the room, though clean, gave the impression of seldom being used. The man running the hotel was entertaining a native girl in his bungalow at the rear, and I was directed to a café in the main street when I asked for food.

The Texas Bar and Café was a barn-like building with a corrugated iron roof; there were a few tables, neon strip-lighting and a small bar attended by a handsome young man who was the son of a local chieftain. A connecting door led to a general store which stayed open as long as the bar. The proprietor, a young Belgian, spent his time equally between the two businesses. He rustled up some ham and eggs for me.

'You are not very busy,' I said to him.

'No one is spending their money here now; they are only hoping to get it out of the country.'

'Will you leave also?'

He shrugged: I was getting used to that shrug. 'I suppose I shall have to. Even if it were safe here, there will be no money for a long time – no opportunities for us.' He looked at me. 'So you are an Australian, Many of our people are trying to go there.'

'It's a good country for young people,' I said.

'Good!' He said it as though he had made up his mind, and held up his beer glass. 'Cheers!' he said. I often wonder if he went.

The Route Royale Congo Nil, which I was now on, stretches right across the north part of the country to the Sudan border and was one of the first roads built in the northern Congo. Today the Congo, contrary to some other countries in this part of the world, has main roads that stay open all the year round. Once across the river from Bongo, the villages came into view more often and there was more traffic. Some of the villages had beautifully constructed native court houses which were over sixty feet long; their walls were made of plaited bark, and the wooden posts and framework were ornately carved. The barns used for storing cotton were, in some cases, equally well built and the diminutive replicas of these were used for domestic purposes to hold the family grain and cotton. Some of the huts were round and roofed with large flat leaves that had dried and curled, giving a light bulbous look, while others were cone-shaped like giant bee-hives. Near the bamboo forests, orderly villages were made entirely of bamboo, including fences of the straight, clean wood, and these enclosed areas spoke of Moslem, *purdah* peoples.

I arrived at Buta ten minutes after twelve and had to wait until two o'clock for the bank to open, to cash my travellers' cheques. Many beautiful villas for the military personnel, European traders and government officials sheltered under the banyan trees. There were several stores along the main street and the largest, known as C.E.D.E.C., was an offshoot of Unilever, as S.G.K.N. had been. A European-style café and several garages with petrol pumps completed the European community. Opposite the bank was a low hotel with bungalows in the garden for the bedrooms, and the price for the room was the same for one person as for two. Here again I was oppressed by the feeling of being hemmed in by the jungle, for there was no escape except by the few roads that cut through the undergrowth.

I lost my way trying to reach a certain village by nightfall. If one leaves the main road, or makes a slight detour, the tempo of life changes; one finds the natives are living untouched, with the same customs and beliefs they have had for centuries. I was uncertain about camping, for there had been many elephant tracks and spoor, more than I had seen before. Just as the light was fading a sudden storm broke and the rain poured down accompanied by flashes of lightning and thunder. Night came just as suddenly and now there was complete darkness. At such times the Congo is too much, with its vitality, buoyancy, tempestuous sudden change of weather and its complete disregard for the individual. You are caught in a whirlpool of the jungle, and the world of the equator becomes a living thing; it breathes, convulses and is a very far cry from the quiet, still desert.

The Land Rover edged along the track that was deteriorating fast. I had obviously left the main track, but it was now too narrow to turn back. Once, I stopped to remove a small tree that had been uprooted by elephants bulldozing their way through the undergrowth, and when I climbed back into the car I was wet through.

Each time the lightning illuminated the jungle there was no sign of a village or of people. What would happen if I stopped for the night and an elephant came along? If he put his foot on my bonnet I would be in a pretty fix. Also, the sect of the Leopard Man came from this area. They make themselves up to look like leopards and, having singled out a victim, track that person down and brutally kill him. Their fanaticism is such that once a person has been singled out they never escape, which is all the more brutal because the choice has nothing to do with revenge.

Now the thunder and lightning was coming simultaneously, for the storm was directly overhead. I ducked at each sharp crack and had never felt so inadequate; the individual, it seemed, had no place in this tempestuous country.

At last, in one of the lightning flashes, I saw two huts and pulled off the track beside them. The storm made its rowdy progress across the jungle, but I, having stopped, suddenly felt safe, as one did in an especial corner during the blitz.

When the storm had passed and the jungle was quiet again, two faces appeared at the window. They bobbed as their owners bowed, and their inscrutable expressions showed no surprise at seeing me alone, but they indicated that I should leave the car and go into the hut near by. It would be hot, very full, and lice-ridden, but they were insistent, trying to open the door, so I climbed out and made a dash across the mud to the hut. It was round, and thatched with palm-leaves, and the roof extended past the walls forming a verandah or *baza* right round the building. The interior was quite large and there was a low bed similar to an Indian charpoi and other matting on the floor. Spears hung from the wall, and the floor was taken up with jars, pots, baskets, an extremely battered European suitcase, and some skins for milk and water. The men, who were Bantu, motioned me to sit down, but conversation was not easy, and before the long business of tea or coffee-making began, I indicated that I would sleep in the Land Rover. They offered me the hut, making it clear that they would retire to the other one with the women and children. But I went outside. The sky was lighter and I could see many figures huddled under the verandah. Climbing back into the Land Rover, I cleared a space, unrolled my sleeping-bag, bid the company 'good-night' and, as the living silence of the jungle settled around us, was soon asleep.

There was an air of suppressed excitement when I woke in the morning. The inevitable bevy of small boys stood around the Land Rover although the women were going about their ordinary chores in the usual way. It was a peaceful scene with the high back-cloth of the jungle behind us. A middle-aged woman squatted on a tiny wooden stool and coaxed a fire, and a young girl was pounding manioc; she was very beautiful and as fresh as the clear morning air; her young breasts were small and firm and she moved in an easy rhythm as she pounded the manioc. It made a picture of youth and supreme health and she had that look of amused superiority one sees on the faces of really beautiful women. All the women wore sarongs and the men had a piece of cloth passed between the legs and held up with a cord round the waist.

As I made tea on the woman's fire and passed sweet biscuits around, the jungle was alive with the chattering of monkeys and fluttering of birds, while a couple of small brown dogs dissipated their energies in locating fleas on different parts of their anatomies. Suddenly, the high green back-cloth of the jungle became a flickering drapery of gold as myriads of yellow butterflies flew across the sunlit clearing and brought the scene miraculously to life. Later a man and one of the boys offered to direct me back to the main road, and the small group stood in a semi-circle as we drove off . . .

The eastern borders of the Congo comprise the Mountains of the Moon, the Edward and Albert Lakes and the protectorate of Ruandi-Urundi. The numerous tribes with their distinctive customs and dances, who live in the beautiful country in these areas, have attracted many tourists just as the pygmies do who live in the rain forests of the Ituri. The late Patrick Putnam, an American authority on pygmies, had a camp hospital in the jungle. It is deserted now except for a few of the little people who stayed on and have become a tourist attraction.

I was looking for pygmies in their natural setting and stopped the car in the forest. A narrow track led through the undergrowth to a clearing where there was a group of small round huts and a jumble of dirt and litter. The group of pygmies froze from their various activities and eyed me solemnly. They were all under five feet, with ungraceful figures and wrinkled, incredibly ugly faces that had odd worried expressions. Their skin was the colour of milk chocolate and all the women seemed pregnant. The children had badly distended stomachs and refused persistently to smile at any of my overtures. The pygmies are shy and cautious, and even today some who live in the deep forest believe they are animals, for this is what the other tribes, who look down on them, say. Soon they would be changing camp, for the surrounding game was nearly exhausted and their camp had become too dirty even for them. They are very clever with spears, using a poisoned tip, though, when game is scarce, they can live on the fruits and berries of the forest. I looked around for their spears because they are known to be rather 'trigger happy', and it would not have been wise to go too far alone into their forests. They spend many days tracking down elephants which they catch, either by making a pit with a cover into which the elephant falls, or creeping up behind him and slashing a tendon of a rear leg; then they follow the wounded animal, for days, if necessary, waiting for its strength to fail. The tragic procession wanders through the forest until finally the great beast falls; and still they sit around waiting for it to die, for it is considered unlucky to put an elephant out of its agony. But the pygmies' greatest, carefree sport is hunting monkeys which they kill with spears, and they delight in the expeditions that take them after the little creatures. Although they breed very fast, pygmies are not increasing for many die from tree falls or from burns which they receive from falling into the fire when they are asleep at night. They suffer a lot from malaria, and venereal disease is spreading fast through the tribe.

The little group overcame their natural shyness and took some sweets, salt and sugar from me. But even the babies were ugly and without charm, though perhaps if they had taken to the trees again the fascination they have for many people might have become more evident to me.

*

Paulis is the most important town in the north and for the first time the Europeans outnumbered the native population. In a garish modern hotel there was a busy bar with a screaming juke box. My room-boy was Mangetu, a tribe that elongate their heads and it gave him an inane, stupid expression. Their women wear a curious cone-shaped headdress over their high foreheads which is more picturesque. The tribe formally practised cannibalism which was carried out to conform with certain tribal rites and, if it is practised now, it is done away from the eyes of the authorities.

Here, as in Equatorial Africa, the practice of circumcision or incision for girls is still practised by some of the tribes although it has been proclaimed illegal. The operation is accompanied by a ceremony and is performed by an old woman who is attended by several young girls. They use a knife, a sharpened stone or the fine edge of a bamboo shoot. The custom dates from the times when men left their women alone for long periods while they were away hunting; they believed the operation destroyed all sexual enjoyment for the woman; others say the operation was performed to make the woman entirely feminine and as little like a male as possible. Most Africans deny that these reasons are the real ones and generally do not know – or will not tell – why they follow the practice.

Beni was the jumping-off ground for the Congo side of the Mountains of the Moon and the hotels had a tourist air. There was a good display of African drams, ebony figures and small pieces of ivory. Some told of the missions' influence, for there were black madonnas and different saints.

At the bar of the hotel a quiet distinguished-looking man of middle age was chatting with the proprietor about the weather, the tourist season and the beauty of the Mountains of the Moon.

'From now on,' said the proprietor to me, 'it is all very beautiful – but there are many tourists. The wild part of the Congo is behind you.'

The elderly man took his leave and went out to an old van standing beside my Land Rover.

'He has a farm near here?' I asked.

'Yes, he is the Kaiser's grandson,' said the proprietor, 'he is a real gentleman. Have another beer – on the house this time.'

It was Easter and, along the Lubero Valley, gaily dressed natives crowded the mountain roads on their way to church. Groups of round thatched dwellings called rhondals clustered together on the sides of the mountains, picturesque in the clear air and making a musical comedy setting. In the hill-town of Lubero, the bungalow-hotel bedroom had holy tracts on the walls, and the boy brought logs and lit a huge fire, to warm the first cold night I had experienced since leaving the Sahara. Next morning he brought breakfast of coffee, omelette, bananas, smoked ham and eggs, cheese and wild strawberries with cream.

The mountain pass leads finally to the Cabasha escarpment overlooking the Rwindi National Park, 3,000 feet below. It has always been a favourite haunt of tourists from both the Congo and near-by Uganda. The park's camp set in the open plain has a main building surrounded by *de luxe* rhondals, equipped with every modern convenience, as sleeping quarters.

A row of large limousines stood in front of the main building, and on the verandah a group of tourists sat looking incredibly clean. I was suddenly conscious of my own dusty appearance. A young woman with a pony-tail who stood behind the reception desk did not like the look of me any more than I did myself. She raised her eyebrows when I asked for a room, and shook her head.

'I *did* want to see the animals,' I said.

She looked at me impatiently, hoping I was not going to make a fuss, and a woman near by started to plead for me.

'There are *never* rooms unless you book,' the girl broke in sharply and turned away, the pony-tail sweeping me out of existence.

It was getting late and, as one is not allowed to camp in the parks at night, I climbed into the Land Rover and headed for Uganda. It was the final example of Belgian disinterestedness.

7

'Garden City Country': Uganda

Be quick to love and slow to die.

Norman Douglas

I should not be able to spend much time in Uganda for my visas for the Sudan and Ethiopia would soon expire and to renew them could take some time; also, if the rains started while I was waiting, the border into Southern Sudan would close against surface traffic. However, to visit Uganda at all was the fulfilment of a life-long ambition for, as a small child, I had had a relative who lived in this far country and bought eggs at thirty for a shilling. My passion for eggs made Uganda a kind of culinary Shangri-La.

Towards the border I passed Land Rovers with the names of White Hunters printed in large letters on the sides and large vans followed carrying the luxurious equipment necessary for Gentlemen Game-Hunters. A pleasant but fussy Indian official welcomed me at the customs post and, as I moved into Uganda, a thunderstorm broke over my head. A strong wind blew the car crabwise across the road and rivers formed quickly, rushing along the side of the road and sometimes across it. This kind of storm signifies Africa, for one is powerless and can only wait hoping that soon the fury will abate; it is a curious, inner cry of hate and turmoil. Then, when it is past, the country looks washed and innocent.

Running through Elizabeth Game Reserve, in the late afternoon, I had been confronted with a sign saying that I did so at my own risk, and others that warned me to 'Beware of Elephants' and 'not to leave the car'. I knew it was necessary either to be out of the park or at the park's camp by nightfall though I had no idea how far I must drive to reach either place. Rounding a bend, I came almost face to face with a very large elephant; he was standing on the side of the road flapping his ears and, as he did so, the folds around them rolled backwards and forwards like the waves along the sea-shore. Had I read that when elephants flap their ears, they are angry? I certainly knew that any *lone* elephant was suspect, but this was my first direct encounter with the species. In all game reserves animals have right of way, so I stopped the car, hoping he would move on. It was impossible to pass him as the road fell away into a deep ditch and also, because of this, it would not be easy to turn the car round if the large creature decided to charge.

There was something pathetic about this lone creature whose pride had sent him off from his own herd, for when a bull becomes too old to defend his females, he leaves the herd and becomes a hermit. Although he generally resigns himself to this state, he may sometimes become uncertain of temper or down-right vicious. In any case, he is always unpredictable. There seemed only one thing to do, for he was not moving; and putting the car in reverse I began to back. Suddenly, attracted by the square grey Land Rover which he may have thought was another of his own species, he began to move after me. Elephants, I had been told, can travel at forty-five miles an hour when charging and, on this narrow road, I could not do anything resembling that speed in reverse. It was difficult to drive, keep an eye on the road behind and another on the advancing elephant. Perhaps there was something, after all, in the pygmies' idea of getting rid of these great creatures. Just as his interest was completely taken up with me, a tiny French car came busily round the corner, tooting its horn loudly, and nearly running into me. The elephant, startled by the noise, gave it a contemptuous glance and turning, lumbered off down the road. No one has since given me a direct answer as to what I should do in an encounter like this.

I rose at dawn, for that is the only time one is likely to catch a glimpse of the Ruwenzori Peaks. Miraculously, they appeared quite near in the crystal-clear air, they were snow-capped and immense, and between, were the orderly hills covered with coffee plantations, while nearer still around me were the gardens of the new Ruwenzori Hotel whose colours deepened as I watched.

'My!' said the African servant who was standing behind with my early morning tea, 'you are lucky to see. There are always clouds.'

I watched as films of cloud began to pass horizontally across the peaks and I knew that I would remember that picture always.

The previous night a young Belgian couple had chatted about many countries and, as I was loading my suitcase into the Land Rover, the man came up to me.

'It has been nice meeting you,' he said. 'We have been thinking, you are not, by any chance, Freya Stark?'

'No,' I said, and as I drove down towards the symmetrical lines of coffee bushes, whose dart-green leaves glistened in the early morning sun, I thought, suddenly, overwhelmingly, what a marvellous thing it must be, to be able to answer 'yes' to that question!

*

If it were not for the high expense of the air ticket from the United Kingdom, Uganda would make an ideal place for a holiday. It has everything that a tourist could wish for; the eastern flank of the Mountains of the Moon form the north-west border and near by at the famous Murchison Falls the Nile thunders through a twenty-foot gap and cascades down a giant stairway of stones. There is the inland sea of Lake Victoria and steamers make a leisurely journey of many days along the Nile. The main roads are good and they lead to national games parks and reserves that have camps and chalets where one can stay and see the wild animals at close quarters, and there is fishing, and hunting for the more sanguine. The hotels, in the smaller towns as well as in the two capitals, Entebbe and Kampala, are quite good, and the people almost universally pleasant. For the visitor it is an ideal holiday place, but holidays need companions and one should not go there alone. There is no real loneliness in deserts or isolated places, for the few people one meets are used to aloneness also; they have time to stand and stare – and to chat.

The four provinces of Uganda are Bunyoro, Toro, Ankole and Buganda, and they all centre round ancient chiefdoms that have been combined by the Europeans into one country. The people of Buganda, whose Kabaka (King) is now restored to them, have had, from the first, more contact with Europeans, for their area lies around the capitals. They are intelligent and quick, taking to the things western civilisation has to offer very readily. Many, also, have become Christians.

Entebbe, the administrative capital, is on the shore of Lake Victoria and, although it is merely a few miles from the Equator, the climate is good as it stands nearly 4,000 feet above sea level. The city was built by the British with orderly official buildings, fine homes and gardens, and a large Government House. The main hotel overlooks the lake and, although not so ultra modern as the French and Belgian ones in neighbouring countries, it is nevertheless first class. The city is extraordinarily clean, quiet with a beautiful setting, but it looks what it is, a city built up entirely by Europeans in an African world and it is rather synthetic – and dull.

Kampala, joint capital with Entebbe, is twenty miles away and has the added colour of the African and Asian populations to bring it to life. The more commercial and bustling city has an erratic hilly skyline of mosques, skyscrapers, Protestant and Catholic cathedrals and the buildings of the famous University College of Makerere. The latter's campus is one of the most beautiful in the world and its students' friendliness and enthusiasm make it seem that the establishing of such fine places has been eminently worthwhile.

The palace of the Kabaka stands on one of the hills and a straight road runs from the entrance, dips and mounts another hill opposite where the Parliament or Council House stands. It is called the 'Loved Mile' and the king's subjects, to show their devotion, *walk* the distance between the two hills.

Here again there are beautiful garden suburbs set on the surrounding hills where the wealthier Europeans and Indians live, and there are several good, but slightly old-fashioned, hotels. Many Indians own stores or work in banks and government offices. In the country towns there are large Indian quarters, for they outnumber the Europeans eight to one. They are great workers and stick together, build and save; if you want anything done you go to an Indian, for no job is too small for him. The aborigine, on the other hand, is not overfond of work, nor has he ever had to do much, for there is always enough to eat in this lush land; moreover, for centuries, many of them owned slaves and it was considered degrading to do manual work; and they still cling to this tradition.

There is a feeling of consistent, solid prosperity about the country; things like tea, sugar, tobacco and bananas grow abundantly, and Uganda is the largest exporter of coffee in the British Commonwealth. The beautiful trees in the banana plantations grow to a great height and the fruit is the main part of the diet of many tribes who appear to thrive on it. Everyone carries a bunch of bananas, some on their heads, others on the handle-bars of their bicycles, on donkeys, or piled high in carts; they are to the folk of Uganda what the long loaf of bread is to the Latin.

The Land Rover Agency in Kampala is owned by the Cooper Motor Corporation, a large and efficient concern which functions in many places in East Africa. The works' manager took the Land Rover away to have it serviced. He was a German and he looked at me speculatively.

'So you come across the Sahara, huh?'

I nodded.

'Have you in your body your appendix?'

'Yes,' I said, mystified.

'So! Always you should give your appendix! During the war I was in submarine. Before we go from Germany we, all of us, take our appendix out. *So, so, so, so, so!*' and he rapped the table several times, disposing, irrevocably, of the offending parts of one's anatomy.

'You go north, alone to Khartoum, huh?'

I nodded.

'You will not get through if the rains start.'

'I hope I shall be in time,' I said, the eternal optimist. 'I will send you a card from Khartoum to let you know.'

'Oh no, you will not,' he said. 'Always they come through here, they say they will send a card, but nobody does.'

But I did, when I reached Khartoum.

It is difficult to believe, as one drives east from Kampala towards Jinga, that no white man had seen this country before Speke arrived in 1862 and that sixty years ago the only way to reach it was to walk in. The road and country-side had a civilised appearance – a veneer of sixty years – which was broken suddenly by a group of women sheltering in the shade of a tree and selling oranges in baskets made of plaited banana-leaf. The oranges had thick green skins but were very sweet and cost two shillings for forty. The women, wearing native *batiks*, were beautiful and graceful. Most of them who moved along the road had babies strapped on their backs while everything else was balanced on their heads; it could be a large basket, a bundle of clothes or a tiny Coca Cola bottle, but its presence, whatever it was, contributed to their graceful carriage.

Beyond the town of Jinga which is on Lake Victoria, the road runs across the Owen Falls Dam below which the water roars through, as the Nile starts its 4,000-mile journey north. I was going to see its waters many times during the next few weeks. By damming the Nile as it leaves Lake Victoria, the lake has been turned into the biggest reservoir in the world, and the turbines generate enough electricity to supply not only the whole of Uganda but surrounding countries as well. The river is known here as the Victoria Nile, but after passing Lake Albert it takes that name, and finally when it reaches the Sudan it becomes the White Nile, and is joined at Khartoum by Ethiopia's Blue Nile.

My route took me in a wide circle round Lake Kyoto to Tororo where I left the main Kampala-to-Kenya road and moved towards the flatter northern province. Just before Mbale the road ran along the foot of Mount Nkokonjeru, which is a spur of Mount Elgon.

This flatter but fertile area has attracted many races from the north and east who came originally as pasturers but settled because of the rich ground. The black-skinned Nilotics came south from the Sudan with their cattle and mingled with the Bantu from the lakes. Some of the lighter-skinned migrating Hamites from Ethiopia settled here, though others of the same race moved further west to the Congo border where, today, they are famous for their long-horned Ankole cattle which are almost identical with the beasts owned by the Gallas in southern Ethiopia today.

There were no hotels after Mbale, and I was advised to stay at rest houses whenever possible. At Gulu I asked permission to stay at the Government Rest House.

'Goodness!' said the secretary at the Provincial Officer's headquarters, 'we're *always* full. You have to book *ages* ahead!'

'Not even a verandah to sleep on?'

'Nothing! Nothing.'

Back in the main street of the flat, dusty little town, I entered a general store run by an Indian. It was a long corrugated iron building with a large stock of everything from automobile spares to cotton dress material. It was very hot and the Indian had no beer for sale.

'No matter,' he said, 'I see you are thirsty, isn't it? I will send out for one bottle. Just sit and wait.'

The jumbled activity outside was very like a trunk road in India, and the store was doing a brisk trade. As well as the locals, people came down from the Sudan to do their shopping, for although they would lose a lot on the exchange, everything is in short supply in that country. The Indian changed the last of my

Uganda money into Sudan pounds and when I finally rose to go he would not allow me to pay for the beer.

'That's quite all right, it is a pleasure,' he said, and was as pleased with the transaction as I was.

It is a good rule never to arrive at a border towards nightfall, but this time I had no alternative. As I drove north the country became desolate, the few people I saw were tougher than the mountain and lake dwellers of the south, they were hard and lean, like the country around them. Men from these parts are often recruited into the army and the police force and, during the last war, they had a fine record; more recently they have been making a name for themselves as footballers, a game which is becoming more and more popular in Uganda.

The sun had lost some of its heat by the time I drew up at the Uganda frontier post of Atiak. Behind the customs shed were three little lavatory buildings and over the doors were the signs: EUROPEANS, ASIANS and AFRICANS respectively.

The Indian official was pleased to see me. 'I'll give you a letter to the customs official on the Sudan border,' he said, 'telling them that a manifest for the car is not necessary. They can be difficult at times,' he added quietly.

This, I was to find out later, was a gross understatement.

He followed me out to the car. 'I'm very glad you have come along,' he said. 'There hasn't been a vehicle going north for ages, and a young man has been waiting all day for a lift. He left a couple of hours ago, but it's not the sort of country where one should wander around on foot.'

Five miles along the road I saw a group sitting alongside the track and with the Africans was a young man who rose as I drew up. He was short, with an olive skin and large brown eyes.

'Could you give me a lift?' he asked in a soft American voice.

'Yes, climb in,' I said, and the little group beamed at me.

His name was Roger Pisani, and he had the quiet, pleasant good manners that natives like. He came from New York of Italian parentage and was hitch-hiking round the world, having already been in the Far East, Thailand, Malaya and South Africa. Now he was making his way to Egypt and finally intended going to Europe.

'I decided to see a bit of the world when I left college,' he said; 'my mother wasn't happy about my going off – but she came round.'

As he was an only son, and very unspoilt, it was no wonder she had raised objections.

At the Sudan border the officer who was tall and good-looking was very drunk. Although he was cheerful, experience has taught me that drunks' moods can change in an instant, so we helped the formalities along as quickly as possible, directing his hand with the rubber stamp to the right pages on our passports.

'Where is the rest house?' I asked as we came out, for it was 120 miles from here to Juba and the light was already beginning to fade.

'The *rest house*?' The situation was magnified as it always is with drunks. 'The rest house?' he repeated. 'It is twelve miles from here, up the hill overlooking the Game Reserve.'

'Thanks,' I said and started up the engine.

He still had to lift the frontier pole for us and he shook his head knowingly. 'Caretaker,' he said almost inaudibly.

'Caretaker?'

He nodded, triumphant. 'Caretaker with the key. Must have key for rest house,' and he pointed *back* along the track we had just come.

'Oh blast!' I said, but there was nothing for it but to go back and find the man.

He was an elderly Arab who was delighted at the prospect of a ride up to the rest house even though he would have to walk back the following day. By the time the three of us had returned to the frontier, our drunk had been joined by another officer who was sober, and there followed a complicated pantomime where we had to be cheerful and carefree with the drunk and serious and business-like with the cold-sober one.

As they raised the pole, the sober officer sprang forward. 'You must not forget,' he said, 'to call at the police station in Juba.'

'I won't forget!' and we shot forward into the Sudan.

I have met Englishmen in many countries who have been soldiers or worked in the Colonial Service in the Sudan at one time or another. Many of them had maintained that the Sudanese react magnificently to training and to the principles of democracy. The Sudan was to them a dream come true, for the idea of training a country to become self-governing was really working here. They spoke with affection of the Sudanese themselves, and even Colonel le Blanc had said, with warmth, that you could always tell a Sudanese by his wide-open smile.

What had happened since independence? How had the internal troubles amongst the people and the systematic anti-British propaganda from their Egyptian neighbours on the northern border affected them? Had they really learnt democracy – or were they just good actors and mimics as so many other nationalities had been?

I drove up the rocky path towards the rest house wondering if I'd be able to find out.

8

The White Nile: The Sudan

Have patience and the mulberry
leaf will become satin.

Spanish Proverb

The rest house was built of stone and a long enclosed verandah overlooked the magnificent view of the Game Reserve plain below where the Nile snaked its way into the distance. Two German hitch-hikers had forced their way into the building and their beds and belongings were scattered along the verandah: they had been waiting several days hoping for a lift to Juba. We installed ourselves in the two tiny rooms beyond, and the caretaker lit a fire and, with a proprietary air, took my pots and kettle and set about preparing a meal. The Arab immediately becomes part of your expedition no matter how short the period may be. As the old man began digging into my tucker box for tea and sugar, I suddenly relaxed for my years of wanderings through Arab countries have left their mark, and it is with these people that I feel most at home. They will look after you and take what you offer in tips and food, pleased, but you are not thanked; for is it not Allah's will that they have received them? Then, they will leave you without even a backward glance.

Later, two Egyptians arrived in a hired car and the rest house became very full. They told us they were professors and had been touring along the border. Their English was extremely good but it became quite incoherent when we asked what sort of professors they were, and what subjects they were studying – (the border, no doubt). And so the old game of Intelligence goes on.

The hill above Nimule added short-lived beauty to the scene, for next morning we ran down on to flat, dull country and, from now on, until I left the Sudan the weather was so hot and enervating that one seemed to be living in a steaming basin. The bright clothes of the Negro had gone and, as we neared Juba, the long white *galabiah*, the fez and the turban took their place. They were clothes that belonged to desert-dwellers.

Finally, about midday we ran along a built-up bund and came broadside on to the Nile. Juba stood beyond the opposite bank where the ferry was filling up with foot and bicycle passengers, all carrying something on their heads. The river, having come hundreds of miles through some of the world's most vivid scenery, now headed north where the country was more fitted to be a desert, which it would be, without the river. The ochre-coloured water was dirtier than when it left the turbines at Lake Victoria. It moved fast but silently with none of the ripple, bubble and chatter of most fast-moving rivers and the heavy silence of the colossal swell of advancing water was curiously ominous.

As I waited, a large, dusty lorry pulled up behind my Land Rover and out of it climbed two young Englishmen in flannel trousers, loose shirts and topees. They were Mark Goodfellow and Derek Partridge, attached to the British Embassy in Khartoum who had been holidaying in the southern province and using what transport they could find to get around.

'We've seen absolutely everything,' said Mark, the more volatile of the two, 'even a white rhino.'

'Oh? And was it really white?' I asked.

'No, grey like the others, but becoming very rare.'

Half-way across the Nile my hand-brake failed and the Land Rover began to roll back into the Nile! Had it not been for dozens of willing dark hands holding it back, we would have plunged down into the depths.

On the other bank there was no sign of customs or immigration officers and finally I pulled up alongside a large car which was coming towards me, flying a standard.

'Could you tell me just where the Immigration Office is?' I asked the Sudanese sitting in the back.

'It's – oh, you'd better follow me as it's difficult to explain. It's right in the centre of the town.' He spoke to the chauffeur and the large car swung round and set off the way it had come.

The car caused a stir as it swept ahead of us, and he was obviously someone of importance in Juba. His speech, manner and whole demeanour were completely English and only his slightly darker skin belied the fact.

He left us at a group of large buildings set around a court.

'Thank you so much,' I said.

'Not at all, it's a pleasure,' and the large car was off.

It was Ramadan, and good Moslems neither eat nor drink in the day during the fast. When it falls during the summer months it is a great trial and one is always warned to have as little as possible to do with officialdom during this time.

Education is coming much later to the southern province of the Sudan and most officials have been imported from the north. They were curiously on the defensive, as though they treated their appointments as a kind of exile and there followed an infuriating twenty-four hours that was made worse by the dry enervating heat. Although I had a visa, it would be necessary, they informed me, to wire to Khartoum for permission for me to proceed. The permission could take several days to arrive and, in the meantime, if the rains started the journey would be completely impossible for the rest of the season. Also, the customs official demanded one hundred pounds as a deposit on the car, even though I had a Carnet for it.

The officials were efficient, well-mannered and spoke excellent English, but *nobody* would move or take the initiative without permission from Khartoum so, having seen a telegram go off from the Police Station, I now sat in the Customs Office not far from the river. Near by was the quay where the Nile steamer starts its journey north to Kosti and Khartoum. I argued about the hundred pounds.

'But you belong to the International Carnet Agreement,' I said. 'Why should I pay a hundred pounds?'

He was looking through a large book. 'We do not recognise Carnets issued by the A.A. Only those with the R.A.C. stamp on them.'

'But it's the same *Carnet*! It doesn't matter if the Wali of Swat issues it,' I said, exasperated.

'We will telephone to Khartoum and ask about it. Come back tomorrow.'

'Tomorrow is Saturday. You close midday.'

'We cannot do anything until we speak to Khartoum.'

I went out into the flat, hot dusty street. Juba is the main town in Sudan Equatoria. It is an overgrown unattractive village and most of its life centres round the river. The surrounding countryside is woodland savannah and even today lions have been known to roam the streets after dark.

During the Anglo-Egyptian *condominium*, foreigners were not encouraged to come to the southern Sudan, and the hotel at Juba is the only one in the entire area. It was a low one-storey building, with another at the rear for the high-ceilinged bedrooms where huge fans turned perpetually. Each room had its private verandah enclosed with wooden lattice work.

In the main building there was a bar and a large, sprawling lounge with basketwork chairs and faded chintz where, in the evening, the few remaining Europeans and the occasional Sudanese sipped drinks and fought the mosquitoes. It is called the Railway Hotel because it belongs to Sudan Railways, but the line is hundreds of miles away. The service was not very good; and one sensed ghosts of the old regime sitting, protesting, in the old basketwork chairs.

The Nile Steamer, going north to Kosti, leaves Juba every second Saturday and it is possible to make the whole journey from Lake Victoria, Uganda to Khartoum by buying a ticket at any railway station. The journey does a kind of leap-frog with steamers, buses and trains. From Juba you board the third and last steamer for Kosti where, on arrival, an over-night train completes the journey to Khartoum.

There had been no reply to the telegram when I called at the Police Headquarters the next morning and, at the Customs Office, the official had not been able to get through to Khartoum on the telephone.

I was in a fix. If the authorities in Khartoum did not grant me permission to proceed north soon and the rains started, I would have to retrace my steps. I went back to the Police Headquarters.

'How about letting me go by steamer to Kosti with my car, today?' I asked. 'Then Khartoum can sort things out when I arrive. If they don't like the look of me they can put me in jail there.'

The tall northerner laughed, thought a minute, and decided. 'All right,' he said, 'but you'll have to hurry if you want to put your car on the steamer; it's Saturday and the men stop working at noon.'

The customs official was not so helpful and demanded the hundred pounds deposit.

'If I have to pay, I'll do so in Khartoum,' I said.

'You must wait until I speak to Khartoum.'

'But how long will it take?'

He shrugged. 'It is not easy – on Saturday.'

'If I miss the steamer, I shall have to wait another two weeks and the rains . . .' Also, I thought to myself, a refusal might arrive from the north. It was the last straw; my lip quivered. I was sweltering and very sorry for myself. *Everything* was going wrong with this journey. Ethiopia seemed further away than ever. My brimming eyes and quivering lips had an instantaneous effect. The official came round from behind his desk.

'If – if you will sign a letter saying that a Carnet issued by the AA is just as valid as one issued by the RAC, I shall let you go.'

'Oh yes! Yes! I'll sign *anything*.'

'Come back when I shall have the letter typed.'

I smiled and my lips stopped quivering; he looked relieved and went back to his desk.

For the next two hours, in the ferocious heat, when even to walk across the quay brought one out in a dripping sweat, I packed, paid my bill, changed money, bought tickets for the car and one for myself, called back to sign the letter – only to find the official had decided it wasn't necessary after all – and finally drove the car on to an open barge beside a crashed military lorry. The journey was costing me twenty-six pounds for the Land Rover and fourteen pounds for myself; it was an atrocious amount for a seven days' journey but I was on my way, at last.

The steamer, with the barges lashed to it, covered an immense area of water. There was the main paddle-boat, the only one with an engine; our first-class barge was lashed to one side and the second-class barge to the other; while in front of us, four other barges were being pushed ahead. Two of these were for the third-class passengers while the others, which were flat like Rhine barges, carried cargo and the vehicles.

Our barge, or steamer, had two decks. The upper for'ard one was wired in and made an observation lounge free from mosquitoes but the wire added considerably to the heat and its ugliness. Amidships were the cabins which were tiny, narrow and very hot. The second-class barge was similar and occupied by northern Sudanese school-teachers and civil servants returning home for their vacation. The third- and fourth-class barges had their entire top decks enclosed in wire-netting or slats of wood, for there were no cabins, and these decks and the open space below were crowded with people.

Roger was a deck passenger and disappeared among the great mass of natives ahead of us, together with the two young German hitch-hikers. The two young men from the British Embassy were travelling first class as far as Malakal and there was also an Indian couple from Kampala, their brother from Bombay and a Canadian doctor who was touring Africa.

The barge ahead kept any breeze there might have been from us, but there wafted into our lounge all kinds of smells, depending on the time of day, which gained in strength as the journey progressed.

The great floating mass set off finally at ten o'clock that evening and, once in mid-stream, the engines had more difficulty in curbing our progress in the current, than in shunting us along.

It was a pleasant prospect; seven days doing nothing but watch the Nile banks go by, through the country of the Dinkas, the Nuers and the Shillucks. We would pass through the Sudd, the largest swamps in the world, an area that had for centuries defeated many who had tried to penetrate it. I could take photographs at my leisure; I could even read. It would be a rest . . .

I woke to find myself on the floor of the cabin and the thermos flask which had been full of iced water in pieces all around me. We had crashed headlong into one of the banks, for the river was now making sharp turns and the paddle-boat's engine was having difficulty in steering the great load round the bends. All night we continued to run, first into one side of the bank – and then into the other!

Breakfast found us rather wan. We were in Dinka country; it was flat and the monotony of the landscape was broken occasionally by a Dinka village where a place had been cleared and curious tall huts made of grass were set in a semi-circle. Not far away, their cattle grazed, magnificent white creatures with huge horns. The first Dinka I saw was standing on one leg with the other tucked at right angles behind it. The extremely tall, slim figure wore nothing but a necklet and even the spear he held was not used as a prop. He stood so still that I mistook him for the black trunk of a tree but there was an air of great superiority in his stance seen even from this distance, as if confirming their attitude that they are indeed superior.

At one of the bends, the current took over completely and we had a deafening crash, when the entire load of passengers lay splay-legged over the decks and the crash of broken glass and crockery would have woken the Pharaohs. The engine was not working properly and could not control the heavy load. We stopped and, after a great deal of discussion between the crew, during which all the passengers gave free advice, it was decided to leave the barge with my Land Rover on it alongside the bank, to lighten the load. They informed me just before they cast off.

'You can't do that!' I said, desperately, but I only had time, firstly to tell the engineer I objected, which did no good at all, and, secondly, to collect a few things from the Land Rover.

I stood watching the Land Rover getting smaller and smaller, as we continued down the Nile. I had an awful feeling of misgiving; it was out in the blazing sun with all my provisions, film and the Uganda oranges I had forgotten which would have been a luxury for the boys.

'It reminds me of the time they sent a turbine down to Juba and it got lost in the Sudd,' said an official beside me. 'No one ever heard of it again till six years later when an "ad" in a local paper announced that a junk turbine was for sale in the Sudd.'

'Oh,' I said.

'The rains started, you see, and the barge drifted up on to higher ground and got stranded out of sight.'

'Oh.'

'Of course the rains are late this year.'

'But they *could* start any day?'

He nodded.

'If only I'd thought of it, I would have got off and camped on the barge,' I said.

'It's too late now.'

'Do not worry,' said the engineer who was really the captain. 'The Land Rover will be waiting for you when you come to Kosti,' and he gave a large Sudanese grin.

However, even with the lighter load, the engines could not control the barges and finally we edged alongside the bank to make some repairs. Near by was a Dinka village, and the men, women and children came to the water's edge to greet us. Dug-out canoes swept across the river at an amazing speed and hippopotami raised their surprised heads to watch us. The people's healthy-looking black skins gleamed in the fierce sunlight; they were good-mannered and exuded happiness; their amusement when I wanted to photograph them made it seem that *we* were the curiosities, not they.

The Dinkas are cattle-breeders and live mostly on milk and blood. They love their animals and seldom kill them, but draw the blood from a vein in the neck which they do with the aid of a fine hollow stick. They are proud, believing wholeheartedly in the rights of the individual and have always reacted badly to any form of outside authority. This authority now means the northern Sudanese, for whom the Dinka has an especial distrust because for centuries they were raided by the northerners and taken off as slaves.

Both the Dinka men and women are well over six feet and have slim, graceful figures. The children looked healthier than any I had yet seen which is a good recommendation for the milk and blood diet. The women wore an apron of leather and sometimes a skin cloak, but the men were completely naked except for attractive but crudely-made jewellery and beads. Most of the men wore a large ivory bangle on the upper part of the arm which contrasted startlingly with the black skin, and some had their faces and bodies adorned with cicatrices. The women's hair was shaved, making them look boyish and extremely handsome.

Cattle are also used as a bride price, and the girl's father can be given cattle worth £1,000 or more for his daughter. The Dinkas walk with the air of kings and, if you would believe that individual independence is the beginning and end of all human dignity, go and see these people before it is too late.

It was still Ramadan and the repairs to the engine were being carried out in a lethargic fashion. They were not wholly successful, but after three hours we set off again, edging cautiously along the bank.

Dawns and sunsets have a curious quality on the Nile. The light arrives with a sudden gush, and then the sun climbs up over the horizon and creeps along the ground towards the steamer while, in the evening, it slides over the side, a giant waterfall of light and colour.

That evening there was a sudden squall and thunder-storm, and the engine, which was still behaving badly, could not cope with the rough surface as well as the current, so we edged alongside the bank and tied up to a tree for the night. There was a great commotion about nine o'clock when a large snake ran along the fastening ropes and climbed on to the for'ard barge. It was voted not dangerous by the engineer, but it disturbed the sleeping crowd who woke and chattered like a tree-full of birds faced with a nocturnal intruder.

The third-class and deck passengers were a great source of interest. Each time we stopped, great quantities of mangoes were brought aboard and sold and the huge earthenware jars were refilled with drinking water. One man had the wooden framework of a *charpoi* and was weaving its mattress as we sailed along. There was a baby gazelle tied by its foot to one of the posts; its owner, a quiet, elderly man who ran a garage in Kosti, offered it to me, but the boys said it would die in about six weeks. One small child sat behind the wire-netting and we became friends by means of signs. She was in the same position for the whole journey and I never heard her cry or complain.

During the lazy, hot hours there was no movement at all on the barges. We sat in the wired-in lounge, reading and talking in fits and starts, for it was too hot to lie down. There was not much of interest along the shore for, like ourselves, the people and animals were resting out of sight in whatever shade they could find; but as soon as the sun lost some of its heat a perpetual stream of people started scooping up water from the river, preparing to wash for the evening prayers. Fires were started on the barges and meals cooked. One wondered that there were no accidents in the crowded space.

Sometimes, in the evening, Roger and I sat on the front barge; it was quiet away from the chug of the engines and there was more breeze, although the midgets attacked relentlessly. Ahead of us, the wide stretch of the Nile was wholly covered by water-hyacinth. This beautiful plant, with its tiny blue flower, grows so fast that it becomes completely out of hand, and several times a day we were forced to stop and disentangle the plant from the paddles. Here, as in America, research continues, to try and find a way of destroying it, for it is costing millions both here and in the USA.

As the sun sank below the horizon, high clouds of smoke rose from the huts on the shore, seeping through the grass walls and roofs making them a smouldering pall as the Dinkas fumigated their huts against mosquitoes and midgets for the night. It was a magic golden land at this time of the evening, despite its flatness, and a great compensation after the ferocious, enervating heat of midday.

'I'll remember this stillness and peace for a long time,' said Roger as the nose of our barge edged its silent way through the hyacinths.

On the third day we stopped beside the bank, for the engine was still giving trouble, and waited for a little tug to come from Juba and help us out. In the centre of the river a great school of hippopotami played in the muddy water, their pink and grey heads turning occasionally towards us with their surprised and amusing look of curiosity. But this was not wild-game country; we had seen a few elephants, crested cranes, flamingos and an occasional cygnet settling on the backs of the Dinkas' cattle, but that was all.

A Dinka family came down to the water's edge, and I fetched my camera.

'Don't photograph these natives,' said a Sudanese school-teacher, thrusting his hand in front of the lens.

'Why not?'

'You must not photograph these people. They are too primitive.'

I looked from the round-shouldered, near-sighted little man at my side to the tall, healthy creature on the shore. 'But if they don't *mind* being photographed . . .' I began.

He cut me short. 'That's not the point, we are ashamed of them. But,' he added, 'we will change all that.'

I put the camera away, realising a little why the British had been loath to hand over the administration of these people to the northerners so quickly.

About midday a little tug came chugging down the river, and attaching itself to our side we set off once more. It was already dark when we arrived at Bor where the tiny wharf was crowded with the entire population. The local D.C. and a northern Sudanese and his family joined the steamer. The wife and children crowded into one of the cabins and were not seen again, while a small boy-servant sat on the deck or ran backwards and forwards with food and drinks for the family. Boys of this age are in great demand as servants for women in *purdah*. Then when they reach adolescence, the women must be protected from *them*!

We stayed late at Bor loading sacks of durra, and a spotlignt from the ship was trained on the quay to give light. I wandered along the quay amongst the crowd of natives whose dark faces were thrown into relief in the spotlight glare. There was bustle, excitement and good humour. Three startlingly good-looking young men stood still in the milling crowd. They made a black fresco, each with an arm on the other's shoulder, their heads back with an expression of unconscious hauteur, but they were completely oblivious of the magnificent picture they made. Around them the animated crowd chattered, passing sacks of grain. How quickly one adjusts oneself! It was only when I was back in the ship that I realised that I, alone, in that vast crowd, had any clothes on.

The next morning we had entered the Sudd, and despite the little tug's help were bashing from one side of the canal to the other. A vast world of floating papyrus grass surrounded us. The Sudd is a mixture of swamp and floating islands of vegetation that stretches for hundreds of miles, through which the Nile passes. For thousands of years it has formed a barrier to the upper reaches of the Nile as nothing could penetrate the jungle of floating vegetation. Many attempts were made to cut a permanent way through but without success, and it was not until the beginning of this century that the British engineering project under Major Malcolm Peake succeeded; and even then the project took four years.

The papyrus grass grows to a great height and crowds the side of the canal. The task of cutting through it seems quite impossible, and in an earlier attempt by Samuel Baker in 1870 the undergrowth closed behind him as he tried to cut his way through. It is a nightmare place, like the great mango swamps of Indonesia, for the whole landscape looks exactly the same in every direction. The curious dingy, misty air that hangs over it accentuates its strangeness and yet, there is a moment as the last rays of the sun catch the light-green thistles of the top grass that it suddenly becomes quite beautiful.

We all became very adept at dodging the bumps, grabbing glasses and cameras from the tables and bracing ourselves against a post or wedging our chairs. The Indians played bridge, the Canadian doctor read *Inside Africa*, Mark 'caught up on his letter writing', Derek seemed mesmerised by a detective story and I re-read my favourite travelling companion, Laurens van der Post's *Venture to the Interior*.

As we neared a small place called Adok, the wharf presented a curious sight, for dozens of naked people stood, each holding upright a high roll of golden-coloured matting which towered above them. The golden matting contrasted startlingly with the black bodies. These were the Nuers, who had shaved heads and, like the Dinkas, wore no clothes. Many had lined cicatrices running across their foreheads. I made my way to the gangplank, for the mats, though crudely made, are useful for sitting on the sand. The northern Sudanese, father of the large family, was at my side.

'You cannot buy those mats,' he said.

'Why not?'

'They are not allowed to sell them. These natives have enough to live on. They do not need to make money by selling such things.'

'Maybe not, but I'd like to have one of them.'

'It's ridiculous their wanting to sell the mats. Why don't they sell some of their cattle?'

'Oh. Have they many cattle?'

'As many as the Dinkas, in some cases, but they won't sell any.' A look of bewilderment crossed his face. How to understand a tribe who had thousands of pounds' worth of cattle and wouldn't sell one of them?

Even the police on shore would not allow me to buy the mats. The Nuers, perplexed at the northerners' attitude, gladly gave me one and treated the whole thing as a lark.

Eventually the policeman and the other Sudanese will win, for it will become necessary to have money and, if they do not get it from the mats, they will be forced to sell their cattle. The situation is slightly similar to the pagans in the Republic of Central Africa who are now forbidden to wear only a bunch of leaves. If they must wear more, then they must make money to buy the cloth to wrap round their bodies; and so they must work – a thing they have never thought of doing!

Many of the land-people had already left, migrating to higher ground before the rains cut them off, but occasionally we passed a couple of huts standing on firmer ground. They looked impermanent and there was none of the untidiness and clutter associated with habitations, for, like the Dinkas, they needed only a few pots, fishing spears, their families and their cattle.

One night the whole sky was lit by a fire. The grass had been set alight so that the next season's growth could come up, stronger and uncluttered. We chugged steadily towards it until finally we were gliding past a great wall of flame. The whole world seemed afire and the magnificent arch of the sky was a great flickering golden bowl.

Towards the end of the Sudd the canal ran into Lake No where, for the first time, there was more water than land around us. Had all of the Sudd been like this eons ago before the floating mass began to pile up on itself? The lake finally narrowed and small villages appeared that were quite different from any we had seen for they were substantially built of brick and corrugated iron. We were turning again towards the western world, the people wore shorts and shirts and Land Rovers ran busily along the tracks. I had crossed the centre of Africa once, going south through the Sahara and had now re-crossed the continent through the equally impenetrable barrier of the Sudd.

It was late afternoon when we arrived at Malakal, the administrative centre of the area and the biggest town since leaving Juba. The Canadian doctor had diagnosed a case of chicken-pox on board and the steamer was not allowed to go alongside until the local doctor came aboard. We waited for some time in mid-stream and were all duly inoculated against *smallpox* before being allowed to go ashore.

There was no news of my Land Rover and the station master, relaxing after his day of fasting, was not very helpful, but good chance led me to Hussein Hamo, the Malakal Commissioner of Police, a pleasant man who spoke with a slightly exaggerated Oxford accent.

'Should I leave the steamer here and wait for my car?' I asked him.

'Shouldn't think so,' he said, 'there is only one rest house and unfortunately it is quite full. I suggest that you go on to Kosti and wait there. Here is my name and telephone number, I will see it through as quickly as possible.'

As we left Malakal the new moon was sighted and so ended the fast of Ramadan. Everyone was in high spirits and celebrations began. Our great mass of floating barges were more erratic than ever and when we ran aground on a sand-bank, the captain of the little tug that was helping us out stood with a large bottle clasped in one hand and the tug's wheel in the other. The tug pushed and pulled and encircled us with the agility of a ballet dancer.

This was the country of the Shillucks who, like the Dinkas, are a Nilotic people. The men had a line of cicatrices across their foreheads that stood out in large globules like a string of beads. The decoration was similar to that on the Boghama tribe near Bongo in the Congo. The work is done by pricking the skin, and when it festers putting ash and dirt on the sore to build up the mound.

The people here were not as handsome as the Dinkas, and they wore more clothes with a great assortment of necklets made of beads, silver and sometimes wire. I was photographing one of the men when a young man, dressed in shorts and a shirt, came up.

'Do not take his photograph,' he demanded, 'those marks on his forehead,' he pointed to the line of globules, 'they are ridiculous!'

But the speaker himself had tribal marks, which were long deep gashes nearly an inch thick, down both his cheeks.

There were Europeans now as well as Africans on the banks, and the high green 'sausage-trees', festooned with long bulbous pods, gave height to the landscape at last. Other craft passed us, and I had the same sense of reluctance I had felt on coming out of the desert to join the bustle and noise of the peopled world.

9

'At Khartoum – turn right for Ethiopia!'

Wisdom should reckon with the unforeseen.

Edgar Allan Poe

Early in the morning we waited for a bridge to open, and half an hour later slid alongside the slanting concrete quay at Kosti. All the tussles with the current, the crashes and the hold-ups, were over, and we realised that for the steamer-folk it was just a routine journey except, of course, that my Land Rover lay somewhere in the hot sun hundreds of miles to the south.

Already the glare made us squint and the heat roared up from the ground around us. The station master tried to persuade me to take the train on to Khartoum without my car, but I waited three days in the boiling Railway Hotel before my Land Rover arrived. By that time all the inhabitants of the flat, dusty little town of Kosti knew of my loss, and the barge was greeted on its arrival by me and most of the enthusiastic population. The car had been looked after very well, and all the men on shore downed tools to get it ashore for me at the first possible moment.

'You are happy now?' asked the old man who had been left on the barge with the vehicles. 'It is better – better when you smile!'

*

These days the journey overland from Kosti to Khartoum need only take one day and the best track cuts due east, running along the railway line to Sennar on the Blue Nile. The country between is desert except for an occasional outcrop of high granite rocks. Sennar was the capital of the Funj Empire whose territory once extended far to the south and east to Ethiopia. Very little remains of the old city and the main region of Sennar today is the triangular territory between the White and the Blue Niles before they join at Khartoum. Most of the triangle is part of the great Gizera Irrigation Scheme, and the canals give the country-side the appearance of a vast draught-board. The grey alluvial soil comes to life when it is watered and the country-side looks prosperous if not beautiful. Driving through the scheme is a chancy business for tracks run along the side of the canals and once on them you must stay for many miles. There are few signposts and, in the flat, featureless landscape, it is easy to lose all sense of direction. Whenever I *did* stop to ask the way I was either insulted or somebody was especially nice to me; there were no half measures.

By mid-afternoon the draining heat was bringing me near to tears. I drove into a small settlement with a shanty town appearance. There were no direct tracks leading out of the village and I drew up alongside a line of crudely erected buildings. In a small café full of men, I ordered a Coca-Cola and asked the proprietor which direction I should take. He slapped the bottle down in front of me and, affecting not to understand, went back to the counter. A middle-aged man sitting near by came over.

'I will show you,' he said quietly, and followed me out to the car. 'You are alone?'

'Yes. And I find the tracks along the canals difficult to follow.'

'Of course. You should not be driving around alone. It should never be allowed,' and he called a small boy over to him. 'He will take you. He lives in that direction.'

'Well, thank you very much,' I said, climbing into the car.

'It would not have been allowed in the old days,' he said quietly.

The whole country seemed definitely divided in their attitude towards the British. The sudden looks of hate, the fanaticism, or the kindly, almost sad willingness to help and play host in their own country.

It was dark when I arrived at Khartoum whose real identity seemed hidden in some curious way under the bustle of traffic policemen, bright lights and overlay of commerce, tourists and swelled air traffic. The hotel situation was acute and across the street from the main hotel an old steamer is tied up in the Nile where, if you are unlucky, you must try to sleep in the airless cabins.

Despite the temperature of 112 in the shade, it was impossible not to go out and explore the city. Along the river road, renamed from Kitchener to 'Neel', the giant banyan trees meet overhead, forming a permanent avenue of shade; and past the bridge that leads to Omdurman the two Niles meet, miraculously continuing side by side for some time, one ochre, the other dingy blue, before they merge. One having come through the endless miles of flat desert and the other through Ethiopia's spectacular mountains.

The large building where I went to settle the argument about the deposit for the car was one of a group of solid British-looking structures set around a court. The officer in charge was charming: he gave me coffee and chatted for a long time. He did not want the hundred pounds deposit at all.

There was the sparkling white 'wedding cake' of a palace where a guard, resplendent in white uniform, posed for a photograph in front of the circular steps just about where General Gordon met his death, and along the river, towards the hotel, there is a flat dais surrounded by lawns that look over the river and it is the place where Kitchener's statue used to stand. They have removed it and given it back to the British.

'There was a ceremony. They did it very well,' said Mark, and there was sadness in his voice.

The country, trying to balance its budget, was importing only the bare necessities, and many things were unobtainable in the stores; there were no torch batteries, elastic, matches, plastic goods, and second-hand cars fetched a very high price.

The end of Ramadan festival crowds had trampled the grass in the famous zoo, so it had been closed and the director took me round himself and spoke to the animals as though they were children. But it was dusty and sad, and the hippopotamus in his little dish of slimy water seemed a far cry from the joyous frollicking creatures we had seen south in the Nile.

There were receptions and parties where beautiful Greek and Armenian women wore the best of Paris fashions. I was taken for moonlight parties on Crocodile Island where the sand was still hot from the sun, and dined in cool, softly-lit gardens.

There had recently been another coup which had started at midnight and ended before dawn.

'We are a police state, we have a dictatorship,' I was told by the Sudanese themselves; 'it is the best thing, as a beginning. It saves a lot of expensive departments, graft and discussions. Democracy is a thing you must grow into, not be given on a plate.'

But hadn't the amicable little coup, with its discussions and terms, shown a certain advance, a certain civilised reasoning?

When I was leaving for Ethiopia, I went to pay my bill. The reception clerk was very busy and had that independent air that perpetually full rooms in an hotel give such people. He had seen me arrive in my Land Rover, dusty, tired and hot and now, as he pushed the bill towards me, he leant over the counter and said quietly, 'I *do* hope it isn't too much?'

I went down the steps to the Land Rover standing under the huge banyan trees. I was beginning to understand what all those people had meant when they had told me about the endearing qualities of the Sudanese.

The journey from Khartoum to Kassala, near the Eritrean–Ethiopian border, is 215 miles if you cut due east across the desert and follow your nose. If you keep to the tracks and follow numerous signposts with Arab lettering, you can cover much more ground. I followed my nose.

The route map described the journey as 'a track, often ill-defined through desert scrub with sandy patches and best negotiated at night on account of the heat. Water, petrol and food should be carried and the local police informed of departure.'

I filled up with petrol and was self-contained otherwise. As for the police, it was too hot to have to cope with any obstructions in that direction, so I carefully avoided them. Driving out of Khartoum, a familiar figure hailed me.

'Wait! Wait! Lady Barbara!' It was Habbib, the Sudanese civil servant who had been with the Colonel's convoy. He looked very different, for he was dressed in a neat office suit, European-fashion.

'Habbib! How are you?'

'Terrible! I am just back from convalescing. When the convoy arrived in Khartoum, I had nervous breakdown.'

'Oh, I am sorry. And the rest of the convoy?'

'They flew home from here. We had a very bad journey from the Sudan border, through Wau – desert most of the way. It was very hot.'

'And Mahommad?'

'He looks now for a new job. You, perhaps, would like a good boy?'

I shook my head. 'I'm off to Ethiopia.'

'You are a lone camel! Well, good luck, better you than me. Come and see my family if ever you return to Khartoum.'

'Thanks, Habbib, I'd like to.' I drove off. City Arabs like Habbib find desert journeys far too strenuous: they haven't the stamina and have also a curious fear of the desert.

Across the river and a few miles east of Khartoum, the sealed road stopped completely and ahead lay the semi-desert, which finally gave way to desert grassland. Occasionally, I drove near a small settlement not much more than a group of mud huts with small hillocks near by, that told of the old Arab habit of building new dwellings near, or on, the ruins of the old. The signposts in Arabic, when I came to them, pointed in all directions, linking up these small settlements. It is a British characteristic to cover the country-side, even deserts, with signposts. One Arab lettering kept occurring time and again, it had the same sweeping stroke one sees on the advertisements for Coca-Cola. As the language is phonetic, I supposed it was a signpost to Kassala.

I kept my compass steadily to the east and towards evening when the foliage had become thicker again I picked up a railway track. Far ahead two round little hills showed on the horizon, tiny sentinels to the majestic highlands of Ethiopia beyond!

The Kassala area has some of the most fertile, unirrigated land in the Sudan, and the town itself is 1,700 feet above sea level. It lies on the River Gash which floods each year and then dries completely from October to June. The floods are used as the main source of irrigation, for the rainfall itself is very light.

Night fell suddenly and ahead of me were flickering lights which disappeared then came into view as the car dipped and rose over the uneven ground. Finally, I pulled out of the soft sand on to a small concrete bridge spanning a dry river bed and ahead of me was a bustling Arab town where people waited with huge bundles and were jostled by donkeys. Amongst this weaving crowd was a fine spine of soldiers who moved with a more purposeful air, and I caused a good deal of comment such as one encounters in out-of-the-way places. I was directed, amid a fine display of enthusiasm, to an English-speaking Greek whose shop stood on a large square surrounded by tiny shops. He took me to the hotel near by where the neon strip-lighting hit us as we entered. The ground floor was a large bare café with a bar, and a friendly, ragged boy led me upstairs to a bedroom, bare except for an iron bed and a bentwood chair. He went away and returned with a key.

'This,' he said, giving it to me, 'is for the boss's bathroom. You cannot use the other.'

Several gay young Sudanese dressed in flowing white *galabiahs* were staying at the hotel and their interest in me deepened as the evening advanced.

'It is better you have dinner up here on the private roof,' said my youthful guardian, watching with disapproval the young men's approaches to me.

For centuries young boys have protected the womenfolk, and it has become an instinctive reaction to guard them, so I dined alone on the roof, as becomes a woman in a *purdah* country. The boy brought a large meal, happily climbing the stairs with each new course. The heat in the town, which is caught in an undercliff of the hills, was terrific and the sudden gusts of wind merely added to the discomfort by spraying everything with grey dust.

Because of the heat, I intended to make an early start next morning. But it was Friday, the Moslem Sabbath, and the immigration and Customs Offices in Kassala were closed for the day, a situation I had never met anywhere else in the world. It took three hours of tracking down and persuasion, to coax the immigration official out of his house to stamp my passport.

'And the Customs Office? Where do I go to have my Carnet stamped?'

'Ah, that is out of the town on the way to the border, which is fifteen miles away.'

The road stopped a couple of miles out of the town and tracks went in every direction. I kept towards the east and finally spied ahead two square buildings of stone surrounded by wire. A naked toddler came towards me followed by his large fat father, and both of them grinned at me.

'Customs?' I enquired.

The father's face fell with alarming suddenness and the toddler's followed more slowly.

'Customs,' said the man, pointing back the way I had come, 'in Kassala, fifteen miles . . .'

'But they told me it was out of Kassala.'

'*Just* out of Kassala. On road.'

'Can't you telephone them and say you will stamp my Carnet here?'

He shook his head. 'No stamp.'

'Well, telephone and ask if a signature will do.'

'No telephone,' he said with finality.

There was nothing for it but to go back. The Customs House *did* certainly stand on the road that led out of the town, but the small sign was almost completely covered by the branches of a tree, and it took an hour to extricate this official from his home.

He was a cheery, wiry little man, also accompanied by a small son, and he spoke good English which he used only to punctuate his own language, in a snobbish fashion as some people use French phrases.

'*What* is the name?'

'Toy.'

'Toy! *Musch mumkin!*' (not possible) and he roared with laughter. 'I'll have to charge you overtime,' he remarked as he cheerfully tore out the appropriate slip.

I parted with the last of my Sudan money, and went out into the hot midday sun. Officialdom in the Sudan had been tiresome, but punctuated all the time by the sudden friendliness and sense of humour of the Sudanese themselves.

The official near the border pointed ahead. 'Follow the dry river bed for some time and you will come, at last, to a built-up road. You will know then that you are in Ethiopia.'

I registered the direction on my compass and plunged down into the dry rocky bed which, when the rains start, becomes a raging torrent that closes the border for many months. Now the earth was rising all around me; bushes and trees were growing with the hardiness of mountain plants. Gone was the uncomplicated simplicity of the flat desert over which I had come. Rocks piled up with healthy confusion and suddenly, jutting out into the river, was a built-up road. I set the car's nose towards it and made a dash, landing on the top with a crash. A good road stretched ahead; it led right into the heart of mountainous Ethiopia.

Part Two

Ethiopia

Encompassed on all sides by the enemies
of their religion, the Aethiopians slept
near a thousand years, forgetful of the
world by whom they were forgotten.

Gibbon

10

Ethiopia by the Back Door: Eritrea

> Mountains never shake hands, Their roots may touch; they may keep company some way up; but at length they part company, and rise into individual isolated peaks. So it is with great men.
>
> Hare

I have watched the light come into people's eyes who have been to Ethiopia, and listened to the lift in their voices as they speak about the country; yet, they are often rather inarticulate. The royal family, they say, claims descent from the Queen of Sheba. Proof? They shrug; whether or no, Ethiopia is unique and, without doubt, beautiful. They stumble over the word 'beautiful' for the quality, the 'air' of Ethiopia is difficult to define. Then they go on to tell of *chiftas*, and that it is impossible to travel alone, or after dark. They talk of endless rounds of permit-queueing, the frustrations and petty officialdom. But this part of the story I know only too well; the light has gone out of their eyes and I am no longer interested.

Ninety-nine per cent of foreigners fly direct to Addis Ababa and see little of Ethiopia's mountainous interior. Would my arrival at this out-of-the-way frontier cause a situation? Would I be held up while they arranged for an escort for me? This was the question that had been on my mind from the start of the journey. Would the effort and expense of the long journey prove fruitless and I merely escorted to the first large town and handed over to a tourist bureau? Now at last I would find out.

The road rose slightly, it ran a spearhead into the plateau ahead, that forms the main part of Ethiopia. From the flat humid deserts of the Sudan, I was climbing quickly towards the great mountains that give Ethiopia some of the wildest and most spectacular scenery in the world, for along the plateau a range of mountains rise from 8,000 to 10,000 feet higher still and run for 400 miles to beyond Addis Ababa in the south. On the east the great mass drops in a sheer wall to the plains of the Danakil and the Somali, while the western slopes ease down on to the high plateau I was now approaching. For many months I was to climb and descend these fabulous mountains.

South of Addis Ababa, the great Rift Valley enters the country from Kenya and runs to the coastal plains of the Danakils; along the valley a chain of beautiful lakes, starting with Lake Rudolph on the Kenya border, stretches in an irregular line to within a few miles below Addis Ababa. Here the Ethiopian scene takes on a more mellow tone and the shores of the romantic lakes make ideal camping and picnic grounds. South of these lakes the mountains peter out and finally run down into the deserts, deserts that surround the country from all sides.

Already, as I climbed, the air was fresher for the higher altitudes give the country a beautiful climate despite the nearness to the Equator, and the big rains between June and September keep it green and fertile. These same rains, however, play havoc with communications and close all but the main roads.

The most important river, both to Ethiopia and her western neighbours, is the Abai or Blue Nile. Its source is a holy spring feeding the Little Abai that runs north into Lake Tsana. On the south-east side of the lake the Great Abai starts its spectacular journey through the mountains to the Sudan. During the rains the river swells and, together with most of the other rivers of the country, drains towards the west to feed the Upper Nile basin. The swelling of the Abai is responsible for most of the annual flooding in Egypt which means that Ethiopia governs the waters of Egypt. If the river was controlled by a couple of small dams in the Ethiopian Mountains, the Aswan Dam would be almost unnecessary.

Ahead of me on the side of the road were two female figures in dark clothes that made a sudden jab of black against the dusty foliage. They waved to me and their thin Semitic faces were smiling and excited. Behind them walked two men whose appearance was slightly familiar. Their slight bodies, thin almost to emaciation, moved with the same bearing as tribes in southern Arabia with whom they probably had some connection, for as early as the First Millennium B.C. tribes from Arabia and the Yemen landed on the African coast and invaded the more fertile highlands. The likeness is still there, the slightly tentative withdrawal of manner, the dignity and the same gliding walk. These men also carried a stick, but it was slung across their shoulders and their hands hung over each end in a way I had not previously seen.

Before the influx from Arabia, the Ethiopians, together with the Somalis and the Danakils of the desert plains below, were of Hamitic stock, related to the peoples of North Africa and Egypt. The highlanders, however, after centuries of intermarrying with the Semitic races from Arabia, assimilated much of their culture, as well as their language, and these are the main origins of the

Ethiopian people today. The name Abyssinia comes from one of the original migrating tribes from Arabia, the Habashat, but today the people prefer to be known as Ethiopians. Although the royal family's descent from the Queen of Sheba cannot be proved, their line has been, except for a few minor breaks, on the throne ever since the country's history was first recorded.

Around the first century the country was known as the Kingdom of Aksum and most of its early history is centred round the northern province of Tigré and the part now known as Eritrea. An old caravan route ran from the city of Aksum on the plateau, to the Greek port of Adulis on the Red Sea. The Ethiopians made their first contact with the outside world by this route; and Christianity came to the country when two small boys made the journey along it from the Red Sea in the fourth century. At that time, a philosopher from Tyre named Meropius was returning from a visit to India and he had the two boys, Aedesius and Frumentius, with him on the ship which put in at a Red Sea port for water. The entire ship's personnel was murdered, with the exception of the boys, and they were taken to the ruling king, Ella Amida, who befriended them. Eventually, Aedesius became King's Cup Bearer and Frumentius, Treasurer and Secretary. The king's son, Azana, who later became one of the greatest emperors of ancient Ethiopia, was still an infant when his father died, and the two Syrians stayed on to govern the country at the queen's request, until Azana was of age. During his stay in Ethiopia, Frumentius, who was the more pious of the two, helped the Roman Christian merchants, and when the two men finally left, Frumentius went to Alexandria and asked for a bishop to be sent to Ethiopia to watch over the small Christian community. No one could be found who could fulfil this mission as well as Frumentius himself, and he was therefore consecrated and sent back to the country.

This step established Egyptian patriarchal authority over Ethiopia and from then on, until quite recently, a bishop or abuna has been selected by Alexandria. Frumentius and King Azana converted the people and established the priesthood all over the country; and it plays a great part in Ethiopian life today.

But Christianity in Ethiopia suffered many setbacks. With the rise of Islam in the seventh century, which was quickly embraced by the pagans of the coastal plains, the highlands were continuously attacked, their treasures confiscated and their records destroyed by the Moslems. They were now cut off from their outlet to the sea and from other Christian countries and for this reason their religion did not develop on the same lines as other forms of Christianity. They retained many old rituals and customs, such as the dancing and chanting of the debteras, the ringing of sistrums, all of which has a certain pagan quality.

Another series of invasions started when the pagan Gallas from the south penetrated into the hills towards the centre of the country. These people, unlike the desert-dwellers who plundered and returned to the desert, came to settle, and many finally became Christians so that now they are barely distinguishable from the Amharas with whom they live. Some of the southern highlanders retreated before the Gallas to mountain strongholds, becoming completely isolated, and they continued to speak the original Ge'ez, very different from modern Amhara although this stems from the Ge'ez.

This much I knew about the kingdom of that absolute monarch, the Emperor Haile Selassie I, King of Kings, Conquering Lion of Judah, but of the people I knew nothing. I had never met an Ethiopian.

The road ran through a jungle of matted doum palms that would become a swamp during the rains. I was hot and tired after the exasperations of the Sudan bureaucracy and stopped to make some coffee with hot water from my thermos. Suddenly, out of the undergrowth, a tall, thin man emerged carrying a stick, curved at one end. He wore a shawl called a *shamma* over the skirt-like *longui* and moved swiftly towards the vehicle, looking through the window. It could be a *chifta*; and I was in a no-man's-land where nobody would think of searching for me. There was a ring through the lobe of his left ear, which is worn only by those who have killed an elephant. He stood watching the hot water coming out of the thermos – it is always a good rule to treat the situation as ordinary until it is proved otherwise – and shook his head with an incredulous smile. He did not look very dangerous and glanced at me with a slight air of patronage before pointing ahead along the road. I nodded. He made a scooping movement with his hands and I realised he thought I had broken down.

'*Tamam*,' I said, patting the steering wheel. He recognised the Arab word for 'good' and grinned back. '*Gowa?*' (coffee).

He put the long stick on the mudguard before accepting the coffee and wrinkled his nose as he tasted it, for all such liquids must be syrup-sweet. He took more sugar and stirred the coffee with his finger crooked, looking at the car, the contents, and me, as he sipped. Finally, passing back the empty cup, he picked up his stick and disappeared into the tangled undergrowth of doum palms as silently and quickly as he had come. I had met my first Ethiopian.

Ten miles further the track ran head-on to a main road, and at the intersection was a small round concrete pill-box with a thatched roof. A soldier, sitting on a stool by the opening, rose and came over to the vehicle. This was my first encounter with officialdom and would probably set the procedure and treatment I was going to receive from such people. He stood there, uncertain.

'Tessanai?' I enquired.

He looked startled that I should even speak, let alone know the name of the place, then he pointed along the road to the right in a southerly direction.

'Keren?' I now enquired.

He pointed along the road in the other direction, then back towards Tessanai. 'Police. Tessanai,' he said, and gave me a jab in the shoulder, before standing back to allow me to drive on.

Tessanai was twenty-eight miles from the border and stood on the spur of a small hill. Below it, on broken ground, were some solidly built structures placed at odd angles, which housed the customs personnel. The Customs House had two high-ceilinged rooms and a verandah. A large fat man greeted me cheerfully.

'I am British,' I said, as I handed over my passport.

'It does not matter,' he said.

'Oh, you speak English?'

'Yes, why not?' and he indicated a seat the other side of a wide desk.

He studied my passport intently, looked at me then blew out his cheeks and shook his head. I wondered, in a panic, if my visa had run out.

'*Na! Na!*' he called loudly, and a smaller, younger man hurried in from the next room. They both spoke at once, in a language that was very strange, before becoming silent as they studied, first my passport and then me. Despite the sunny warm air I felt cold all over. Was I going to be turned back before I had even entered the country? Were those thousands of miles all for nothing? I could stand the tension no longer.

'What is it?' I asked.

The larger man studied me intently. 'Is *this* your age?' He jabbed his fat finger on to the open page.

'Yes?'

'But you are older than I am.'

This was a shock, but I regained my manners. 'Yes, I'm sure I am.'

'You look younger.' His tone was accusing.

'I don't really, you know.'

'How do you do it, when you travel such rough places?'

'I only look younger at first glance, it's because I'm small – skinny really.'

'Skinny?'

'Thin, like desert dwellers. Also, I have nothing to worry about,' I added.

He nodded. 'You are not married.'

'I am a widow.'

'It is the same.'

'My – my passport is all right?' I asked.

'Oh, yes.' He stamped it with a flourish, his mind obviously still on the unfairness of age and size. 'Where do you arrive tonight?'

'Keren.'

'*Melcome* (good). When you come to Asmara, the Customs Headquarters will arrange for your Land Rover.'

It was as easy as that! But as I moved towards the door there was sudden chaos as a roar was set up through the building and both men ran, first to the door, then to the windows, banging them shut. With his back to the shuttered window, the fat official heaved a sigh of relief.

'*Chiftas?*' I quavered.

'No. A whirlwind. It will pass, but if it comes in we could be weeks finding the papers.'

Outside an odd humming could be heard. It came nearer, then the shutters and doors began to tremble. With a final crescendo of noise the air was suddenly filled with sand; it was there with us, like a child swept aside during carnival time. Just as suddenly all was quiet and the sand began to sink slowly to the ground.

'Phew!' The official and his companion opened the door and the windows. 'Now, you can go.'

It was a fanfare, a fitting welcome to the beautiful country that lay ahead of me; my spirits rose and quickly I was out in the brilliant sunlight again.

All the buildings along the spur of the hill were painted white and they glared back at me in the stark light. A spick-and-span petrol station was shaded by a huge peppercorn tree. Near to a long low building was a café owned by an Italian whose wife was a local woman. She was heavily pregnant and sat alongside a high, shaky bar while two small children played at her feet. The cheery Italian husband did the cooking and was serving as well. There was the chatter, bustle and humanity of the Latin countries, for most of the tables were occupied by Italian lorry-drivers who had stayed on after the Italian occupation ceased, allowing the exigencies of politics to pass over their heads.

In the Moslem Sudan I had been an oddity, but here I was a woman to be looked at, commented upon, and even given the wolf whistle at times. Ice-cold beer was served without the furtive sense of sin that accompanies the serving of liquor in Muslim countries; and the food, especially the spaghetti, was excellent. There was that easy indefinable atmosphere that is found in countries where people live and work by their own initiative.

Nobody had mentioned my requiring a permit or pass, nor cautioned me about driving at night. Had I asked if a permit was necessary, somebody would have had to answer the question, and it would have caused trouble and delay while somebody procured that permission. Had *I* not treated my arrival here alone as perfectly ordinary, they too would have found it unusual.

Ahead of me a back-cloth of blue and purple hills stood up in strange shapes; high pinnacles piling one behind the other were mountains of sheer rock of the most vivid colours. Some, flat-topped with perpendicular sides, called *ambas* were to become a familiar sight. The fierce flood waters of the summer rains cut deep into the mountains and plateau making not only wide valleys and narrow gorges, but these flat-topped *ambas* which, with their sheer sides, have been used for centuries as fortresses, prisons and monasteries. Even today, monasteries perch on their flat tops and one of the most famous, Debra Damo, has cliff sides so sheer that everyone has to be hauled up by a rope. This *amba* was previously used as a Princes' Prison, for it was the custom to imprison all the princes of royal blood, except the heir, and an *amba* was ideal for this purpose.

The road skirted this great canopy of rock, and suddenly over the high peaks rolled huge black clouds that swept down towards me as the whirlwind had done. There is something personal in everything that nature does in this country. Then the clouds burst around me and I edged slowly forward in the deluge. They had brought with them high winds and the anger that all African storms have. It passed as quickly as it had come, leaving the landscape more vivid than ever.

I drove on through the deserted mountains where, if there were people, they kept well out of sight. Gross baobab trees grew to an enormous size, their thick deformed-looking trunks gleaming in the afternoon sun. On the outskirts of Agordat, a little town set in a shallow valley, I was pulled up. A soldier inspected the car, studied my passport and indicated that his colleague would like a lift, as he had to deliver a letter to Asmara. The young soldier climbed into the Land Rover carrying a large rifle and an old skin-bag. He was obviously nonplussed by me, but kept the rifle at the ready, watching the undergrowth intently. As he was the enemy of *chiftas*, this made us, I felt, a sitting target. However, the enervating heat of the lowlands had gone, and with it, all feeling of tiredness and frustration, I had been told about the magic of the country and this was already beginning to work on me.

Keren was 170 miles from Tessanai and, by contrast with the hills, was bustling with people. It stood on a little hill in the middle of a wide fertile valley full of gardens and fruit-trees. The Italians built a fine road through the remote mountainous country from Asmara, opening up this little-known area, and they made Keren the centre of a large colonisation scheme. The town's history is one of many sieges and battles; the Egyptians seized it in 1872 when the rest of Ethiopia was weakened by civil war, and they in turn were defeated by Ras Alula, a local chief, who was ousted finally by the Italians. Again, in our time, it was the scene of a famous and bitter battle during the last war, and two miles from the town is the British Cemetery where some of our men lie. The narrow gap and fortified hills where the British and Indian troops made their brilliant attack, is commemorated by a plaque. It is a beautiful valley, wooded and sunlit, and the air is clear and brilliant; there could be no lovelier place in which to be buried.

We stopped in the hilly centre of Keren near an Italian-style coffee bar and a crowd gathered around. The soldier did not know the town and the excitement of the crowd had reached fever-pitch by the time a tall Egyptian in *jellabah* and *tarbush* had edged his way through the crowd and informed me that he spoke English.

'You want 'otel?' His dignity was accentuated by his concentration, as he tried to find the correct words.

'Yes, please,' I said.

He spoke to the soldier, pointing up the hill. 'It is above,' he said to me, 'the *askari* will show you,' and he moved off through the crowd.

The hotel opened on to a tree-shaded square which was set unevenly on the side of the hill with one corner towards the summit. The one-storey building was full of old people, children and the smell of newly-ironed linen. An inner court was used as the dining-room and bushes of hibiscus and an orange-tree grew between the tables. A large cage full of small birds, all brilliantly coloured, completed the lively scene. The hotel café overlooked the square and had its own piazza. There was an espresso machine and a juke-box, and many people, children included, sat on the piazza playing cards and yelling above the din.

'Well!' said the Italian proprietor expansively, as he regarded me. 'You must 'ave first a *sabanya* (guardian) for your Land Rover and you must also take everything out of the Land Rover during the night.'

'Everything?'

He nodded fatalistically.

'But surely if I have a watchman, that is enough?'

'It is *not* enough, but . . .' he shrugged; for it is the white man's burden to live in countries where stealing from the foreigner is the natives' national sport. I decided to risk it.

By the time a night-watchman had been found and my overnight luggage taken to a bright room full of chintz, the entire clientele of the café had joined in the operation. There were Italians, Greeks and both Moslem and Christian Ethiopians. Greeks were amongst the very earliest traders to come to the country and there is an Ethiopian saying: 'Turn over a stone in Abyssinia and you will find a Greek under it.'

A young Italian boy with a crew-cut and skin-tight jeans had a guitar-like instrument which he played every time the jukebox stopped.

'He is Georgis,' the proprietor confided to me. 'He is clever and will one day go to Italy and become a star.'

Georgis, draped elegantly over the chair opposite, began to play the sentimental *Anema e Core*; when he stopped he leant across the table towards me. 'You come from the desert like a whirl of wind,' he said softly, 'you pass and nothing is behind.'

'Oh,' I said.

'I am also poet.'

'Do you live in Keren?' I asked.

'My father grows fruit. It is very healthy and all the people are virile.'

'Yes, I am sure.'

'But I shall go to Italy where they make the best films. Do they also wear crew-cut in England?' But he did not wait for my answer and started to pick up an off-beat tune that was blaring forth from the juke-box.

Far into the night, as I lay surrounded by the bright chintz, *Anema e Core*, together with the more strident juke-box tunes, floated through the shuttered windows and disturbed the peace of the first cool night I had had in weeks.

11

The Queen of Sheba Passed Here: Asmara and Aksum

Trust instinct to the end, though
you can render no reason.

Emerson

Next morning I came out of the hotel and the *sabanya* was sleeping peacefully beside the Land Rover. The soldier arrived as I started the engine and climbed in beside me, having left both the rifle and his dispatch on the seat.

We drove through the cool morning air, out of the valley of fruit-trees and through high mountain passes. The rugged broken country spoke of wild animals, feuds and guerilla warfare, though all the inhabitants of the mountains kept out of sight until suddenly we were amongst beautiful women as we entered a village of the Beni Amer. They were tiny, dark-haired and vivacious and dressed in brilliant blue velvet. Their hair was done in tight plaits that stood out forming a halo around their small heads. They could have been some beautiful blue gentians come suddenly to life as they stood, confident in their beauty and smiling at the wonder on my face. And it was even more amazing that their clothes were exact replicas of those worn in the harems of the

Hadramaut in Southern Arabia; though these delightful creatures had a freer air than the *purdah* women.

Sixty miles after leaving Keren we drove into the bright clean city of Asmara which stands 8,000 feet above sea level. At last I knew what was meant by the expression 'the air is like wine' and in Asmara one asks for nothing better than to just go round *breathing*. The clear bright air makes the brilliantly-coloured flowers glisten and the inhabitants walk with a spring in their step.

The city's ancient ruins are well buried beneath the modern Italian-built city. The re-named Haile Selassie I Avenue in the centre of the town is a beautiful dual-carriageway promenade with modern shops, parliament buildings, pavement cafés, a Roman Catholic cathedral and various modern office buildings. Off the main avenue there is a large Mosque and a very modern Coptic church which seemed to combine something of both Moslem and Christian architecture. The cinemas show American, British, Italian and Arabic films to meet the needs of the polyglot community. Many of the Italians left when the country regained its independence, but they still predominate. Much of the bustle and the commerce has gone, however, from the city whose size now seems too large for its population.

The main hotel, C.I.A.A.O., pronounced 'Chow', was patronised by tourists and USA men from the hush-hush Military Radio Base near by, but other smaller hotels were much less expensive and served better food. At sundown the entire population of Asmara paraded, Italian-fashion, along the wide promenade or sat in the pavement cafés. Horse-drawn gharries transported people for a few shillings along the avenue which was curiously free from heavy traffic.

The Customs Authorities demanded £200 deposit for the Land Rover while it was in the country, and two days were wasted dealing with this. There were numerous interviews that started with the office clerk and ended with the Chief of Customs himself. He was a pleasant man with quiet manners, who moved in an aura of great importance; at every interview he held court, and underlings ran in and out at his bidding. I was kept waiting the suitable length of time necessary for an audience with such an exalted person, for position is an important and serious thing in this country. Finally, it was agreed that I should be given a letter to the authorities in Addis Ababa and take it up with them when I arrived at the capital.

When the Italians captured the main part of Eritrea in 1880 and controlled the coastline from the ports of Massawa to Assab, they cut Ethiopia off from the sea as she had been in olden times. The Emperor Haile Selassie made immediate demands for the return of the territory after the liberation of Ethiopia in 1941, although it was not until September 1952 that the Federation Agreement was finally concluded.

The road running from Asmara to Massawa drops sharply from the plateau to the hot desert plain below, and the change in temperature is just as sudden. Massawa, the port for Asmara, is seventy miles away and was built by the Italians as a naval base. It is the biggest port in the north of the country, and small islands are joined to the mainland by bridges which make it as picturesque as Zanzibar. It has a humid and enervating climate and the women are among the most beautiful in the world.

On the outskirts of Asmara, near the edge of the escarpment, is the city's rubbish tip, which is invaded at night by hyenas. They are never shot or destroyed for they dispose of the refuse overnight, and by the morning nothing remains. It is not wise to go alone at night to see the hyenas, for as well as the animals there are human scavengers who live in shanty huts beside the tip.

I left the road to drive towards the tip that made a platform jutting out from the sheer side of the escarpment. Dark figures came towards me from the huts; they were boys of all ages and wore an odd assortment of black rags. They ran swiftly like black fauns uttering no cries or words but giving curious grunts as I drove towards the edge. There was the excitement of the chase in their black eyes and they circled the car with the enclosing movement of vultures. Their excitement reached fever-pitch when they saw I was alone, and each tried to outstrip the other, almost snapping at each other. The animal-like quality, with the sharp intake of breath and curious grunts, unnerved me and I kept the car moving, making a circle round the tip before turning towards the main road again. They followed but, as I gained speed, were outstripped. This was a kind of wild creature I had never met before.

I drove slowly back to the city. There had been none of the shouts of children, and the boys' silence and animal-like stalking made them seem less than human. It was a new kind of wildness, and the encounter shocked and set me wondering what the deeper interior would hold. The inaccessibility of such parts, the months of isolation during the rains, the reluctance of the church to relinquish its hold to the state and to education, would all tend to keep such parts of the country backward. There were tribes in the more remote areas who knew loyalty only to their local Ras or chief, and it would be reasonable to expect that little had changed in their way of life. When James Bruce, the Scottish Traveller, came to the country in the eighteenth century hyenas cleared the dead from the streets at night; and books written in this century speak of the dead still being cleared in this way. Travellers journeyed with live oxen and fresh steaks were taken each day from the living animal; today, raw meat is hung up and guests cut thin strips, eating it direct from the carcase. How far then had the centuries merged? And did it matter if they had not? Even in those other days Alvarez, Bruce and other travellers had been welcomed and protected with traditional Ethiopian hospitality. A bad encounter could happen in *any* country, I argued to console myself.

It is obviously better, if you are not a V.I.P., to be as inconspicuous as possible in Ethiopia; and the most important thing is never to get a direct 'no'. For this reason I went warily about obtaining information for my journey south. There is a main Asmara-to-Addis Ababa road running 650 miles down the centre of the country, but I intended going south-west to Aksum, the first-known capital, and on to Gondar which lay north of Lake Tsana and had been the capital from the sixteenth century. If no road existed round the lake, I should have to retrace my steps 230 miles and join the main Asmara-to-Addis Ababa road again.

I called at the tourist office in Haile Selassie I Avenue to enquire about a map.

'Map?' The young man regarded me dubiously, for most people went by air. 'I don't think we have a map.'

Above the counter was a gay poster advertising the government-owned Ethiopian Airlines, which read: 'Ethiopia, the land of the Queen of Sheba'.

'Is that so?' I asked. 'Did she come from here?'

'Of course. If you go five miles out of the town towards the club you will see the place where her son was born.'

'The son she had by King Solomon?'

'That is right.'

'Is there anything to commemorate it?'

'No. Just a few ordinary stones, but it is the place,' he said with conviction.

'Nonsense,' said his companion, 'it is an old legend.'

'Everybody knows that it is so! Everybody knows His Imperial Majesty is descended from Solomon and the Queen of Sheba. It says so in the *Kebra Nagast*.' Then he pointed to the poster: 'And, there, look at that!'

Another man had joined us. 'It is not the place where the son was born,' he said, outraged, 'everyone knows it is near Massawa.'

'English poppycock,' said his Italian companion, 'you are all children.'

I left them arguing – and without a map. To mention the Queen of Sheba, I found, always started an argument.

Finally I made my way to the headquarters of the Imperial Highway Authority, the organisation that has the gigantic task of building and maintaining the mountain roads.

'There is certainly a good road through Aksum to Gondar,' said the Italian surveyor, 'but there is no road around Lake Tsana. Our men go through occasionally and you might be able to join one of their convoys.'

'Thanks,' I said, making a mental note that if a convoy could get around, so could I.

He looked at me quizzically. 'What *are* you doing here?' he asked.

'Well, I've come from Khartoum and I'm trying to reach Addis Ababa by this . . .'

'You come from the Sudan; no one stops you; you have no permit, no escort . . .'

'Please!' I interrupted, for his voice was rising, 'I am just going along, minding my own business. Please! I want to go this way.'

Suddenly, he looked almost sad. 'I know. And we all help you because we would like to do the same. But somehow – we don't.'

'Perhaps it is the reason why people *do* help me so much. They like to know that it *can* happen.'

'That's about it. Well, here is a map of the roads already built; eventually another one will run down the eastern shore of Lake Tsana to Bahar Dar and connect with the road south to Addis Ababa.' Then he laughed. 'The best and safest way to go to Gondar is still to fly there, you know – everyone does.'

I nodded. 'Thanks, for everything,' I said.

The Ethiopians have gone almost direct from the mule and camel to the aeroplane and they are all very air-minded. Government-owned, the Ethiopian Airlines has opened up the country and keeps it open during the rains. This remarkable institution which has a unique influence and place in the lives of everyone in the country was founded in 1945 and operates by an agreement with T.W.A. The pilots come from the USA, and the Ethiopians are trained as co-pilots and radio operators. Everyone concerned combines a business-like efficiency with a rather endearing *laissez-faire* attitude, necessary when operations cover such terrain. It says a great deal for the company and its personnel, that, over this dangerous country, there have been no fatal accidents since operations began in 1946.

Next morning there was a knock at my door. A small boy entered. 'Madam,' he said, and bowed.

'Yes?'

'You want to know about Makeda?' His eyes were wide and he was breathless with information.

'Makeda?' Oh yes, that is what you call the Queen of Sheba.'

He nodded. 'It is so. I hear they talk to you at the Tourist Office. I will take you and we shall see the place.'

'Do you mean the place near the club or the one near Massawa?'

'The place near the club, of course. Could we now go in your Land Rover?'

It is always amusing to hear them pronounce the word Land Rover which is more common with them today than the jeep.

Past the club there were just a few stones and nothing else to indicate the historic spot. Grass grew round the grey stones and the clear air was hush still. Why had this spot been chosen? Had they believed the Queen of Sheba was going to Aksum on her way from the north, even though there is no record that the city existed in her day? Had she, however, passed through 'with a very great train, with camels that bear spices and very much gold and precious stones'?

The small boy beside me looked up expectantly. 'Is that what she had?' I had quoted the line aloud.

'Well, that is what it says in the Bible,' I said, 'and it also says, "The King Solomon gave her all she desired whatsoever she asked and so she turned and went to her own country."'

'Then it is as I say,' he said, looking round, 'and here, it is called *Mai Bela*.'

'Why do they call it that?'

'It means, "give me water", and that was the first thing she said after the baby was born,' and he spread his hands out as though he was giving me the facts, the whole truth.

I looked at his wide eyes. 'So,' I said, for before such faith it is well to believe.

A more colourful version that enlarges on the Old Testament can be found in the Ethiopian Book of Kings, the *Kebra Nagast*, which is the history of the country. The standard edition dates from the thirteenth century, though it is believed that earlier written copies existed about the sixth century. It states that the Queen of Sheba, known as Makeda, ruled over Tigré and, having heard of the great wisdom of Solomon, made the long journey to visit him. She arrived with a magnificent court and fine gifts, and was received and entertained royally. She stayed long enough to be converted to the worship of Israel, and when she finally prepared to return to her own country the king, by a ruse, possessed her. Solomon, on hearing of her intention to leave, invited Makeda to a farewell feast at which he served hot dishes made from peppers and paprika. When the feast was over the king invited her to sleep at his palace and the queen consented on condition that he would swear not to take her by force. Solomon agreed if she, in her turn, would not take anything that belonged to him. She agreed and they retired, evidently within sight of each other. Makeda awoke with a great thirst caused by the peppers she had been eating, and thinking Solomon was asleep, took some of the water in a jug near by; whereupon the king who had been feigning sleep sprang up and demanded that as she had broken her vow, he was released from his. She had no alternative but to agree and 'he had his will with her and they slept together'.

Makeda returned to her own country and when a son was born of the union she called him Menelik. The boy when he became a young man was sent by his mother to Solomon who instructed his son in many things, and when Menelik finally wished to return home Solomon gave him twenty young men, sons of the noblemen of Israel, to accompany him. Legend has it that Menelik and his companions carried off the Ark of the Covenant from the Temple and escaped to Ethiopia and that now it lies in the church at Aksum. 'Thus were the religions and laws of Israel established in Ethiopia by Menelik who, as King Menelik I, waged many wars and conquered much land.'

Many other legends and incidents have been added to the original story. Makeda was reputed to have the feet of an ass, and Solomon, to verify this, had a floor of glass placed in a reception room, and she, thinking it was water, raised her skirts to reveal two perfect feet. And there are also many tales of Arwe the serpent, worshipped by the whole country, to whom it was necessary to make an annual offering of a virgin. On one occasion the virgin was rescued by a stranger who killed Arwe and married the girl who later became Makeda, the Queen of Sheba. The legends about the King Serpent are known all over the country and perhaps the dangerous overpowering serpent represents the violent flooding rivers that rise and destroy, but were finally conquered by the invaders from Arabia who introduced ingenious terracing, bunds and irrigation systems into the country.

Although there is no absolute proof that the Queen of Sheba ruled over Tigré, the story is romantic and the royal family's claim to the direct descent from the Solomon line has a unifying effect in establishing His Imperial Majesty's right to be King of Kings.

Chifta Country

News came through that *chiftas* had held up a busload of people coming from Gondar to Aksum and killed four passengers. Everyone was shocked, and if the authorities discovered that I intended going along this road they might stop me. So I set off early the next morning.

The plateau was dry, dusty and bare except for an occasional sycamore tree whose spreading branches attracted whatever humanity there was on the landscape. The people made their way from one tree to the next, following humped cattle or merely carrying a stick or a tiny fibre parasol. These incongruous little parasols, together with the flat spreading trees, made a landscape reminiscent of a Chinese print. Some of the dwellings on the plain burrowed into the ground and were half covered with earth, but the more typical Tigréan house, which is the most solidly built of all Ethiopian homes, is made of plaster and stone with an outside stairway.

The villages stood on raised ground, and the men and women alike wore the *shamma* which is a hand-woven toga-like shawl about three yards in length. There is a language of the *shamma* which is worn in different ways to denote respect towards acquaintances, for Ethiopians are very socially conscious and rank is most important. During formal gatherings in olden days it was continually being adjusted as people of different social standing appeared. Underneath the *shamma* the men wore cloth tunics and trousers similar to jodhpurs while the women's full-skirted dress came to the ankles. Some of the men wore hats made from the same fibre as the parasols and shaped like an outsize bowler.

At a village called Adi Quala there was a confusion of routes, and I pulled up beside a soldier to enquire the way. He immediately asked for a lift and climbed into the Land Rover with a rifle and a large sack of grain. He scanned the landscape intently as we drove towards the edge of the plateau where we dropped sharply into the deep valley of the Mareb River. Near the bottom there was a jumble of large red boulders and the steep cliff sides were honeycombed with caves. Bushes and wild fig-trees grew amongst the rocks and a long, red iron bridge spanned the river which, at this time before the rains, was merely a tiny trickle of water following a zigzag course between fillets of white sand.

I stopped on the bridge to take some photographs. The soldier followed me, his gun at the ready and peering uneasily into the undergrowth and cliffs, for the valley has always been a favourite haunt of *chiftas*. During unsettled times chiefs, who did not wish to join the battles or take sides, disappeared into the valley here, where they took to banditry in order to live. It was the main route from the north to the plain of Adowa and Aksum, and those who wished to make the journey waited until they could join a rich merchant or Ras who had his own bodyguard. The caravan might consist of hundreds of people and stretch for miles down the mountainside. It was often accompanied by itinerant Azmaris or strolling players, who cheered the travellers with music and songs of gallantry and love. The Azmaris exist today and are mostly married couples who wander around the country attending all festivities, including marriages; the man plays the *Masinko*, a one-stringed instrument, or the *Kra*, a crude kind of lyre, and he improvises the songs while his wife dances.

In these valleys, guerilla warfare and banditry were carried on against the Italians when they occupied the country and caused them great trouble; the *chiftas* were heroes then, but today they are feared by the local people and are gradually being stamped out.

The soldier pointed out wide rock wells built by the Egyptians who, in 1875, were attacked by the Emperor John on this spot. He did some realistic mime of wholesale slaughter and then hurried me back to the car.

Deep in another valley which was so narrow that the light filtered down to us, opaque and lifeless, the soldier motioned me to stop. Near by were two low huts that made his home. Three children and their mother came towards us. The children looked like little honey-coloured cherubs with their hair shaved except for a tiny top-knot reaching to heaven. The woman was beautiful with finely-drawn features and light brown skin; her hair was braided in many tiny plaits which were then caught at the nape of her neck. A full white skirt showed beneath her *shamma* and she walked barefoot with a fine grace towards us under the trees.

I left them and climbed steeply, running on to the plateau again where a great back-cloth of peaks and mountains confronted me across the Adowa Plain, famous as the scene of the Italians' defeat by Menelik II's army. The clearness of the air sharpened the colour of the *ambas* and spears of purple and blue rocks; the world seemed to fall away behind them.

A family with their cattle were moving towards the east, dignified, unhurried. On their way from Aksum, twenty miles to the west, they were following the old caravan route to the coast just as their ancestors had done 2,000 years ago. On their way they would pass Yeha, older still than Aksum, where there are the remains of a walled city. It was known to the Ptolemys, and in the present village near by there are sections of stones belonging to both Sabaen and Byzantine periods. Beyond, on the plateau of Kohaito, is Koloe, a once beautiful city where rich merchants and nobles from the humid port of Adulis had their summer villas. In the heart of the old city there is a dam dating from Sabaen times with a wall 200 feet long forming one side of a large lake that was filled from a near-by stream. Leaving the cool city the caravan route continues to the coastal plain and finally reaches Adulis.

Aksum is at the other end of the caravan route and stands in low hills overlooking a wide plain, which in the days of the city's greatness was part of the centre. To my right as I approached, a tiny peaked hill with a small, round thatched chapel perched precariously on its summit, looked gay, picturesque – and rather unpractical.

Sycamore trees and a Euphorbia bush, which stood like a giant candelabra, grew on the slopes and the road led directly to the Cathedral of St Mary of Zion, the holiest shrine in the country. In its sacred enclosure criminals were safe from arrest for, once gaining the sanctuary of the cathedral, they could, on ringing the bell on the porch, announce their intention of taking refuge here.

From then on, so long as there were friends to feed them, they were safe.

The cathedral was destroyed in the sixteenth century by the Moslem invader, Mahommad Ghan; and the present smaller one was rebuilt on the former foundations a century later by King Fasilidas. Francisco Alvarez, chaplain of the first Portuguese Mission to Ethiopia (1520–7), describes the original building as 'a very noble church with seven chapels'. Some pieces of early Byzantine work are incorporated in the present structure which had medieval Portuguese influence, for that country's craftsmen were employed extensively up till then.

I viewed it from afar, for women are not allowed in the sacred enclosure; the wide, square façade had a crenellated surround and a bell-tower. Steps led to the wide corridor formed by the outer pillars which faced the front, and it is along here that the *debteras* dance and chant during festivals and ceremonies. The Ark of the Covenant is reputed to be in the cathedral's *Makdas* or Holy of Holies.

Smaller churches, the treasury and houses of the clergy surround the cathedral. Many things of value were brought here for safe keeping and placed in the vaults of the treasury and in the cathedral. There are many crowns of the Ethiopian emperors, some magnificent treasures, others merely gaudy. Here, also, are beautiful examples of Ethiopian craftsmanship in silver, and embroidery on fine velvets, and many fine manuscripts.

In a far corner stood a curious group of stones, grey and crudely cut. There were four, forming posts for a canopy over an equally crudely cut stone throne; and it was here that the ancient Ethiopian emperors were crowned. Above them, casting a stringy shade, was a group of eucalyptus saplings, recent arrivals from my own new country on the other side of the world.

From the cathedral an old processional way leads directly to the obelisks, the most extraordinary monuments in Ethiopia. Terraces of stone ran along the shallow valley where several of the obelisks had been erected on foundation stones. One was still standing, and it rose to a height of seventy feet, while another larger one had crashed to the ground and broken into many pieces. There are no inscriptions on the stone and their origin has not been definitely placed, although it is believed they were erected in the pre-Christian period. All of them were made of a single piece of granite and some are over a hundred feet high. The standing obelisk was elaborately carved to depict a building of several storeys, and it tapered to a round and fluted top. On the 'ground-floor' there was a carved door with a lock realistically executed. Near by some of the fallen parts of the obelisks had been used as foundations for the present buildings just as the Byzantine pieces were incorporated in the cathedral. I climbed on to the broken fallen pieces to examine the carving and it needed the help of several small boys to get me there. It would be a major operation to shift even one of the broken pieces today and it is difficult to understand how the whole piece of granite was quarried, brought to the site, and erected. I looked from the great monuments to the insecure-looking *tukuls* of present-day Aksum and wondered if, after all, tales of giant ancestors were all that tall!

Other obelisks, merely crude stones, some of them phallic symbols, stand half buried on the plain, and every time it rains coins are washed up that date back many centuries; these tell of the city's great age and give a hint of what probably lies beneath the earth. Many civilisations influenced Aksum's style of architecture; the Sabaens, the Himarites, Greeks and later the Portuguese all contributed something to the final style, that is seen also in the monolithic churches of Lalibela and the castles of Gondar.

A boy deacon led me along a path which was backed by a high wall, and we entered the courtyard of a round thatched church. After removing our shoes we entered the outer circle or ambulatory called the *Kene Mahlet*. All around us on the straw-strewn floor, men and women sat, and the noise of prayer and chatter resounded round the walls. Many prayer sticks lay heaped to one side and a beautiful ceremonial drum glowed golden in the half light. We passed into the next circle or *keddest* where the walls were covered with crude and brightly-coloured paintings depicting many scenes of martyrs, St George and the Virgin Mary. No one except the priests enters the *makdas* or inner sanctuary where the consecrated piece of wood or stone symbolising the Ark of the Covenant and the Tables of the Law are kept. We picked our way over the feet and came at last into the open.

'You must pay two dollars,' said the boy deacon, 'for the church.' He took it and disappeared into the church again.

The traditional Ethiopian church is circular with a thatched roof supported by pillars and arches. To the east there is another small house called Bethlehem where the bread and wine of Sacrament are stored; and another building holds the vestments of the church and other things belonging to it.

I inspected my feet carefully for 'jiggers' or moyale which are small insects that get under the skin and lay their eggs there. If one scratches, for they cause acute irritation, and the egg sac breaks, the eggs hatch and spread. It is generally agreed that an Ethiopian is by far the most expert at removing the sac complete.

The Land Rover bumped up the shallow valley, past the old stone reservoir that can still be used, to the rock tombs on the summit. A young boy sat beside me, delighted at the very rough journey as we cut across the stony fields. We stopped at last, defeated by the high boulders, and scrambled to the top where the underground tombs of the emperors Caleb and his son Gabra Maskal lay. Caleb ruled in the sixth century and he crossed the Red Sea to south Arabia to protect his Himyar Christian subjects, for at that time Ethiopian territory extended that far. He established order and returned to Aksum where he eventually abdicated and became a revered monk who was known to Greeks, Latins and Arabs alike. The tombs were of cut stone, beautifully interlocked and without plaster, similar to those outside Palmyra in Syria, and the big caverns with alcoves for mummies stood as the others had done, empty now but not oppressive. One passageway disappeared into the darkness and I peered ahead. Several small boys who had raced across the fields stood around trying to control their short breath and excitement.

'Where does the passage lead to?' I asked.

'Judith!' said my boy.

'Judith. Is she buried here?' Judith was the Falasha queen who sacked the city in pre-Christian times.

They shook their heads. Judith, the legend goes, was finally routed by the Ethiopians and disappeared down the passageway which came out on the plains below the plateau near the coast. But such tales are endless, and another relates that Menelik I when escaping with the Ark of the Covenant, used such a tunnel to leave the Holy Land and reach his own country.

'And Makeda?' I asked.

With one accord they pointed to the west, where seven miles away French archaeologists had recently excavated a small summer palace. There is nothing to substantiate the boys' claim, but Makeda is associated with any place whose origin is in doubt. Alvarez heard and read about Makeda during his stay in Aksum and quoted from books that were subsequently destroyed when the cathedral was sacked by Ghan. The queen, it is stated, built her city here and called it Debra (Mount) Makeda. When she was preparing for her journey to the wise Solomon: 'seven hundred and ninety-seven camels were loaded and mules and asses innumerable'. She would have passed across the wide plain below me, towards the great canopy of blue and purple mountains. Later she returned and graciously said: 'I went through the door of the treasury of wisdom and I drew for myself the waters of understanding.'

The time of Aksum's splendour is recorded from the first century and continued until the sixth century. It is not definitely known that the kingdom was in existence during the Queen of Sheba's time, but who can dispute that this country might not have been a colony of Arabia for its territory was known to extend across the Red Sea; just as part of Southern Arabia belonged to Ethiopia in the Emperor Caleb's time?

Six miles to the west of Aksum on the spur of a hill known as Mount Gobederah there was a large granite rock with the fine carving of a leaping lioness in low relief; she sprang with realistic vigour towards a disc-like sun. All around on the hillside were great rocks of granite, and it was obvious that the stone for the obelisks had been quarried here. How the rocks, some weighing 500 tons, were moved and erected, remains a mystery.

On the outskirts of the town there was a small hotel run by an Italian woman. Lorry-drivers called at all times of the day and night for a meal and a few hours' rest; they travelled in convoy because of the recent *chifta* tragedy, and were carrying salt from the coast to the interior and bringing back grain.

'So!' said the proprietress, 'you go to Gondar.'

'Yes,' I said.

She sighed. After all, it was not her business and she had warned me that to obtain permission for most things was difficult.

'Then you must not stop, *at all*!'

'Not even to take photographs?'

'Least of all to take photographs. Then you are – target!'

'All right.'

'However,' she edged nearer to me, '*if* someone challenges you, even if they are not in uniform, you must then stop, *pronto*!'

'But if they are not in uniform, surely I should not stop?'

She hesitated. 'They will be soldier, just the same.'

Perhaps she was trying to say it would be safer to stop if challenged by *chiftas* as they are very good shots and had killed the people in the bus as they were driving away. But it was better not to get into too many discussions.

'I shall be all right,' I said, 'I shall start early.'

She nodded vigorously. 'Every minute of the daylight!' she said and gave me a long steady look. 'Such a nice signora, no trouble at all,' I could hear her saying later, should I be wiped out by the *chiftas*!

12

South to Gondar: Gojjam

> Day follows the murkiest night; and when
> the time comes, the latest fruits also ripen.
>
> Schiller

Starting early from a sleeping town is the loneliest moment of travel. The town is still, uncommunicative, and the only living thing astir is the odd waiting animal, or the first ruffling bird in a tree. This morning the one remaining obelisk was facing the dawn as it had done so many thousands of times before; it had stood there as the first cry of a child broke the morning stillness, and decades later as the midnight wailing told of that same person's death. Dawn plays a large part in my lone journeys. I forget it in the western world, but often now I anxiously await its arrival for the dark can hold terrors; at last it arrives, always different, always quite beautiful.

The road ran west across the plain where much of the city of Aksum and its suburbs lay buried, and after thirty miles turned south towards the first spur of the Semien Mountains, Ethiopia's highest peaks. The grass, acacia trees and solitary Euphorbia bush gave way to tangled vines and a crush of thick foliage which grew on the sloping sides of the gullies as they deepened into gorges.

Running towards the brink of a particularly large gorge, a magnificent road dropped 3,000 feet into the valley of the River Takazze and wound down in tortuous curves and hairpin bends. On the other side across the valley, the road could be seen quite clearly winding up in a similar manner. It was perfect road-block country, for it was possible to hear and see, for many miles, the approach of anyone from the other side.

At the base of the valley there was a military road-block where a soldier looked at my passport, took the number of the Land Rover and asked my destination. He seemed a little uncertain what to do, reasoning perhaps that as I had come so far I must have permission to do so. I gave a quick nod and moved on, relying on my bush-jacket, which has a slightly professional look, to help me pass as either a doctor or a missionary.

The Takazze Valley road was merely a forerunner to the magnificence of the Semien Pass. Here hills towered around me and there were high peaks of every shape and colour that made crazy patterns and a strange but beautiful skyline. Snow falls on the highest peaks of the Semien and many early explorers had their words doubted when they returned with this piece of information, for it was not believed that snow could fall so near the equator.

Once again, it was the Italians who were responsible for the building of the road, for they planned to make Gondar the capital of their Amhara colony. Unlike the concentrated Takazze Valley road, it climbs the great spur of the mountain face, winding in and out and rising in a series of wide curves while the scenery around is open and far reaching. Half-way up the mountain the road circles an *amba* where, on its surface of bright green, a couple of *tukuls* sat. Nearer the top, a spring, coming out of the mountain-side, had been made into a rather ostentatious drinking fountain in the Italian style; and still higher was a memorial to those who had lost their lives in the making of the road,

I disregarded the hotel proprietress's warning and stopped the Land Rover. Far below, on the vivid green *amba*, a man had just driven a red cart stacked high with golden logs and, in the fold of the mountain, a thin line of blue smoke curled up as someone smoked out a hive of wild bees. The clear air gave a kind of unreality to the scene; the picture was too perfect, no cloud, no wind and now, even the owner of the cart had disappeared into one of the *tukuls* – the world was still and I had never seen such magnificence . . .

There was a rustling in the undergrowth behind me and out of the bushes scrambled a woman and two men. They were a happy, intimate trio with light skins, wide-set eyes and aquiline noses. The woman moved with an air of great confidence and well-being, and the men, I noticed with relief, carried only sticks and no gun. They were Falashas, known as the Black Jews, who live in the Semien Mountains and the area north of Lake Tsana. Legend has it that they are descended from the Israelites who accompanied Menelik, the Queen of Sheba's son, when he returned from his visit to Solomon; though it is more likely that they are a pre-Christian Aksumite group who resisted Christianity and retreated to the mountains. For centuries they have been isolated, fighting for their independence and belief. Their religion now is a mixture of paganism and Judaism of which many old customs have survived and even today they practise incision for girls, as well as circumcision for boys.

The younger man spoke a little Italian, and he asked me, with the help of realistic mime, why the woman had no children and also what could be done about the sore on the older man's lip. I supplied some salve for the lip, but it was more than language difficulty that prevented me from giving any practical advice on the other problem.

Finally they left, continuing down the steep mountain-side, spurning the flat surface of the mountain road. They waved back at me, happy and secure in their mountain fastness.

I turned towards the great fertile plain that leads to Gondar, and life here was more orderly, for the lush fields stretched far ahead and groups of golden *tukuls* clustered together on the gentle slopes. In some of the trees long cylinder-like bee-hives hung, and occasionally a copse of juniper trees surrounded a church. Even if the church had crumbled the trees remained, for they are never destroyed on Holy Ground. Here, the Goreiza or colobus monkeys had taken sanctuary, and they swung from one tree to the next. The monkeys were in danger of becoming extinct but they are protected now, although it is still possible to buy the circular black and white skin mats from the street vendors in Addis Ababa. Near a church there was a crude wooden frame, and from it hung long pieces of granite that are struck to summon the congregation to church service.

Finally, ahead, in a wooded green basin lay Gondar, once a capital of twenty palaces and over thirty churches, though, all that could be seen now were a few white buildings amongst a thick growth of eucalyptus trees. I disturbed a pair of large spur-winged geese before dipping down into the final valley to the town. They took to the air heavily and were the first unusual birds I had seen.

The town spread over small hills and valleys, and the main street climbed in a steep winding spiral past derelict Italian structures that had been built more for show than style, and led to a small modern hotel overlooking the walled castles of the Ethiopian kings. The high rounded tower of King Fasilidas' castle could be seen beyond the great encircling wall, and high stone arches ran from the outer side of the wall and spanned the modern street below.

The hotel was small and modern, with a swimming-pool in the garden. The reception desk was deserted, and in the lounge a young woman sat near the window reading. She looked up and smiled.

'Can *I* help?' she asked in a soft American drawl.

'I want a room, that's all.'

'They'll be along soon. They kind of like to sleep in the afternoon.'

'It's a very good custom,' I said.

She had the quiet assurance of the American woman, and her face was familiar, but this is a trick of mine, to think I recognise someone whom I am going to know very well.

'Just where have you come from?' she asked, glancing through the door at the Land Rover.

'From Aksum.'

'Alone?'

I nodded.

'My!'

She was Margaret Mabbott, and her husband, Lyle, was the chief engineer on the Sources of the Nile project. The job took him over much of the wild country through which the Abai flows, and he was away for weeks on difficult and often dangerous journeys in a Land Rover or a helicopter. They had a home in Addis Ababa, efficient servants and, while her husband was away, Margaret had little to do. She had flown to Gondar to be near him.

'I'll be glad to show you Gondar,' she said, and we set off that afternoon to see the first of the palaces.

King Fasilidas, whose reign began in 1632, established Gondar as his capital, and it remained so until the middle of the nineteenth century. There had been no permanent capital for some time as the country was still suffering from the wars of the previous century, and the kings set up camp wherever they halted. This makes Gondar unique, for nowhere else in the country, except perhaps at Lalibela, are there such large and solidly-built palaces and churches of the periods. Fasilidas is also remembered for having finally squashed the Jesuits' attempts to establish their religion in the country. Finally, it was he who revived the old custom of imprisoning all the princes of royal blood, and he used Amba Wahni for this purpose.

The walled enclosure of the palaces was over 1,000 feet long and the buildings ran from south to north in order of succession, starting with the largest palace of King Fasilidas. The rectangular structure, made of golden limestone, was three storeys high with round turrets at each corner. An outer stairway rose to the first storey, and the whole affect was extremely picturesque. The medieval-style towers and the high windows owe a lot to the Renaissance, and despite the fact that by this time the Portuguese had been banished from the country, much of their influence in architecture still remained.

Margaret and I climbed to the high parapet. 'This reminds me of the *rheims* (enclosed roofs) of my house in southern Arabia,' I said, looking at the crenellated edges.

There are many foreign influences, and ghosts of strangers who brought something of their country, or who wrote about Ethiopia when they left. Many of the explorers, missionaries and artists, however, who came here were never allowed to leave, for the Ethiopians were notoriously loath to let them go. Some were confined to prisons, but the scholars and craftsmen were put to better use either to teach or build. The Venetian painter, Nicholas Brancaleone, who came to Ethiopia in the fifteenth century was never allowed to leave; he worked for forty years and his influence is seen in many paintings, and the miniatures in the churches' manuscripts. Some travellers were forced to move around with the king, even accompanying him to the wars, and they were known as the 'King's Strangers'. James Bruce who came to the country to discover the source of the Nile in 1768 became a 'King's Stranger' and resided with the court at Gondar. There are echoes of them all, Alvarez, Brancaleone, Bruce, Poncet and even John Bell and Walter Plowden, the English friends of the Emperor Theodore who came to the country in the nineteenth century.

The walls and windows of the palace were decorated with the hard blue-red tufa stone and it was cut into square tiles covering the lower floor. The palace had been carefully restored but little remained of the interior decorations that have been described as 'magnificent with tapestries, mirrors, ornaments and buffalo horns'.

Near Fasilidas' palace were two smaller ones known as the Library and the Chancellery, and tucked away near the outer wall was the smaller crumbling palace of Jesus II which must have been a little gem. At the far end of the enclosure was the palace of King Bacuffa. It is a long bare structure, that made a fine banqueting hall but has since been used as a barracks for which it now seems eminently suitable.

King Bacuffa is a popular figure in Ethiopian history and there are many tales about him, for he was extremely energetic and a great builder. He escaped from Wahni, the Princes' Prison Mountain, but was recaptured and had the tip of his nose cut off. This should have excluded him from becoming king as no mutilated heir could succeed to the throne. He was, however, finally brought down from the mountain and crowned, after his brother, King David, had been poisoned. He reigned from 1719 to 1729 and suppressed many court intrigues. He used ingenious methods to gain his objective, often feigning death and, when his enemies showed their hands, he would reappear and punish them. He also travelled through the country-side in disguise in order to discover his rivals; and on one occasion he fell ill and was nursed by the daughter of the local lord of the village. She was the beautiful Berhan Mogasa whom he finally married and gave the name Mentwab (The Beautiful). It was their son who became King Jesus II; Bacuffa was also very superstitious and he worried for years about a prophecy that foretold a woman named Wallata Giorgis would have complete control during his heir's reign. After the birth of their son, he repeated this story to Mentwab who told him that her own first two baptismal names were Wallata Giorgis. The prophecy was fulfilled for she became regent while her son was still a minor, and concealed her husband's death for some time so as to establish firmly her son's succession. There was never a dull moment, one feels, during Bacuffa's reign.

Mentwab lived for years after her husband's death, and Bruce heard many of these tales from her. He speaks of her as being still beautiful in old age and with a very light skin of which she was inordinately proud.

Near to Bacuffa's was Mentwab's own palace, a curious high block with falling wooden verandahs and ornately decorated niches inlaid with tufa.

'Let's go and see Mentwab's summer palace of Kusquam,' said Margaret. 'It's a little out of the town.'

We passed the remains of pavilions and smaller palaces, and a solid building with vaulted rooms that had been Bacuffa's stable. Above it was a flat roof along which the horses paraded. The large circular church was locked and the priest with the key could not be found. On the apex of the roof a finely worked maskal or cross had each of its points tipped with an ostrich egg which is, no doubt, a fertility symbol.

Outside the palace enclosure the branches of a wild fig-tree spread shade over a vast area and people sat on a stone platform that surrounded the trunk. Until recently *chiftas* were hanged from its tough branches.

In the curve of the valley and encircled by a beautiful old wall was Fasilidas' own summer palace. The ornate little building was set round a pool whose water came from the tiny River Kaha near by. Standing apart was a solitary little building which was the tomb of the king's favourite horse, and we wondered what tales of endurance and gallantry could be told of this four-footed friend.

During the ceremony of Timkat, which commemorates the Baptism of Christ, all Gondar makes its way to this enclosure and the Ark of the Covenant is brought from each of the churches, to the pool. The bishop dips his cross three times into the water and then blesses the congregation, sprinkling them with water taken from the pool. This is a cue for the priests who follow suit and bless those around them; finally all the small boys jump right into the pool and everyone is wholeheartedly blessed and gets very wet. After the ceremony each ark forms a procession as it is conveyed back to its own church, followed by the choirmen or *debteras* who with prayer stick and rattle stop, from time to time, to perform the Dance of David. They chant and shuffle backwards and forwards accompanied by the drummer who stands between the two rows of dancers. And so the day goes by with each slow procession finally reaching its own church.

Now the enclosure was quiet and deserted and the small palace with its tiny causeway was reflected in the undisturbed waters. Kings, however, have been known to push irritating subjects into these same still waters.

Up the slender valley near by was Mentwab's Palace of Kusquam which was a little community of palaces, chapel, church and official buildings surrounded by crumbling walls. Along the wall's length, picturesque turrets, set at intervals, were used by the monks as dwellings. We stopped the car near giant juniper trees that are as old as the buildings themselves. Jesus II built the palace for his mother who retired here towards the end of her life, and James Bruce spent much of the latter part of his visit here, for he became disgusted with the many excesses of the disintegrating court. The high walls made a wonderful sun-trap for the many buildings, and an inner wall surrounded a large stone church that had been badly damaged just before the final collapse of the Italians during the last war. Now everything of value had been taken from it and the inner sanctuary was crudely boarded up. Monks were praying in a small chapel that clung to the high outer wall, and near by in the shade of more juniper trees an old man sat weaving fibre parasols. He sold us one for a few dollars.

'They make fine lampshades,' said Margaret, and went off with the light flimsy thing over her head.

Ethiopians are very proud of their light skins and protect them whenever possible. Someone will certainly tell you about when man was created and colour was a problem. Experiments were carried out by putting him in an oven; the first person was overcooked and very black so he was the negro; the second was undercooked and white; but the third was the Ethiopian and he was just right, being a perfect delicate brown.

Most of the walls of Mentwab's own palace had fallen and we climbed the one remaining turret, slipping over the vines and crumbling stones. Below us was a jungle of trees and bushes where a garden had been, but the buzzing of bees was the only sound and sign of activity in the deserted place. Another building where

Bruce spent much of his time had highly decorated arches and carved windows with surrounds of tufa which gave a slight idea of the place's original grandeur but, when we tried to penetrate further, we were forced back by the undergrowth. We wandered round, unwilling to leave, for much of Kusquam's charm still lingers in there being no restorer's mark, no face lift; and in the memory of the lovely Mentwab.

Right on the other side of the town is the rectangular Church of Debra Berhan built by Jesus the Great, whose reign was amongst the most spectacular of the Gondar period. The church has been described as 'truly magnificent' and fine paintings, which were later destroyed, covered the walls of the Holy of Holies. The encircling turreted wall has a majestic archway with huge wooden doors ornately studded. A sermon was in process but a boy deacon led us past the priest, who sat on the floor surrounded by the congregation. They took no notice of us and very little of the sermon, and the friendly atmosphere was slightly reminiscent of a mosque. The interior walls were bright with decorations of paintings and carved woodwork and hundreds of rounds, vivacious faces, most of them looking sideways to denote virtue, covered the ceiling. The boy deacon uncovered a fine painting of a Byzantine-style Madonna near the wall of the inner sanctuary and the sermon still continued as we made our way out into the sunlight again.

Several damp patches on the ceiling were destroying the paintings.

'Have you no money to repair the roof?' I asked the boy.

'When the Emperor comes to Gondar, we shall ask him for the money.'

'And will he give it to you?'

'He gives many things,' the boy said simply.

*

There is a great variety of designs in crosses worn or carried by the Ethiopians and the finer ones come either from Gondar or Aksum, for these two towns are famous for their metal work.

We made our way towards the market section of the town where in the narrow cobbled streets the silver workers had their tiny shops. We passed long frames where cotton was hanging out to dry and people and donkeys jostled each other in the friendly atmosphere found in such markets. Some of the shops were closed and we waited while the owners were sent for. Margaret had made many friends and we stopped and chatted in the shops even if we didn't buy. The craftsmen made crosses, the chains to go with them, a few bangles and ear-rings and occasionally *tej* pots that were beautiful and very expensive. We were offered many crosses of inferior workmanship, but if we waited long enough better ones were brought out from drawers and cupboards.

The market square was cobbled with large blocks of granite and deep draining-ditches ran around it. Many different types wandered between the piles of merchandise; there were itinerant monks in cloaks of skin, Tigré women with tightly-braided hair caught at the nape of the neck, women from Shoa with their hair shocked out like Struwwelpeter and women whose hair was shaved as a sign of mourning. There were a few Negroes from the south and Moslems in baggy trousers, while the more sophisticated Ethiopians wore tunic, jodhpur and *shamma*.

Two soldiers were sitting on the rampart walls playing *gabatta*. Between them, on the flat surface of the wall, eighteen grooves had been hollowed out and three small stones were placed in each hole. The men passed the stones from one groove to the other, sometimes slowly and then with a sudden rush, when they became very excited.

We watched, mystified. 'Maybe it is like draughts,' said Margaret, at last.

'I've seen it played in all the countries across Africa,' I said, 'perhaps it scores like "shove ha'penny".'

'What the heck's "shove ha'penny"?'

'It's a game we play at home with a ha'penny.'

'And what's a ha'penny?'

'A ha'penny? Half a penny.'

'Oh,' she said, 'you mean a half-penny.'

We were disturbed early one morning by the beating of drums, and climbing the high road near the Governor's palace saw a procession coming towards us. It was the Sunday in early May when the Ethiopian Coptic Church celebrates the Nativity of the Virgin Mary. The Ethiopian year has the same number of days as ours but it is divided into thirteen months; twelve have thirty days and the thirteenth has five. The first month is Maskaram, which is around September.

Priests in their devotional robes moved beneath a canopy of brilliant umbrellas, and a large cross also had its own umbrella, while small boy deacons in cloaks of bright colours were enveloped by equally large ones. The velvet and gold glistened in the clear early light and the procession, followed by a large proportion of the inhabitants of Gondar, had a carefree and festive air that accompanies all ceremonies in Ethiopia. The long line of bobbing umbrellas, cross and the occasional itinerant priest in his rough wide cloak of skin seemed to be walking towards us right out of the past. The procession turned off the road and entered the high gates of the Governor's palace which closed behind the Head Priest and his retinue. The rest of us waited outside while they breakfasted together.

In Ethiopia invitations for breakfast have been the usual thing for many centuries, and the country's turbulent history has taken many an erratic turn after this meal, for while some such invitations were mere social occasions, others had a more sinister motive. Enemies, discarded lovers, unwanted kings, foreigners or priests were invited to breakfast and poison was served. Today the custom still persists though the motive is not so sanguinary.

Finally the high gates opened again and the priest emerged. The procession continued, with dozens of brilliant umbrellas, and the high ornate cross bobbed its way down the tree-shaded road.

13

No Road South to Shoa

Travel teaches toleration.

Disraeli

Margaret was flying back to Addis Ababa and I began making enquiries for continuing my journey south. Gorgora was forty miles south of Gondar on the northern shore of Lake Tsana and a small steamer left there every week for Bahar Dar on the south of the lake, calling at some of the islands on the way. There are monasteries on some of the islands, and women are forbidden to land there; some have drowned from floundering craft rather than set foot on the islands. The lake is very treacherous, for sudden squalls turn it into a rough sea. The local people build long canoes that are not much more than a bundle of reeds woven together; they sit low in the water and skim across at a great speed which is necessary for they finally become waterlogged and sink.

The brigand King Theodore lived on one of the islands as a child and his story and fate were linked with the two Englishmen, John Bell and Walter Plowden. In 1848, previous to Theodore's spectacular rise to power, Plowden, accompanied by Bell, had been sent by Lord Palmerston to Ethiopia with a trade agreement which Ali, Ras of Gondar, signed. When Theodore came to power in 1854 the two Englishmen became his friends. Plowden tried to obtain help from Britain to restore the port of Massawa to Ethiopia, and he made many protests about the cruelty of the Egyptians towards the tribes on the western borders. In 1860 Bell died fighting beside Theodore during the Tigré revolt and Plowden was murdered as he travelled towards the coast. His grave is near the Church of Ghamgiabiet in Gondar. After the death of his friends, Theodore's character changed and his life became altogether dissolute. Notwithstanding, he wrote to Queen Victoria suggesting there should be an Ethiopian Embassy to Great Britain (it has been rumoured that he suggested marriage between the Queen and himself) and by some oversight the letter was never answered. He took this as an insult and imprisoned Captain Cameron, Plowden's successor, together with any other Englishmen he could find, and later an expedition was sent out under Sir Robert Napier to rescue the prisoners. They landed at Massawa in 1867 and together with elephants, camels and mules started on the difficult 325 miles' journey to Magdala, Theodore's capital. It took nearly a year to reach the capital, and when the Emperor realised that defeat was inevitable he shot himself. Napier released the prisoners and, having obtained his objective, returned to the coast after a long and very costly expedition, taking no spoils except a gold chalice that is now in the Victoria and Albert Museum, the Abuna's crown that was returned to the present emperor in 1925, and the royal copy of the *Kebra Nagast*. The next king, John IV, pleaded to have this, for he said: 'My people will not obey my orders without it.' And this also was returned from the British Museum.

I decided against putting my Land Rover aboard the tiny steamer and went in search of the office of the Imperial Highway Authority.

'You might find a way round the lake,' said a plump little man, 'if you take an interpreter. There are two rivers to cross and also the Abai, just outside Bahar Dar; there they are building a bridge for the visit of the Emperor; until it is built, you cannot cross the river.'

'When will it be finished?'

'We do not know. But the Emperor comes to Bahar Dar soon.'

'Do I go from here to Gorgora? And then follow the lake around?'

'No, you must take the airport road and continue for two and a half hours until you come to the village of Addis Zemen. From there you turn south across the country. But you must take an interpreter,' he added again.

It was enough information, and next morning at six o'clock I slipped out of the hotel to the resounding battery of guns, for it was Independence Day. From now on, a place was always so many 'hours' by Land Rover or mule and the times, subject to breakdowns, were generally correct.

The route ran along the north-east corner of the lake and over the many valleys that sloped towards it. The villages had a festive air because of the Independence Day celebrations, *tukuls* had been built as feast-rooms and there were processions assembling that would finally lead the holiday-makers to picnic near streams and waterfalls.

Addis Zemen was a long straggling village that climbed gradually towards the hills, and to my left a high-peaked hill overlooked the village. Beyond it, through the overlay of hills, Wahni, the Princes' Prison Mountain, lay five days' mule journey away. Had the princes coming from Gondar been taken to this old village on their way to the mountain? And when they returned, as Bacuffa had done, also passed this way?

I stopped in the centre of the crowded village where several men were mounted on fine horses; their colourful harness and bridles made a brilliant splash of colour in a gathering of white *shammas*. To my right the ground fell away in rocky fields and ditches and beyond there was a jumble of boulders and hills. A soldier came up and many people gathered round.

'Bahar Dar?' I enquired.

The soldier looked blank.

'Bahar Dar,' I repeated, pointing south, and a small boy, quicker to understand, pushed forward.

'Bahar Dar,' he said, and nodded.

'Which way?' I asked, pointing at different parts of the field, but the soldier gave a sweeping movement as though it was immaterial which direction I took. The small boy pushed his face up to the window.

'I come,' he said, and there was a hush of delight from the crowd.

'Oh, you speak English. Good!'

He grinned back, climbed in and we dropped down off the road into the field of stones.

I was now moving south in the province of Gojjam. From some miles north of Gondar to beyond Addis Ababa in the south, the people are mainly Amharas who, though in the minority of the total population, are the most dominant. Their language is now the official one and they are smart, intelligent, quick to learn and have many of the high positions in the country.

We bumped over the rough ground, past clumps of bushes, spreading acacia, fig-trees and stumpy olive-trees. Stretches of dried grass camouflaged deep irrigation ditches. I fell into the first one and when the car was finally back on firm ground, proceeded more cautiously. At the top of the hill, the boy stopped me and climbed out. He pointed to some whitewashed stones. *If* I could find them, they would lead me to the River Reb. I gave him a couple of dollars and he bowed solemnly.

'Thank you very much for your help,' I said.

'Thank you,' he bowed. '*Tenasterling*.' Each time I turned he was standing there, and each time he bowed from the waist.

After the Little Abai, the Reb and the Gunmara are the most important rivers that flow into the Lake Tsana; they run parallel to each other and can only be crossed in the dry season. I came suddenly on the Reb which was a deep muddy gash in the plain. The bank fell away sharply to the water below which made its way through grey alluvial silt. I stopped the car and went down to test the ground. The bank opposite looked reasonably firm, so climbing back into the car I drove to the edge. We dived sharply off the bank, and, as we ran to the base of the river, the weight at the rear swung the back wheels sharply to the left in a bad skid. With a sickening squelch she sank deep in the wet mud. The wheels began to spin and I was completely stuck!

I climbed out into six inches of mud to review the situation. The front near-side wheel was on firm ground, but both the rear wheels and the far-side front one had settled in the mud. I squelched around in the mud but every time I dug it away from a wheel the gap filled with water. I was in a fix. I had not seen a soul since leaving the small boy and if it should rain in the hills the river would swell and either submerge us or sweep the car into the lake.

Half an hour later I had moved most of the cargo out of the vehicle and was completely covered with mud. The Land Rover was a few inches further down in the mud, and now, on the high bank, a row of boys stood watching me with interest. As in the desert, they had appeared as if by magic. Finally I beckoned the spectators towards me and set about organising a line of workers to bring stones to make a quarry. It would take a day or two and probably use up whatever money I had, but it was my only chance.

At this moment two men in a red jeep appeared at the top of the other bank. The large dark-skinned driver looked down with surprise at the bogged vehicle and the mud-covered woman surrounded by children. It was an I.H.A. vehicle and the men were making a dash for Gondar to pick up a spare part for a lorry. The driver, a Sudanese, greeted me with a wide grin.

'You are lucky,' he said, 'you might not see a vehicle here for weeks.'

'I know, I *am* glad you have come!'

They put a tow-rope on the Land Rover and she was out in a matter of minutes.

'Just what are you doing in this part of the country?' asked the driver when I was safely up on the other bank. He gave me a speculative look and shook his head. 'You British women. Mad! Quite mad!' he said and, before I could answer, he had climbed back into the jeep and was making a giddy ascent up the bank opposite.

The flat plains had been ridged with mounds of earth for the planting of Tef (*Eragiostic Abyssinia*), that is the cereal used to make the pancake-like bread called *injera*. The harvest had gone while the hard ridges remained. Tef is a tiny grey seed that is almost a grass. From the trees hung large bundles of maize that looked like giant bee-hives; and wild coffee grew in the copses and near any cultivation for, as well as using the beans, the local people make a pungent drink from the husks.

The Gunmara River was deeper than the Reb and made many tortuous curves so that it was in turn flowing north, south, east and west. I stopped at one point where the bank fell away making thirty feet of sheer cliff. Below a group of people were watering cattle and small boys clambered up the banks towards me. They insisted that Bahar Dar was away from the river and to the east, so I set off again across the ridged fields. Soon I was completely lost and for two hours wandered round seeing no one. There were bunds and deep ditches that set me off on long detours.

Quite suddenly a cattle track appeared ahead and led to the river again. It was wider here and the water ran faster. In the centre a pile of stones made a wet island where men, women and children splashed and played. The large, slippery boulders were the only connection with the bank opposite and I would probably get straddled across one of them if the fast-moving water threw me off course. A small boy volunteered to guide me to the other side. He moved ahead, scrambling over the stones as the water curled in high folds over his small body. I drove steadily into the water, keeping my foot on the accelerator, for to raise it for a second would mean trouble with water in the engine. The car lurched and swerved against the strength of the current and I swung her sharply to the right. We crashed over one boulder after the other, bouncing up to the top of the pile of stones; the boxes, the tripod and other tins made a frightful din, and we finally ran out to the other side.

It was just luck that we had not stuck or become straddled on one of the boulders. I roared up the steep side of the muddy bank and the crowd gave a cheer and came streaming after me, pleased that I had got through.

There were other rivers with high sharp banks that would have been too deep and narrow for a longer vehicle to cross. All I could do was judge the distance and depth, as well as the solidness of the bank opposite – and make a dash for it.

Now Lake Tsana came into view stretching west towards the horizon like an ocean, and I weaved through thorn bushes, acacia and an occasional Kosso Tree (*Hagenia Abyssinica*) whose branches were hung with red-brown flowers. It has a more mundane purpose than its beauty implies for it is used by the local people as a purgative against tapeworms; a common complaint in a country of raw meat eaters.

Finally, I came to the new bridge that was being built across the Abai where it starts its journey from the lake. The bridge's surface had been covered with palm-leaves and a bulldozer was emptying the last load of red earth on the top as I stopped. An American in a jeep, who was attached to the road survey unit, pulled up beside me.

'What the heck are you doing *this* side of the river?' he asked.

'I've come from Gondar.'

'You don't say! Well, you're some months too early, the road's not built yet.'

I looked at my muddy Land Rover and my filthy dress. 'Yes, I found that out for myself,' I said.

The lake-side village of Bahar Dar was in an uproar preparing for the first visit of their Emperor. The small hotel was being repainted to receive the royal guest, and the lesser mortals had been forced to camp in the grounds. There were European and Ethiopian personnel attached to the Sources of the Nile project, a German engineer who serviced the steamers on the lake and several other Germans and Americans working on the road survey project. They were a few of the many 'tame Europeans' who have for centuries been employed by Ethiopians. The airstrip runs right into the village and planes fly in twice a week from the capital. Rumour has it that Bahar Dar may one day be turned into the capital and this would certainly open up the centre of the country, though the little straggling native village seems, at the moment, far too poor and unprepared for such grand schemes.

I drove along a rough track to the beautiful Tisisit Falls which are twenty miles along the river. They fan out over a circular basin and drop again into a narrowing gorge almost at one's feet, before disappearing from view. The Governor sent his secretary to show me the way, and we stopped at each road gang who were trying vainly to fill in the pot-holes just in case the Emperor might wish to see the falls.

But Bahar Dar was not very hospitable and the hotel guests were finally asked to leave the grounds. Tents were packed and people moved out, either to set up camp on the airstrip or along the lake.

'Come back when it is all over,' the proprietor said to me, 'and we will give you every comfort.'

I broke my camp in the hotel grounds and set off early in the morning. Addis Ababa was 360 miles away and the road was very rough. Gangs were working on it as far as Debra Marcos in preparation for the royal visit. Forty miles from Bahar Dar a good bridge crossed the Little Abai and a rocky valley ran off towards the source of the Nile. To reach it is not easy even today and how much more difficult it must have been when James Bruce made the journey nearly two hundred years ago!

A few miles further on, past the small village of Dangela, there was a sign on the side of the road that read 'Sudan Interior Mission'. I drove into the compound past two small whitewashed buildings, one a dispensary and the other a school. Beyond were two bungalows and a round-faced little woman came out on to the verandah of one of them as I drove up.

'Why, come in!' she said, smiling broadly. 'I'm Betty Warhanik from Canada.' She was the schoolmistress and she laughed when I told her I was an Australian.

'Minnie will be pleased, she is from Melbourne, Australia. I'll send for her.' She spoke to a small boy in Amharic and he set off across the compound towards the dispensary. 'Minnie's the sister here,' she said as she led me into a small bright sitting-room.

Dangela becomes cut off during the rains when the airport is underwater and the road impassable. To the west, towards the Sudan border, there are primitive and hostile tribes and few people have penetrated there. At the moment the two girls were running the mission alone, except for local helpers.

Minnie Bratt came in at a rush. She was fair and slim and had been nursing in Ethiopia for five years.

'You must stay here for the night,' she said. 'The other bungalow is unoccupied and we are going to a local wedding this afternoon.'

'Yes, you can't miss that,' said Betty Warhanik.

'We have men passing through occasionally,' said Minnie, 'but never women, it's marvellous!'

They brought out special things for lunch which they had been keeping for an occasion and displayed with great pride a new refrigerator that Minnie had brought back from Australia after her last leave.

'Friends clubbed together and bought it for us,' she said. 'We've had ice-cream every day since.'

After lunch we set off across the fields with the dispensary dresser, a young local boy. It was sloping fertile country with many fields under cultivation. At last a cluster of *tukuls* came into sight. A new one, its thatch still golden, had recently been added. *Tukuls* are easily and quickly made. A circle of earth is dug up, generously watered and trodden on until it becomes hard; then it is smoothed over. A circle of stakes are now stuck into the ground enclosing the prepared floor and mud is taken inside and thrown at the wall of sticks. Finally it is smoothed out by hand. Rafters meeting in the centre form the roof. They are lashed together and then thatched. On the apex there is either an ostrich egg, a miniature thatch or an upturned bowl of brown clay. Doors are rarely used but a shield of thorn bush is put across the opening at night to keep wild animals out.

Two of the sons and a daughter were being married, so the wedding was a large affair. The two boys were bringing their brides to live with the family and the daughter was going to her husband's home. A separate place had been prepared for the *farangis* (foreigners) between two *tukuls*. A roof of straw spanned the two structures and skin mats covered the ground. Minnie gave the skins an especial glance.

'There has been a lot of anthrax about lately,' she said. 'I want to see the skins are not recently cured.'

Each woman arrived with a pile of *injera* which she gave to the mother of the family and then disappeared into another *tukul*, while the men congregated in the open, under a shelter similar to ours.

We were given glasses of *tej* which is made of honey, water and the leaves of *gesho* (*Rhamnus prinoides*). Some of the men drank a kind of beer made from barley, called *talla*.

'Let's go into the main *tukul*,' said Minnie, 'they will be making the *wat* in there.'

The mother greeted us as we entered; she was a fine-looking woman with light skin and was dressed in a long full white robe. Her greying hair was cut short giving her a modern appearance. Now that our eyes had become accustomed to the dimness and the smoke, we could see the *tukul* was very roomy and the roof rose to a great height. Two women sat near a huge iron pot just inside the opening. The pot was full of bubbling *wat*, the national dish of the Ethiopians. One of the women stirred it occasionally and the other fed the fire beneath, with dry twigs. There can be as many as twenty spices in a good *wat*, and they must be added at different times during the cooking to give the right flavour. The dish is a highly spiced stew that is almost a soup and properly cooked it is delicious but like everything else in cooking, there is *wat* and *wat*!

The father sat in the shadows and behind him was his daughter, the bride, a child of thirteen. She was dressed entirely in white with a *shamma* draped over her head and shoulders and she would remain here until the bridegroom came to fetch her. The best man arrives with the groom and the three depart together. In some parts of the country the best man stays with the bridal couple during the first night. The young bride sat impassive and still, a touching little figure in the smoky bustling dimness.

When the *wat* was ready we returned to our places and coffee was served in tiny handleless cups. We were each given a large circular round of *injera*, neatly folded in four, to be eaten and used also as a table-napkin, and plate as well. A large bowl of *wat* was placed in the centre of the floor and we helped ourselves, breaking off pieces of *injera*, and dipping it into the bowl.

Injera is made of *tef* mixed with water and is poured thinly on to a wide hot dish made of clay and dung which is set on an open fire. A curved cover is placed over it and the mixture, forms into myriads of bubbles as it strikes the heat; these finally burst and a good *injera* must have thousands of these 'eyes' as the Ethiopian woman says. It is a dull grey colour because of the *tef*, but white *injera* made from ordinary wheat is considered inferior and given only to servants and slaves.

Our *injera* was very light and delicious, but the *wat* was so hot that we had to alternate each mouthful with gulps of water. Several young men who shared our *wat* bowl passed special titbits to us. A long bantering argument was going on which was directed at Minnie's dresser.

'What is it?' I asked.

'My dresser is trying to get out of being best man,' she said, laughing, 'because it means walking ten miles to the bride's house and back again.'

Out in the open a boy began to beat a drum, and the conversation became more animated as the women left the *tukul* and grouped around him. As the beat quickened they clapped their hands, and a young woman was thrust forward; she was an exotic creature in a long white dress startlingly embroidered in vivid blue. She began a simple rhythmic dance that quickened with the beat of the drum. The clapping became wilder and the *tukuls* were pulsating with the noise and rhythm. Suddenly she stopped, looked almost shy and turned and disappeared into the crowd. Another took her place and the dancing continued.

From a far *tukul* the two bridegrooms appeared. They were in their early teens and dressed in jodhpurs, jacket and *shamma*. One of them, a sulky youth, had a white cloth tied round his forehead and he picked his nose as he waited for his horse to be led up.

The boys were mounted and each given a glass of *tej*. A mortar had been set on the ground and the horses were led around it. The older groom, raising his hand high, dashed the *tej* glass with a violent gesture into the receptacle, where it broke. Immediately the men guests who held sticks pounded the glass at the bottom to make sure that it was broken. Then the whole procedure was repeated with the other bridegroom.

'Why do they do that?' I asked.

'It signifies that the bride is a virgin and that she shall be broken.'

The ceremony was now over and the bridegrooms set off accompanied by the best men. We watched them straggling off towards the horizon and the desultory groups showed none of the haste or ardour expected from such processions. The dresser, looking slightly smug, was still with us, and before the bridegrooms were out of sight, the rest of the company had returned to their seats and their glasses of *talla*.

'They will not be back until nightfall,' said Minnie, 'when there will be more festivities, but we cannot wait.'

'What about the daughter?' I asked.

'She must stay till her bridegroom fetches her and he lives many miles away. It will be a very long day for her.'

I looked into the large *tukul* as we passed; the bride sat alone now, a little white pyramid in the empty hut; only the steam and bubble from the huge iron pot gave the scene any movement at all. We left some dollars, which is the custom, and took our leave of the mother. Behind us the chatter and laughter continued.

On our way back we stopped at the dresser's own group of *tukuls*. 'My young cousin has had a son today,' he said; 'would you like to see them?'

'Is that the one whose husband left her?' Minnie asked, and the boy nodded.

Marriage can be an elastic affair in Ethiopia, although it is gradually falling into line with other Christian countries. Many people marry by exchange of vows, and either party can divorce just as easily. This is often practised with people previously married. Others sign a paper which is more binding; it sets out a list of jewels and clothes the bridegroom is giving the bride; also what possessions he has and how they will be divided in case of divorce. It states that the bride loves her husband and will be a good wife, even though the marriage has been arranged by the parents. Finally, there are those who marry in the church and these seldom divorce. Children of broken marriages stay with their mother while they are small and later go to the father if he wants them. Concubinage, which was widely practised, added to the confusion of parental and hereditary rights. Extremely young girls are sometimes married by their parents to elderly men and before the wedding night the mother cuts the child's finger-nails quite short so that she cannot scratch her ageing husband. Women inherit and own property just as men do, and this independence in their family life gives them an especial 'air' that all Ethiopian women seem to acquire.

We entered a small dark *tukul*. The dresser kindled the fire with eucalyptus leaves, it flared suddenly and we saw the child-mother, who was fourteen, sitting cross-legged on the floor with the new-born baby across her lap. The girl's face was a tiny oval and very beautiful and her skin glowed the colour of wild honey. She could have been the Byzantine madonna in the church at Gondar. When the dresser spoke she looked towards us with no interest in the eyes drained of emotion. Her husband had left because he had lost his oxen and had no means of supporting her and the child, so she had come to her nearest relation.

'Shall I rekindle the fire?' asked the dresser as the picture faded, but we moved out into the daylight and walked on towards the mission, rather subdued.

'Those were fine movie shots I took of the wedding,' I said, breaking the silence. 'Thanks a lot. It was all very easy.'

'Yes, but it can be difficult. A French journalist was shot dead a little while ago near here when he was taking photographs.'

I gulped. 'Well! That just shows how useful it is, to be with the right people!'

*

Next morning Minnie gathered all the passion fruit from their one vine and made a drink for my breakfast.

'How marvellous,' I said, 'I haven't tasted these since I left Australia.'

'That's what I thought,' and she smiled.

They said a prayer for my safe journey and came to the gate to see me off. It was holiday time for the school children but a large crowd was already sitting on the ground outside the dispensary waiting for Minnie.

There was a fleeting look of regret on her face. 'Wish you didn't have to go,' she said. 'It's been such fun.'

But before I had driven from the gateway on to the road, she had turned and was already moving towards the waiting crowd.

Towards the Capital

The heavy rain during the night had made the red earth very slippery and the car skidded badly so that it moved crabwise over the mountain passes. Several times the car slid downhill again and all I could do was pray it wouldn't go over the edge. I was completely occupied most of the time with keeping the car on the track and saw little of the magnificent scenery around me.

It was 4.30 p.m. as I drove into Debra Marcos, a little town set on a spur of the plateau. Here, the excitement over the preparations for the royal visit had reached breaking point. Arches were being erected and crowds, who had come in from the surrounding country, walked along the streets with an aimless holiday air. As I tried to edge the car through them I became, for the time being, their main attraction, and they jostled and fought to look at me.

Debra Marcos was 185 miles from Addis Ababa and the only hotel was a place of ill repute that did not want me. The Governor, flying past in his Land Rover, pulled up with a jerk when he saw my car surrounded by the crowd. He looked worried and harassed.

'Where to sleep?' he echoed my query vaguely.

'Should I, perhaps, go on to Fitche?'

He looked relieved. 'That – er – would be better. There is a mission near Fitche where you could stay.'

'It is all right to drive after dark?'

'So long as you keep driving. But try to arrive there before it is dark,' and he cleared a way for me to drive off, pleased to be relieved of this extra problem.

Fitche was 120 miles away and I had no chance of arriving there before dark. From now on there were no more road gangs, for the Emperor was flying to Debra Marcos. The plateau was deserted and the road dropped off it as from a table into broken country. Late in the afternoon I came to the great canyon of the River Abai. It had left Lake Tsana as a wide stretch of water surrounded by flat fields, but here it cut a great cleft 4,000 feet into the mountains. Down in the gorge a bridge spanned the river where there were crocodiles, and the hot still air was a sudden contrast to the coolness of the highlands. The valley was covered with a layer of curious pink dust and as I climbed to the other side I was leaving the province of Gojjam and entering Shoa. Half-way up, two lorries were parked near a spring and the drivers were washing, while two armed guards stood near by, protecting the merchandise.

Darkness came suddenly. At nightfall everyone disappears and there is no one on the road. Even the lights in the villages are shrouded and one drives through a black world. It was eerie and I hoped that I would not have a puncture. The distance seemed interminable and the tension began to play on my nerves. Finally, I came to a long line of dimly-lit dwellings. No one ventured out of the huts until I called, when a young man moved cautiously towards the car.

'Fitche?' I enquired, pointing ahead.

The youth nodded. 'Fitche.' He pointed at the dwellings near by.

I had arrived! 'And Mission Anglais?'

I had missed the turn off to the mission for it lay three kilometres back and, turning, I finally found a rough track made of large granite blocks, that was set high above the surrounding ground. The track disintegrated at times into ditches and the night was so black it was impossible to judge what sort of country lay around me. The track was becoming a rocky gorge. I had obviously lost my way, and was contemplating stopping, despite *chiftas*, and waiting for the dawn, when suddenly, near a clump of eucalyptus trees, several men moved back quickly, each shielding his body with the trunk of a tree, which is the age-old caution of their race against a newcomer. It was not till they heard my voice, that they would leave the shelter of the trees.

At my enquiry a young man, wearing a heavy brown cloak and carrying a long staff, leapt across the deep draining-ditch and offered to show me the way. We made several attempts to climb the rocky road and often he ran ahead to direct me around the yawning ditches. With his wide flowing cloak flying behind and his long wild hair, he could have been some strange spirit of the mountains.

'This cannot be the way,' I called at last, 'we have been going for hours. I shall return to the road!'

'That is not possible! Please to go ahead.' He grew more excited and urged me on. We wound through avenues of trees and finally cut off across an open space towards a thick forest. There was no further track and we had to stop.

'What now?' I asked, looking with dismay at the forest ahead.

My companion climbed out and motioned me to follow him into the wood.

'I want the mission,' I said, 'I am not going to walk through the wood.'

He became very excited. 'It is correct! You come with me into the wood!'

But I shook my head. He pranced about in the car's headlights, his long hair streaming, his cloak caught in the wind. The tenseness and enthusiasm were almost fanatical.

'Stay!' he said, coming up to the car and holding his staff high, 'stay, and I shall return.' He disappeared into the forest so quickly and completely that I began to wonder if he had been real, after all.

I sat and waited. Was this really the mission? Or what lay behind the deep forest of trees? I could not turn back for the journey had been so long and complicated that I had no idea where the main road lay. What *was* I doing here? I had been told so many times not to be out after dark in this country. Why had I not had the sense to stay on the main road?

Suddenly, ahead of me in the woods, there was a voice.

'Hello?' It was a very English voice. 'Have you come to stay with us?'

'If I may,' I called, and a slim English woman moved into the car's lights from the woods beyond.

'Oh, what fun. How very jolly.' It was the most beautiful greeting a tired traveller ever had.

'I wasn't certain that the boy was bringing me here,' I said.

She laughed. 'He's a friend of one of our boys; he's a good boy.'

The girl was Vera Jarvis, one of the teachers at the Bible Churchman's Mission. We entered a large old house and came finally to a comfortable sitting-room with old chintz-covered armchairs and a lived-in atmosphere. Barbara Gibbons, also of the mission, and four English schoolteachers from Addis Ababa, were sitting round having tea.

A bed was found for me and a quiet prayer said for the travellers before we retired. Suddenly there was no feeling of loneliness and one's safety seemed important. The long day, the skidding car, the crowding excited people at Debra Marcos, and the long tiring drive through the uneasy darkness; it was all over. Tiredness fell away in the peace of being with good people.

The morning light revealed the forest as being a thick plantation of eucalyptus trees which surrounded the schoolhouse and dormitories. We bought some cloths made by the children with lions rampant and Ethiopian proverbs sewn with slightly unsteady hands and, after an English breakfast of tea, toast and boiled eggs, the schoolteachers and myself said good-bye to our hostesses and set off for Addis Ababa seventy miles away.

We had not reached the main road before the smaller of the two cars broke down.

'I had better tow it,' I said, and it was hitched to the back of the Land Rover.

Some distance to our left ran a deep valley and occasionally magnificent vistas came into view, and on a spur jutting out into the valley lay the famous monastery of Debra Lebanos which was founded by the Saint Takla Haymanot in the fourteenth century. We kept our distance, for no woman is allowed near the monastery, and the monks have a reputation for being extremely rude to visitors. This mistrust goes back centuries, for the place has a long history of invasions and massacres, right up to the time of the Italian occupation when many monks were murdered. Much of Ethiopia's later history centres round the monastery, and in the

Church of the Cross is their most treasured possession, a piece of the True Cross.

We lunched together under a spreading acacia tree with an audience of a dozen or more small boys, who waited patiently to be given the empty tins and bottles when we had finished. In the more remote parts, such things are a form of currency and it is possible to exchange a couple of empty fruit-tins for a chicken and an oil-tin will produce half a goat.

One of the teachers, a tall red-haired man, who kept up an amusing commentary on the ways of the Ethiopians, lined the children up and gave each a tin. None of the boys put out his hand for a second gift, but turned, the object held high, and streaked off across the field towards a group of *tukuls*.

The traffic thickened as we climbed gradually into the Entotto Hills and then suddenly the road swung round to the left, and Addis Ababa, the 'New Flower', lay cradled in the beautiful valley below. Patches of smoke rose from the blue-grey haze made by the Tasmanian eucalyptus trees that grow all over the capital.

Still with the little car in tow, I prepared to brave the city's traffic, and the red-haired schoolmaster sat beside me to guide the way. We quickly dropped 2,000 feet and came to the first roundabout where the large circular Cathedral of St George stood facing the statue of Menelik that had replaced the city's hanging tree.

'That's the King George Bar,' said my companion, at the next roundabout. 'If you sit there long enough, you'll see everyone in Addis Ababa.'

It was the Piccadilly Circus of the city with modern buildings and a concentration of traffic. We turned down a steep hill leading to Churchill Avenue flanked one side with business houses and impressive government buildings and on the other by a long row of tiny *tej* houses run by youthful proprietresses who are willing to supply more than just the drinks.

We passed the Opera House and the statue of a curious granite Lion.

'That is the Ras Hotel beyond, where you will stay,' as we turned off and climbed another hill. 'Brought you this way just to show you.'

'Thanks,' I said.

'Don't toot your horn,' he advised as we climbed along a high wall having dipped down into another valley, 'it is the Imperial Palace and noise is illegal.'

In front of the palace gates was a monument commemorating the Italian massacre of the people of Addis Ababa as a reprisal for the attempted assassination of General Graziani. Imperial guards stood at the palace gates, and in a circular wooden building opposite the royal lions were housed. A fine avenue led to the modern University College, the Old Trinity Church and the more recent New Trinity. On a little hillock beyond was the old palace or Ghibbi which dominated the city in early times and around which much of the country's turbulent history of the last few decades was centred.

We dipped into gulleys again and American limousines edged past horse-drawn gharries and donkeys that were stacked high with grass or clay water-jugs. Occasionally a gentleman of high rank, mounted on a fine horse, rode along the footpath preceded by his manservant. Modern bungalows and fine houses alternated with tiny *tukuls* and rocky unkept tracks led to exclusive houses set behind high walls, while in front of them people gathered round a well. And above all, the blue-grey eucalyptus shed its stringy shade and in the air was the tang from the scent of their burning leaves.

Finally we swept off the road into the grounds of the English school, and I eased to a halt, the little car still behind me.

'A stone was thrown up by your wheels and it has broken my headlamp,' said its owner accusingly to me.

This was all the thanks I received for my rather harassing journey.

14
Addis Ababa: The Capital

> You cannot instruct a wise man,
> you cannot strike a lion.
>
> Ethiopian Proverb

Most foreigners going direct to Addis Ababa by air are less tolerant, less able to understand and forgive the many incongruities and irritations than those who already have some knowledge of the country and its people outside the capital. *I* was already a little besotted by the beauty of the country and the charm of the people – I could never be so critical.

The Emperor holds all the reins and his personal effort and will-power in improving his country and educating her people has an overall unifying effect that outsiders don't always appreciate. One is always conscious of H.I.M.; he *is* the country; it is his vast household and he pays for much out of his own pocket. Despite the grudges, one never hears anything said personally against this astounding little monarch.

The one-man show, however, leads to delays in official departments, for no one has, or will take, responsibility, and everything is passed on to someone else. There are queues at government departments and permits are needed for everything, even for moving around the country. The queues go on, in some instances, for days and the 'waiting treatment' is well known and a sore topic with foreigners. It is no wonder that the newcomer frets, for he does not understand that the sheen of the twentieth century is, as yet, not much more than a façade; but those who really know the country will invariably say 'give them time'.

Haile Selassie I, Conquering Lion of Judah, King of Kings and Emperor of Ethiopia, was born near Harar in 1892. He was the son of Ras Makonnan, soldier, diplomat and Governor of Harar; and his grandfather was King Menelik II. By the time Haile Selassie was twenty-five he was Vice-Governor of Harar, being known then as Ras Tafari. When Menelik II died, Lij Yasu, one of his grandsons, succeeded him. Yasu was a weak character with leanings towards the faith of Islam which made him unpopular both with the people and the church. There was an uprising in 1916 when Yasu was deposed and one of Menelik's daughters, the elderly Zauditu, became empress with Ras Tafari as regent and heir to the throne. A very troubled time followed for Ras Tafari who had to consolidate his position against Yasu and his followers, and other rival chiefs. As regent he visited Europe in 1924, and to solve the problem of leaving many troublesome chiefs behind – who had been waiting for just such a chance – he took a dozen of the most ambitious with him on the tour!

When he finally negotiated Ethiopia's entrance into the League of Nations it gave him great personal prestige, and in 1928 he was proclaimed King of Shoa. He was already striving to modernise the country and educate the people despite some opposition from the church, and when the old empress died in 1930 he was crowned Emperor Haile Selassie I. His stubborn resistance against the Italians when they invaded his country, his final departure *and* return four years to the very day, after an exile spent mostly in England, is recent history.

Despite the Emperor's single-mindedness of purpose, he is very human and is seldom seen without some of his grandchildren. Two of his own much loved children died tragically, the adored Princess Tsahai in child-birth at the age of twenty-two and the Duke of Harar who was killed in a motor accident a few years ago. The Queen is a retiring person and is not often seen, for she has been in poor health in later years.

The Crown Prince has the difficult task of following a great man, but he is quiet, humorous and understanding. Ethiopia is lucky in her heir although, at the moment, it is perhaps difficult to see past the brilliance of the throne. The royal family play an active part in the life of Ethiopia. The princes and princesses and their children are modern-minded, royal without being inaccessible, well educated and intelligent. They have extremely light skins with finely-drawn features. The princesses wear modern sports clothes and smart European styles for parties. They drive cars and are seen socially as well as officially. Many of them work untiringly on welfare and hospital work.

The Empire today covers more territory than ever before, and the work of consolidating it still goes on, though one could argue that its strength lies in its dis-unity. There is a parliament, and although the last word still rests with the Emperor, the foundations of a democracy are there.

From the time of the Emperor's visit to Europe in 1924, education and medical improvements have been his biggest aims. The large campus of the University College, which runs off Miazia 27th Square, started with one building in 1950 and now has a network of buildings including students' quarters, laboratories, classrooms, library and museum; it is run by French-Canadian

Jesuits and there are many nationalities amongst the teaching staff. Some of the scholarship students have studied abroad, come back with degrees and now hold senior appointments in the country. The free education that is being thrust on the young Ethiopian, who already has a great sense of superiority and independence, adds to an egotism that is often out of all proportion to his capabilities and it creates problems, for there are not enough 'white shirt' jobs to go round. The Ethiopian, together with those from other newly-awakened nations, thinks that having been educated, it puts him well above his fellow countrymen. He becomes restless when he is not given a top job and feels he is disgraced when sent to a provincial one. He is being taught to think, but in the hiatus between the past and present-day standards, is not given enough to do with his mind; and education, for some, is merely a way of doing less for more money.

Addis Ababa lies 8,000–10,000 feet above sea-level and has a beautiful climate, though some people find the high altitude plays tricks with the heart. The mountains surrounding the city become a familiar sight. Wachacha lies to the west, with far Managasha beyond the Yerrer, and further still stands the sacred volcano of Zukwala. On the top of the Entotto hills which rise sharply above the city are Menelik's two churches, Entotto Mariam and Entotto Raquel. This was the site of the king's headquarters before Addis Ababa was built and the view from the top is magnificent.

All over the sprawling city there are churches, some old, others modern and bizarre. The large circular St George's Cathedral on Menelik Square is being decorated by the Emperor's young protégé, Afewerk Tekle, with a giant mosaic, and he is also painting two huge canvases, one of the Emperor's crowning and another of the Queen of Sheba's meeting with Solomon. The most popular churches are the Old and the New Trinity both near the old

Ghibbi, but one comes to tiny *tukul*-like places of prayer in many parts of the city.

In the modern shopping-centre there are a couple of large stores and many small but smart Greek and Italian shops. Near by are the small businesses of local traders which have pictures of their trade outside to cope with the language problem. The popular Ras Hotel on Churchill Street is the meeting-place of the city's polyglot population. It is inexpensive, always full and efficiently run. The Ghion Hotel is more luxurious with a large swimming-pool in the grounds. The largest restaurants are in the hotels, and the few night-clubs do not seriously compete with the popular *tej* houses. In the streets, vendors try to sell mats made from the skins of colobus monkeys and also colourful strip-pictures depicting the life of the Queen of Sheba. Despite the latter, and the acceptance by the local people that the Royal family was descended from the Queen of Sheba, there were seldom any tales of her having been as far south as the new capital; Tigré, Aksum and the northern parts of the country remained persistently the areas with which her name was linked. I enquired about her from the librarian of the National Library. He smiled at my question.

'I have recently received a pamphlet from Nigeria,' he said, 'and it states, most emphatically, that she came from those parts. Also, her name has been linked with the mysterious ruins of Zimbabwe in Rhodesia.' He shrugged. 'She travelled, it would seem, as much as you do!'

There are newspapers in English as well as Amharic, and censorship is very strong, which is understandable when it is realised that until recently the only book read by the Ethiopians was the Bible – every word of which he was taught to believe implicitly; he therefore believes everything he reads in the papers as well.

Previously the country attracted a wide variety of foreigners; the adventurer, political refugee, or the man who for other reasons wanted to change his name; and also the ordinary people and scholars who fell in love with the country and wished to stay. There are many of the latter who live here today and they add to the country's air of success. There is also the large community of foreigners in jobs that cannot yet be done by the Ethiopians, and who teach them. No one race is given the tasks indefinitely, the Swedes trained the Imperial Guard, the Ethiopian Police and the military air force; and the military training has been switched to American, British, Canadian and Indian, at different times. The American community is increasing, and they work with the large organisations such as F.A.O. and I.C.A.; also as advisers to the Imperial Highways Authority and the various agricultural and educational colleges. And lastly there is a large business colony of Germans, Swiss, Greeks, Norwegians, British, Italians and Armenians.

The prosperity of the city is generated by the foreigners, for they are the most substantial consumers at the present time, and a great amount of foreign capital also comes into the country in the way of aid. When the Emperor accepted credit for 400,000,000 roubles from Russia, it threw the Americans into a state of gloom, but nothing has yet come of this for the credit has not been taken up; and the Emperor is well known for his ability to balance one policy against another when dealing with foreign affairs.

Climbing one of the city's steep hills, I came to the home of Brigadier and Mrs Sandford. The old bungalow with its long verandah was in great contrast to the modern villas springing up around it. A fire burnt in the grate and the large lived-in lounge held many mementoes of the Sandfords' exciting and varied life in the country. They settled here years before the Italians made it necessary finally for them to leave in 1936, and later the Brigadier, then a man of nearly sixty, became one of the advance guard for the allies' entry into the country when he reconnoitred behind the enemy lines. Later he became the Emperor's political adviser. Among other things Mrs Sandford started the English school which is still flourishing, and they have a farm at Mulla eighty-five miles from Addis Ababa where they grow fine crops of vegetables and fruit, and their strawberries are famous.

'Come and see us at the farm before the rains start,' she said as I was leaving, 'because we are cut off then and the only way across is by a rubber boat.'

The old *sabanya* who had been with them for many decades guided the Land Rover through the gates, glancing up and down the road at the ever-increasing traffic.

It would seem that the country has an especial attraction for the British. There is also the Reverend Mathew who, though retired, lives in Addis Ababa and is translating the Old Testament into Amharic; and on the other side of the city lived Sylvia Pankhurst, famous suffragette and writer, who has since died. She was a great friend of the Royal family and ran the monthly *Ethiopia Observer*.

At first it was difficult to learn the geography of the city, and trying to find the British Embassy I became completely lost. Finally, stopping a horse-drawn gharry, I enquired from the driver.

'I will show,' he said. 'Please to follow.'

We crawled through the hills for some distance before he stopped on Queen Elizabeth Street and directed me to keep straight on.

'Thank you,' I said, 'and how much do I owe you?'

He shook his head, bowed. 'It is nothing. You are welcome.'

The British Embassy compound covers an area of over ninety acres which was given to Queen Victoria by King Menelik II. The various buildings are beautifully set beneath the tallest, straightest eucalyptus trees I have seen. Menelik II introduced these trees, that grow at the rate of twelve feet a year, to supply fuel and wood for the capital when the slower growing junipers had almost disappeared. But for the introduction of the trees, the capital would have moved to a more wooded site. The Embassy has a reputation for hospitality, but to me its greatest claim to fame is that the modern explorer, Wilfrid Thesiger, was born in one of the original *tukuls* on the compound.

I had been bidden to the Embassy for a luncheon party and telephoned the Information Officer, Alex Laurie.

'Must I wear a hat?' I asked. Hats do something to me, they spoil my enjoyment and make me feel as though I am under a lid.

'I should think so,' came the quiet voice from the other end, 'if you have one.'

I admitted, reluctantly, that I did have a woolly thing that *could* pass for a hat; and spent the next hour turning it inside out, pushing it around and completely ruining my temper and my hair.

At the Embassy I was directed into the garden, for the company was lunching under the trees.

Our Ambassador, a tall slim man with kind eyes and an easy manner, and his elegant wife, greeted me. There was an Anglican bishop from Khartoum, Stephen Wright the authority on Ethiopian history, the First Secretary and his wife, and a couple from Kenya. The women wore hats though theirs were wide graceful things.

After drinks we moved to the table set under a large tree. As I passed under one of the boughs a twig caught my woolly hat, whisked it off my head revealing my tousled hair. I picked the hat off the bough, stuffed it into my pocket, ran my fingers through the offending locks, though it made no difference, and resolved that in future I either refused such invitations or flaunted convention and went bare-headed!

Addis Ababa is a very social place; the European colony entertains freely and mixed parties of both Ethiopians and Europeans can fill most evenings of the week; while a visit to a *tej* house, though not strictly for women, can be great fun.

Lyle and Margaret Mabbott's house lay up a steep rough track with deep flood ditches each side. The house was set in a high wall and they lived in great style with two servants and a *sabanya*. The head boy, his wife and two children occupied a small bungalow at the rear, and the *sabanya* lived in limbo never moving far from the house. He was a *Gurague*, which is a tribe from south of Addis Ababa, and they are generally employed as gardeners, *sabanyas* and porters. Lyle Mabbott had rescued the old man after the police arrested him as a vagrant, and now his whole life centred round the Mabbotts and their home. Ethiopian servants, once they enter your household, feel they are there for life. Centuries of slavery has given them this sense of security and the feeling that they are your responsibility. The only *completely* carefree and happy people I saw, were pointed out to me as being slaves. Slave trading, which has been widely practised for centuries, became illegal when Ethiopia joined the League of Nations. The tribes bordering on the desert traded in slaves and obtained many from the *Guragues*; others were escorted through the country from Central Africa and the Sudan on their way to the gardens and harems of Arabia. These slave caravans were big business for the various chiefs en route, who took tolls and safe-conduct fees. Because of this great source of income, it was not easy to stamp out the custom. Domestic slavery has always been an institution, although the slaves were not sold but exchanged or given as presents, and many a young girl received a companion of her own age in this way, as a wedding gift. No doubt there are some 'slaves' today amongst the more wealthy families, and they lead a good life of security as family retainers.

I had been granted an audience by Prince Sahle, the Emperor's youngest son, and his young bride. The Government Press Officer, who was an Englishman and a friend of His Highness, drove me to the shining modern palace with its high glass tower, which was just a couple of houses away from Margaret's. A fountain played in the entrance hall and I was left alone for a few seconds in a tiny 'withdrawing-room', which was bright with white paint and chintz, and then we crossed the entrance hall and entered an oblong room furnished in the Louis Quinze period. Two glass cases held treasures which His Highness had collected on journeys abroad, and amongst them were a few worthless mementoes, obviously kept for their sentimental value only; and they were a revealing clue to the pale-faced young man whose brittle manner covered a certain shyness. But time does strange tricks in Ethiopia for, looking at the Prince's pale skin and shock of hair worn high, I thought of that other prince who became Jesus I, for he was described in just this way.

His Highness's bride was dressed in a well-cut afternoon frock. She had a flawless skin and large eyes beneath a beautiful brow. They spoke excellent English in the slightly bantering manner common to a certain type in England. We were served with drinks from a modern trolley and finally they rose to go.

'Have to excuse us,' said His Highness, 'we have a date. But do stop and have another drink,' and they were gone.

'They always dine with H.I.M.,' said my companion, as we finished our drinks and went out into the glistening hall.

*

Everyone meets at the airport, for it is a social must to welcome and see everyone off. Limousines from the various embassies, government departments and business houses come and go all the time; and the greatest occasion is the arrival or departure of His Imperial Majesty. He was leaving on a trip abroad and I pushed my way through the crowds and, aided by the professional look of my movie camera, was ushered on to the tarmac amongst the press. The Ethiopians have an ease of manner that extends to all formal occasions, and it is taken for granted that everyone will behave.

A brightly-coloured open marquee had been erected and a throne placed in the centre. A long line of priests in devotional robes stood in rows making a square, their brilliant glistening umbrellas catching the sunlight and beside them was a huge ceremonial drum. It was a startling scene.

Near by stood the tall Ras Abeba Aragai, a lion of a man who personifies all that is romantic, loyal and brave in the Ethiopian warrior. He became a national hero during the Italian occupation for he organised a large group of resistance men in Eastern Shoa and did much to harry the enemy and help in their final defeat. Guerilla songs tell of him, and it was his men who lined the streets when the Emperor made his triumphant re-entry into the capital in 1941. I little thought, looking at the incredibly handsome and soldierly Ras, that he would be amongst those so senselessly shot by the rebels in the Royal palace a few months later. The songs about him no doubt still echo through the deep valleys in which he fought.

A black Rolls Royce swept on to the tarmac and came to a halt in front of the marquee. The Emperor stepped out followed by several small princes in dark European suits. The Emperor moved along a line of notables, shaking hands and chatting before finally coming to the throne where he continued to have little asides first with the American Ambassador, then the Soviet one.

At the far end of the tarmac was a small raised platform and a contingent of the regular army were drawn up for inspection.

There was a stir from the marquee as the Emperor made his way on foot to the platform, and his followers withdrew, leaving him alone on the dais to take the salute. He was a diminutive figure on the vast tarmac, and I was reminded once again that greatness has nothing to do with size.

The rest of the press had withdrawn and were congregating at the far end of the line of troops, so that the Emperor and I were isolated. He started down the carpet and was forced to leave it to inspect the near end of the line. He walked directly towards me and as I stepped out of his way, smiled. His dark eyes were those of a visionary, but he summed me up with much shrewdness. He would, I felt, remember me again.

I was very grateful for the marvellous photographs I had taken, but security had been foolhardy and lax in allowing a complete stranger, with no credentials, to stand isolated and alone with the Emperor on whose shoulders so much rests.

15

Journey to Harar: Rimbaud's City

After the Hyena has passed, the dog barks.

Ethiopian Proverb

Harar is the most romantic and colourful city in Ethiopia. It lies in the south-east hills on the edge of the desert and much of its medieval wall still stands. For centuries it was predominantly Moslem and completely separate from the rest of the country, for the Hararis had their own language and coinage as well. They were brilliant business people – the Phoenicians of Africa – and they became very rich. When Menelik captured the province at the end of the last century, it brought a rich and fertile area into the kingdom.

As early as the seventh century people from the Yemen who migrated to Somaliland came into the hills, and in the thirteenth century both Arabs and Persians settled here. Mahommad Ghan the 'left-handed', whose headquarters were in Harar, made several attacks on Ethiopia from here and his successor Nur built the present wall, to withstand the attacks of the Gallas and Somali tribesmen. These attacks continued spasmodically for 200 years, and during that time some of the Gallas infiltrated into the city so that today they are barely distinguishable from the original

Hararis. The Egyptians captured the city in the nineteenth century, although they were forced to withdraw during the Mahdi uprising, and two years later Menelik II, King of Shoa, conquered the city. The present king's father was governor of the province until he died in 1906.

The walled city with its red buildings has attracted many explorers and adventurers. The first European to visit it was Richard Burton who came disguised as an Arab in 1854. Rimbaud, the French poet, spent many years here and the house where he lived still stands within the city walls.

The ordinary journey from Addis Ababa to Harar is by plane or train to Diradawa and then by road for the next thirty miles. Few people attempt the complete journey overland, for the track is almost non-existent and closed during the rains. I decided to make the journey overland, and Margaret was coming with me. I had been issued with a permit to travel and an open letter which stated that although a permit to photograph was not necessary, I was however allowed to take photographs. We set off at midday and, twenty miles south of the capital, passed the fashionable holiday resort of Bishoftu where there is a large hotel built on the rim of a deep crater lake. Down at the water's edge were bathing sheds and a diving-board, making the most unique swimming-pool. Near by the Emperor has a summer residence which is a replica of the house he occupied when he was in exile in Bath, England.

'Doesn't look very English,' said Margaret.

'We have some new houses as well, in England,' I said, but she wasn't really convinced.

Not many miles after the flat dusty town of Nasreth we left the good road and started on a track that was to become one of the worst I have encountered. It was dry, flat bush country and finally we came to a long wooden pole which ran across the track.

'It's the Emperor's game reserve,' said Margaret.

'Well, we won't bother about the pole,' I said, and drove off the track into the rough ground to by-pass it.

At this moment a guard appeared amongst the bushes. 'Get out! Get out!' he shouted belligerently, waving at us.

'Out?'

'Out of the car! Get out!' he shouted again.

We had been warned that the guards unloaded everything looking for fire-arms, or that they expected a bribe to refrain from doing so; but egged on by the sublime confidence of the American woman, I didn't move.

'No,' I said firmly.

He eyed us as we sat frozen with outraged dignity and was obviously surprised to see two women in the vehicle.

'Out,' he murmured again, but it was so deflated that we nearly laughed outright. An older man, arriving on the scene, helped him out.

'Women!' he said, smiling conspiratorily and motioned us on.

We were coming away from the spectacular scenery of the high plateau and the flat scrubby country was similar to much of my own native land. We saw no people at all though now there were many animals. Wild boar with light coats and straight tails that stood upright ran across our path, and many female ostriches merged into the dingy landscape. A couple of baboons leapt from boulder to boulder, their long hair billowing as though they were underwater. We saw many Grant's gazelle and a great oryx, while tiny dik-dik with their fat hindquarters streaked through the undergrowth in all directions. Huge flocks of guinea-fowl with shining blue heads made a sudden dash of colour and they seemed completely unafraid, while the brilliant blue starlings darted from tree to tree.

We stopped for lunch near a wide river-bed where a mere trickle ran over round grey stones, although the high banks told of torrents in the rainy season. The weaver birds' nests hung from the acacia trees like little golden balls, and the birds fluttered above us unconcerned. We cooled our American tinned beer in the cold stream, and a yellow-billed pelican watched us cautiously from the high bank.

If people lived here they kept well away. High cracks split by floods appeared down the centre of the track so that I was forced to drive with the deep chasm below us. Margaret took it calmly but I, not used to the responsibility of another person's safety, found it tiring. It was the volcanic country of the Rift Valley and great boulders of black basalt lay each side of the track, while below in the huge crater of Mutte, which was filled with black rock, a thick forest of bright green trees grew; it was a strange sight.

At last we descended a rough pass built by the Italians, and the hot air of the lowlands came towards us as we ran towards the plain. Ahead, walking through the bushes, was a thin man dressed in a *longui* and *shamma*. A long curved knife hung from his waist and he carried a gun.

'It's a Danakil!' said Margaret.

'Are you sure?' Danakils are dangerous, and many early explorers who were trying to penetrate into the highlands never got further than the desert for they were murdered. Some Danakils still kill and mutilate to procure trophies as a sign of bravery, and some cannot marry until they have done this.

'He's a Danakil all right. Lyle has taken photographs of them,' said Margaret.

'He has a gun,' I said.

'Mmmm. But he may be the only one we see,' said the keen photographer.

'He doesn't look so fierce and, after all, we're not much use, being women.' I slowed up as we drew parallel with him. 'Let's take a few shots before he makes up his mind what to do.'

Taking our cameras we jumped out of the car. The Danakil, seeing us, turned away, holding the gun close to his body. He looked accusingly, almost remorsefully over his shoulder at us; it was a shy, girlish gesture.

'Well! so they've got them – even out here!'

We offered an empty bottle, some bread and an orange, and the Danakil edged towards us with a sideways movement. He accepted the oranges and empty bottle but had no use for the bread, for the Danakils live mainly on blood and milk. He took a long draught of water that would probably last him for days and stood quietly while we photographed him; and then, raising his hand above his head with the familiar gesture of the Arabian nomad, walked off.

'So much for the dangerous Danakils,' said Margaret as we climbed back into the car.

A few miles further on we came to a disbanded Danakil camp. The great migration to the hills was nearly completed, for they dare not be in the lowlands when the rains start. There was a wide circle of thorn bushes, and inside, frames made of saplings to hold the skin tents still stood. The skins had been removed, rolled up and taken away on the camels. The sapling frames, the low fence of thorn and the little piles of ashes were all that was left; there was no rubbish or litter; the Danakils, we confirmed, kept their countryside cleaner than we do in the western world.

The light was already beginning to fade when we arrived at Awash Railway Station and bumped over the rails to the Railway

Hotel. Beyond lay the last deep chasm of the Awash River before it strikes out to the desert beyond. The hotel was a small bungalow and the bedrooms were in adjoining bungalows in the garden. There were iron bedsteads, a couple of rough tables and chairs; and the electric light went out at ten o'clock. But it was clean, and an attentive young boy who brought us tea was clearly delighted with his unusual guests and their odd way of travelling.

At nine o'clock that evening the train from Djibouti arrived and the little village of Awash suddenly came to life. As the passengers climbed out to stretch their legs, enterprising locals rushed up with bowls of steaming *wat*. A couple of first-class passengers disappeared into the hotel to have a meal, for the stop allowed for this. There was the smell of the dry desert in the crowded compartments where people sat, hot and listless; but by the morning they would be in the cool clear air of Addis Ababa. What a Shangri-La these mountains must have seemed to the traveller, making the long journey across the desert by foot, in the days before the railway was built!

'The two things the Italians do really well is retreat – and blow up bridges,' I murmured sourly next morning as the Land Rover crashed over the dreadful surface.

A short bridge had taken us across the river to the south side of the Rift Valley and during the next 120 miles to Diradawa we were to cross 153 rivers, most of which had blown bridges. We dropped down into rocky gulleys, through water and over boulders, running along the river's base looking for a way out, and in one narrow river-bed we were forced to make a rush for the bank opposite. Climbing it, we crashed down almost on top of a lorry which was stationary, for the driver had stopped for tea.

'We do not expect to meet another vehicle,' he said as he cleared a space for us to pass.

'Have we much more of this sort of thing?' I asked.

'It is just as bad until you come to Errer where there is a small hotel – after that, you have no more troubles,' he said. 'Watch out for baboons!' he called after us as we drove off.

The Errer Hotel was built beside some thermal springs, and we crawled the high steps to the verandah of the hotel, still pitching and tossing from the motion of the Land Rover. The Greek proprietor gave us one look.

'Would you like a hot spring bathe?' he asked. We nodded.

The bath-house had two deep pools, and the hot water was splashing into them as we entered. A large step led down to the water which was almost too hot to bear. For some time there was complete silence except for the flow of the water.

'I've heard it is good for rheumatism,' Margaret's voice came from the other pool.

'It's about the only reason for coming overland by car,' I said; 'it is marvellous.'

We stayed in the beautiful bubbling water for an hour and, returning at last to the hotel, sank on to our beds and went off into a blissful sleep.

Two miles away, near the railway station of Gota, is the Emperor's experimental fruit farm. His manager, Blatta Zelleka Negotou, called next morning to show us around. He was a quiet scholarly man with an air of authority, and he led us along an avenue of kapok trees where men and women were gathering the heads into piles which would later be sent by train to Djibouti.

The farm covers an area of nearly 250 acres, and there were many plants not previously grown in Ethiopia. The Blatta showed us mandarins from Japan, oranges from Kenya, grapefruit from the USA, kapok trees from Kashmir and avocado pears from the Congo. The banana groves were irrigated by the waters from the rain forests in the hills, and there were many kinds of trees being grown to meet the afforestation demands. We finally left laden with bananas and a large 'Heart of Blood' fruit.

Within an hour we were in Diradawa which has been the terminus of the railway for many years and the most important centre of the Harar province. It was a mixture of Italian and French, with curb-side cafés, small European shops, tree-lined streets with high white walls – a pastiche of sunlight, flowers and the heavy shade of trees. Behind the town an odd story-book type of palace with a picturesque approach that wound up to the high entrance, gave the town a slightly film-set effect.

The final thirty miles took us several thousand feet out of the lowland heat to the fertile plateau where villages hugged the road and camels were now seen as often as mules. During the last few days we had come through the uninhabited no-man's-land that lies between the Amharas and the near-desert Hararis, and it was possible to understand why the division between the two provinces had remained for so long.

A wide avenue led towards Harar's walled city and we passed the Grand Hotel, the Military Academy, the Emperor's summer palace set in an incredibly colourful garden, the Vice-Governor's office and the House of the Duke which is now used as the Municipal Government Headquarters. Many of these large buildings were erected by the Italians, but unlike those in Gondar, were being used.

Many travellers and explorers speak of their first glimpse of the city of red houses lying in the curve of the hills, for that approach from the south-east is very beautiful. We, however, were coming from the other side and ran directly towards the old city wall which looked, to our surprise, rather flimsy and decorated with an unusual crenellated top and a mellow design in rust red. Far to our left stood the well-known landmark of Mount Condudo mentioned both by Burton and Rimbaud as the first thing they saw on approaching the city. There is a bite out of its flat top which, you will be told, was made by Noah's ark when it touched bottom.

We drove through the Gate of the Duke into the old city. Originally there were five gates that were locked at night to keep hyenas and robbers out. The street narrowed immediately and led to the Faras Magala Square. Ahead of us was the Mehani Alem Church and we passed through the high arch into the enclosure where a priest was conducting a class of small boys under the trees. An itinerant priest, complete with prayer stick, showed us around. The octagonal church had two roofs, and the lower one extended over the surrounding verandah. The eaves of the roofs were highly decorated with filigree woodwork and at the apex there was an elaborate ten-pointed maskal and on each tip an ostrich egg.

Across the square was Ras Makonnan's Palace, a large wooden structure also with a double roof, for this was a feature of the buildings of the Menelik period in Harar. The palace had been used for receptions and audiences, and consisted mainly of a large bare hall which was now falling into disrepair. Ras Makonnan's own house, where the present Emperor spent most of his childhood, is beautifully situated on a hill outside the walled city, and is now used as a rest house for the teachers from the University College in Addis Ababa.

Margaret had known the manager of the Grand Hotel when he was a waiter at the Ras Hotel in Addis Ababa and his brother worked for one of her friends.

'Every man has a brother,' she murmured as we followed the manager up the broad staircase and were ushered into a large bedroom. High French windows opened on to the main road and a small group of boys were passing; they wore garlands of leaves on their heads and were chanting as they walked.

'What are they doing?' I asked.

'They are praying for rain,' said the manager. 'I shall send up some water in a bucket. There is not any left in the taps.'

The hotel was preparing for the influx of French tourists who come from French Somaliland during the summer months. Formally, French was the second language in Harar, and it is still the most useful. In the nineteenth century, French missionaries came and set up schools and an orphanage, and later some of these orphans became priests. They also established the leper colony that stands on the north side of the town; it is a collection of gaily painted huts set under trees, and cured lepers help in the running of it. Moslems and Christians live amicably together, and many married couples have children, for, with the help of Avlosulphon, the parents are almost completely non-infectious when the children arrive. Now there is no longer the stigma and feeling of horror attached to those suffering from the disease.

The city has a mixture of Christian and Islam influences, and is very different from the other cities of the country. In fact, each city takes on a character of its own that is individual, just as the Ethiopians themselves are. In the narrow cobbled streets many of the wooden houses leant across and almost met, for their first storey overlaid in the medieval manner. A steep street led down to the market square where the first European traders, Rimbaud included, conducted their business. The square was filled with Somalis, Hararis, Gallas and Arab traders, all of whom sat under improvised shelters on the open cobbled ground. The pure blood

Harari has extremely light skin, finely-drawn Semitic features and straight light hair. The men wear robes similar to the Arab, but there were very few of the original Harari woman's dress which is a voluminous black garment embroidered in a diamond-shaped design around the neck. It is worn with long tight trousers, and the hair is dressed in two huge buns set low on the neck behind the ears and covered with a coarse black net. The Galla women now have copied this hairstyle so that it is not so easy to tell them apart. Today the clothes are brighter with lots of blue and an attractive tone of rust red.

We passed through an old gate into a tiny courtyard where several women sat in the sunlight bending over large bowls of brilliantly-coloured dyes. They dipped raffia in and out so that the colours splashed in the bright sunlight, and they chattered incessantly, making a lively scene. We climbed an outside stairway to 'Basket Mary's' house; she had recently died, but the business was being carried on and women sat on the floor working on all kinds of basket ware. The *injera* baskets are built on a stand and make very good coffee tables. Margaret bought a large bride's basket with a high-pointed top that was decorated with leather and cowry shells. In it the bride puts all her personal possessions when she makes her first journey to her husband's home.

The winding Rimbaud Street led off the Faras Magala Square and we passed an ornate old archway, very Arab in character, with faded lettering announcing that it had been the Ottoman Bank in the last century. Rubble lay beyond the arch now but it conjured up pictures of more colourful times when Burton and Rimbaud passed beneath the arch. We came to the Mosque of Jamai, with its twin minarets mentioned by so many travellers and where, as a reminder of olden days, there is a plaque warning the inhabitants to 'beware of the attacks of the Gallas'.

Opposite the Mosque was a small house with a gabled roof, and a jaunty little clock, painted on its eaves, was set at eleven forty-five, though no one could tell us why.

On the next turn of the road we came to a two-storey house of wood with a verandah running its entire length and overlooking a courtyard that was reminiscent of an Arab *khan*. This was the house belonging to Arthur Rimbaud, the enigmatic young poet who stopped writing at the age of nineteen and turned gun-runner, and yet as pioneer of the Symbolist movement in France, his work has had a tremendous influence on modern poetry.

The house is now a Moslem school and the courtyard rang with the children's shrill voices. Diagonally across the street, in a magnificent old wooden house, there is a Christian school and during recess the narrow road becomes the scene of a fierce but hilarious juvenile religious war, from which it was best to beat a hasty retreat.

A procession was moving quickly up the narrow street, headed by four men carrying a flat piece of wood on which was a body covered with a white cloth. The followers were forced to break into a trot now and then to keep up with the leaders who made their way quickly past us to the Mosque. It was a curious, hurried, yet silent procession, different from the usual Moslem funerals when the chanting and wailing of the women can always be heard. We wondered if perhaps it was the death of a leper. Before we had moved far down the road, the little procession was back again with its pathetic burden, hurrying past and disappearing down the stony street.

Above us a narrow track led to the ruins of the Castle Anbesa (Lion) built by Ras Makonnan for Menelik II, though the king was never able to visit it. During the Italian war it was damaged and now a friendly Harari family live in a few rooms on the ground-floor. We risked the falling stairway to explore the pleasant, almost intimate, rooms above and to gaze at the beautiful city below. Carved lions, which give the castle its name, look down from the high parapet.

Outside the East Gateway was the *qat* market where women sat with freshly-picked leaves in their laps. *Qat* (*Celestrus edulis*) grows wild in the hills around Harar and is being cultivated in preference to coffee beans for it brings in a better income. The leaves are chewed when they are fresh and give a slightly intoxicating and stimulating effect, though addicts tend to lose their appetite and become thin. About 4,000 kilos are flown each day to Aden and the Yemen, and it is becoming a substantial source of revenue to the country. Experiments are being made by a German company to find out if the leaf can be used as a tranquilliser. We watched a man negotiating with a woman who held the light-green leaves in her apron skirt. The bargaining was long but he finally procured a whole lapful for two shillings, a very low price in comparison with that paid in Aden.

Beyond the Shoa Gate a larger market took place every day, and as well as vegetables and fruit, camels and donkeys were sold. People came from the surrounding country, and many seemed a little wary of venturing within the city walls. The women had the freer air of the *bedu;* they chattered and laughed, while the beautiful Somali women walked like goddesses through the crowds. We recognised the lean Danakils and the Kutu Gallas who made a startling picture with their frizzy hair reddened with clay and glistening with ghee. They swept round in wide coarse cloth cloaks of the same red, conscious of the fine picture they were making. The Amharas are imported to take official jobs and are immediately recognisable. They are the ones who make a fuss and enquire about permits to photograph, thus disturbing the sense of well-being that we had been so carefully fostering.

The Military Academy buildings spread all over the outer town. The academy trains officers for the Imperial Ethiopian Army and the Imperial Bodyguard, on a three-year course that includes arts and science as well as military subjects. The principal was a colonel from the Indian Army, but he was away in Addis Ababa, and his second-in-command, Colonel Sen, also from India, showed us round the well-equipped buildings. The same principle of having various nationalities as tutors is practised here for the army had, up to date, been trained by British, Swedish, Canadian and USA officers.

The students' sense of superiority and independence was much in evidence here also. An American sports personality who had flown from Addis Ababa especially to lecture to the students was boycotted because he would not give the same lecture twice. Students of two colleges refused to attend together in one hall, even though it was large enough to take everybody!

'Would you care to visit the hyena man?' the manager asked us, the night before we were returning to Addis Ababa.

'*What* is a hyena man?'

'He is a great friend of the wild hyenas. Would you like to visit him tonight?' he repeated.

We said that we would.

The old city looked mysterious in the blackness as we drove across it and turned out of the Berberi Gate, running along a path that followed the line of the old wall. The place was deserted except for hyenas who were converging on the town's rubbish tip near by. The lights from the car picked them up as they were slinking into the shadows with a curious cringing gait.

Finally, at a spot where the wall had fallen, we turned into an untidy courtyard with a rough *tukul* in one corner.

'Hassan lives here,' said the manager and, as we climbed out, a small thin man came out of the *tukul.*

His clothes were the colour of the dung-like walls and hung in rags around him. He had a silent and withdrawn manner. We sat near the wall on a rough seat made of old pieces of wood. There was a cleared space in front of us and Hassan settled on the ground, shielding us from the opening in the wall.

A woman came out of the *tukul* carrying a small lamp in one hand and with the other she grasped the corners of her apron. She placed the lamp beside Hassan and let the apron fall so that several bones clattered to the ground in front of him.

'We shall have to wait a little, until the hyenas get used to strangers being here,' said the manager.

Hyenas are desolate animals who have no friends. They turn on each other or any weaker animal and are reputed to attack sleeping people, eating their faces away. But they are part of the Ethiopian scene and have been so for centuries, for they not only clear the streets of rubbish, but until quite recently cleared away the dead as well. When Bruce complained to the Emperor that his path at night was obstructed by hyenas at their grim meal, the Emperor replied: 'The hyena never meddles with living people, he seeks carrion and will soon clear the streets of those encumbrances that so much offend you; people say they are the Falasha of the mountains, who take that shape of the hyena, and come down into the town to eat the Christian flesh in the night.'

Hassan had been feeding the hyenas for ten years, and many of them slept with him in the compound. At times there were as many as fifty sleeping round the *tukul,* enough to kill many men if they became disturbed. Hyenas, the old man told us, always have two cubs at a time. Occasionally as he talked he would pause and call out: 'Ha! Ha! Abdul! Birolle! Zacheria!'

'Is he fond of the hyenas?' I asked.

'He says they are his friends.'

'Abdul! Abdul!' Hassan threw one of the bones to the edge of the circle.

'It is better that we do not speak,' said the manager.

The old man put a piece of cardboard to shield the lamp light from us and we sat waiting in the gloom. There was no noise in the hot still night until suddenly the bleak cry of a hyena made us all jump.

'Abdul! Hah! Hah!' This was more of a command, and two eyes appeared, glistening as the light caught them.

'Abdul!' The old man threw a bone and the ungainly creature moved forward. Their scruffy spotted coats and slinking hind legs personify all that is mean in the animal world. With a quick and stealthy movement the hyena grabbed the bone and disappeared into the shadows. Others, encouraged by the first one's attempt, moved into the pool of light, and one of them, standing facing us full on, looked almost pleasant, but then he grabbed the bone and slunk off with the same unpleasant gait.

From outside the walls came the high-pitched cry as other hyenas joined the pack, and one after the other they moved into the light. Some took the offering direct from Hassan, and now the crunching of bones mingled with their cries.

'Isn't it most unusual that they have become so tame?' I asked.

'Yes,' said the manager, 'I have never known it happen before. It would not be easy to trust them.'

Finally all the bones had gone and the old man stood up. The hyenas moved back slightly but did not scatter until we moved also, then they flashed past us into the night.

The old man stood back while we climbed into the Land Rover, and thanking him we drove off. As we turned on to the track, many pairs of eyes reflected in the lights, and their owners were waiting for us to pass so that they could return to the quiet old man who had made them his friends.

16

The Kleenex Trail to Lalibela: Lasta Province

No road is long with good company.

Turkish Proverb

Lalibela in Lasta Province is famous far beyond the country for its rock-hewn churches. It was the stronghold of the Zagwe kings who took over power in the tenth century when the country had been weakened by a period of civil war and the unity and strength of Aksum had fallen under the devastation caused by the Falasha queen, Judith, who sacked the country and killed many of the princes and priests. The Zagwe kings came from the ancient Agau race and controlled the provinces of Lasta and Waag, claiming descent from Moses rather than David as the previous rulers had done. With the Zagwes' rise to power there followed a great religious revival and a period of artistic splendour during which time the capital was established at Roha, a mountain stronghold in Lasta. King Lalibela, one of their most famous kings, was responsible for many of the rock-hewn churches and later the place was re-named after him. His wife, Maskal-Kebra, was a sovereign ruler in her own right of Bihat in the Tigré and so the territory over which her husband ruled was greatly extended.

The Zagwe dynasty was finally overthrown and the original Solomon line restored. However, the group of rock-hewn churches, because of the very nature of their construction, are amongst the few things that withstood the plundering of both Moslems and Gallas. Although the present ruling family do not recognise the Zagwe Dynasty, King Lalibela has been canonised and his old capital is now a place of pilgrimage.

Until now, to reach Lalibela, it had been necessary to make a two days' journey by road to Waldia on the Addis Ababa-to-Asmara road and then trek for four days on a mule into the mountains. Now, however, the Ethiopian Airlines were inaugurating a new flight to Lalibela, and Margaret, Thedia Barnes, another American, and myself decided to take the first flight. A rough airstrip had been prepared in the valley a half-day's journey by mule from the churches. Three days later the same plane would call back for us; *if* there had been no rain in the meantime.

Thedia and Don Barnes had recently been transferred from Burma to Ethiopia, and Don was in charge of the Sources of the Nile Project. This giant undertaking, which is in the hands of Americans and Ethiopians alike, was making an aerial survey of the country and also testing and gauging the waters of the Abai in all seasons. Not only the main river but all the tributaries were being explored and tested. Helicopters as well as Land Rovers were being used for the job. Thedia and Don had a large house on the outskirts of the capital; they were both fair and good-looking with an insatiable interest in people and places.

Despite the addition on the airline's printed itinerary of the Lalibela flight we had to obtain permission from the Governor of

Lasta province to visit Lalibela and arrange for mules to meet us at the airstrip. Dejazmach Berhane Maskel Desta, Governor of Lasta, was in Addis Ababa; he spoke excellent English and had the easy manner of most Ethiopians. He not only gave us permission but agreed to send the High Priest of Lalibela, who was also in the capital, to look after us.

The Addis Ababa airport was awash with people of every nationality as we lined up at the desk to have our bags and tickets checked. Europeans and Americans were either leaving, arriving, seeing off or welcoming friends; High officials and priests held court, while woolly-haired Gallas and elegant Amharas mingled with the crowd. There was the communal 'live and let live' feeling that epitomises all crowds in Addis Ababa.

'Why do you have three cameras?' Thedia asked as I was piling my equipment on to the counter.

'One's for colour, another for black and white and the third to take snaps for reference.'

'Reference?'

'Yes, just to remember types of clothes, houses and things. They're generally awful pictures, not planned in any way.'

'Ah!' said Thedia who had borrowed a camera for the trip, 'that's what I am – a "reference photographer".'

The Governor arrived and introduced us to the young priest who wore a long black coat and a high black cap. He was more amused than interested in our jaunt.

'Have you brought a tent?' enquired the Governor.

'We had hoped to use one of the *tukuls*,' I said.

'That might be difficult. I shall instruct them to lend you my tent. It is a new one and will be suitable.'

We thanked him and moved out to the waiting Ethiopian Airlines plane with its coloured stripes and Lion of Judah rampant.

With us also was a young Ethiopian from the airlines office who was coming to Lalibela to look after us and see what arrangements could be made for any subsequent passengers.

We climbed over the great gash of the Abai Valley, grey and stark now, before the rains, and came to incredibly green uplands just before the pilot flew lower to find the landing place for Dessie. The tiny airstrip had a couple of sheds and was surrounded by heavily-wooded hills. Two missionaries were leaving the plane here and we all stood round chatting with the driver of a Land Rover who had called for them.

Finally we took off again heading for Lalibela. The green mountains sloped away in a series of ridges like giant half-circular shells. We passed *ambas* where little groups of *tukuls* stood, picturesque and fairy-like, and on one of them was a church shaped miraculously like a cross.

The American pilot from Oregon asked Thedia to go for'ard and have a better view as we neared Lalibela.

'Take Barbara,' she said generously, 'she's the photographer.'

The pilot opened the window of the cockpit for me and then dived towards Lalibela so that a fantastic sight presented itself. The whole brow of the hill was mottled with reddish-pink carving that stood out sharply against the dark green of the trees, for the earth had been dug away around the red rock leaving it isolated and carved into the shapes of churches. Passageways could be seen leading down to the sunken courtyards that surrounded each church, while up on the normal ground level there were the *tukuls* of Lalibela's present-day inhabitants.

We circled twice before turning back to the valley below, came down to the strip, rushing past a group standing beside a small shelter, and made a bumpy landing on the uneven ground. Near by under a tree several mules and their owners waited to take us to

Lalibela, and the little reception committee moved out to greet the priest as the plane taxied in.

A large weighing machine was unloaded from the plane and placed in front of the shed with an air of ceremony. Now, without a doubt, the Lalibela airport was open!

There were more mules than passengers, and a general scramble ensued while we mounted and our luggage was apportioned among the other mules. Thedia, who was by far the tallest, had the smallest mule and was having difficulty in keeping her feet off the ground, and a large straw hat on her head. Margaret's mule was always ready for a stop and a chat, while mine, the largest of the lot, made repeated overtures to all other mules.

Getachew, the airlines official, astride a brisk mount, came up jauntily as we started off. 'It's the first time I've ridden a mule,' he said brightly, 'it's very amusing.' At this moment his mule, catching sight of Thedia's hat, shied badly and unseated Getachew who went sprawling on to the rocky runway; while the mule beat a quick retreat to the shelter of the trees. Finally he was caught, and Getachew, slightly subdued, sat silent, grasping the saddle pummel.

We travelled in single file as we neared the mountain path. The mule owners who had not succeeded in getting passengers, and the priest's retinue, had gone on at a reckless speed and were already out of sight.

Our mules, all exhibitionists, had a habit of suddenly wanting to lead the convoy and would break into a brisk trot, by-passing the leader and often nearly throwing their respective passengers. As the morning wore on, Thedia's mule lagged behind and a couple of followers on foot stayed with her, while a tall lanky youth came with Margaret and me.

We dipped down into gulleys and ran along steep banks, while the high mountain ahead, on which Lalibela lay, came slowly nearer. It was pleasant for the air was invigorating and completely still.

At the foot of the final steep climb, Margaret and I stopped to wait for Thedia. The mountain towered, almost sheer, above us, bare and covered with loose stones.

'It looks as though we'll have to get off and walk up there,' I said, straining back to have a look. To the right the skyline stood up sharp and clear – and incredibly near in the still air. We took photographs to pass the time, but still Thedia did not come.

'Perhaps we should go back for her,' said Margaret, 'she may be having trouble.'

'Maybe. I hope there aren't any *chiftas* in these parts,' I added, as a horrible afterthought.

But at this moment, our escort pointed above us at the skyline where a string of people were moving. In the centre was a tiny mule, and on its back a large straw hat.

'Thedia!' The tiny procession moved along unheeding – to be in Lalibela half an hour ahead of us.

Lalibela is a place of miracles, and several were performed as our mules carried us to the top and then took us through Roha's market which sprawled over the slope of the hill. The surprise value of our appearance was not so great as Thedia's had been, and we passed on to a collection of small houses surrounded by a high bamboo fence which was the priest's compound.

Thedia and the priest were already installed on chairs behind a crude wooden table in the square building, which was made of wood and mud walls, with a corrugated roof. It had none of the charm of the older type of building and none of the conveniences of the new. Several elders were sitting on the floor, and people came in, kissing the priest's hand and trying each time to prostrate themselves before him, but with a gesture he restrained them. A young boy deacon was kneeling on the floor washing the priest's feet. We were given drinks of *talla* in horn containers, and a little later, small heavy cakes were brought in and the chattering stopped as the priest rose to pray and bless the cakes. Then they were handed round to the company.

In a flash, a young minstrel was standing in the doorway; he had the bright free air of the nomad and in his hands was the one-stringed fiddle called a *masinko*. With a gorgeous smile he began to strum on the instrument, improvising a song of welcome.

Later, we made our way, armed with cameras and torches, towards the churches, and Getachew and a young schoolteacher came too. Getachew was delighted at the prospect of seeing the famous churches.

'We always want to come to Lalibela,' he said, 'but until now the journey has been too long and difficult.'

As we passed through the market men and women, sitting behind little piles of grain and large blocks of salt, watched us with interest. Most of the selling, except for tobacco leaves, is done by the women although men were sawing off portions of the salt for prospective buyers. Sometimes coins were used as weights on the tiny hand-scales, but more often, we were surprised to see, a tiny sample packet of Lux soap was used for this purpose. There was little to buy and the market was as much a meeting-place as one of commerce. We were offered horn drinking-mugs for a shilling, and a donkey for the equivalent of two pounds.

Donkeys, relieved of their loads, stood with the air of a grudge common to the breed, and one poor creature had his backbone completely skinned and raw from the harsh saddle; when we enquired, we found there was no doctor or veterinary surgeon in Lalibela.

Beyond the market were five old juniper trees which had been planted in King Lalibela's time. The huge silver trunks are leaning now, but centuries ago, spectacular processions of High officials of the church carrying brilliant umbrellas, and priests in ecclesiastical robes of gold embossed with precious stones, passed beneath their branches; their colourful regalia, glistening in the sunlight and dust, stirred by hundreds of richly-jewelled horses. This was the splendid mountain stronghold of the world of Prester John!

Finally we came to the side of a sheer drop where below, in a deep square courtyard, stood the Church of Emanuel. The rock and earth had been excavated to make the court and the stone in the centre was carved into the church. A steep ramp led down to it and people were moving in and out of the rock church. The exterior was finely carved, and inside high pillars and rounded arches had also been carved to form the aisles, an elaborate frieze, and the ceiling. A boy deacon removed a cloth from some fine Byzantine-style pictures of St George and the Dragon and the Virgin Mary and Child.

I was the only one with a flash bulb. 'If you stand beside me while I use this,' I said to the others, 'you may be able to take a photograph with the same bulb.'

We lined up in front of the pictures.

'Ready?' They nodded, and I counted, 'One, two, three – go!' There was a flash as cameras clicked and our audience of boy deacons gave a start.

'Guess I was ahead of you,' said Thedia, but Margaret, who was by far the best photographer of us all, was dead on time. The curious spectacle of three women, draped in cameras, light meters, tripods and notebooks, standing side by side while one, the smallest and most heavily laden, counted 'one, two, three – go!' before the blinding flash, drew a heavy crowd as we went from church to church.

Two main groups of churches are joined together by passages and underground tunnels, while the large St George Church and the Abba Libanos stand apart, each facing the valley at different angles. It was an eerie experience passing in complete darkness through the long tunnels under the earth, feeling the rough wall as we moved ahead. Some churches were set imposingly in wide courts while others, cut deeper and narrower, gave a feeling of claustrophobia. We looked down into the deep cut where the Church of St Michael and Raphael ran diagonally across the court. The only way to reach the church was to walk across the trunk of a tree that had been thrown over the narrow abyss. It led first to the wall opposite the church where a passage and archways had been cut; from here, a more perilous journey across longer logs took us to the church door which was set high above the base of the court. If the logs were to be removed it would turn the church into a fortress that was completely cut off.

'If you can cross,' said the schoolmaster with mock seriousness, 'then you will go to Heaven; if not, you will fall – and go to the other place!'

'It is a challenge!' said Getachew, stepping off first, but he almost lost his balance, panicked, and had to be rescued.

We were finally across, followed by the large retinue of boys. The interior of the church was bare and dark, and smelt of bats. Below in the courtyard the ground fell away to one corner where slippery steps led to a subterranean spring and the river 'Jordan'.

This spring also added to the church's safety in times of siege, and one wondered how many more tunnels lay deeper still under the hill. But the church and its setting was grim and unattractive and we crossed back from 'Heaven' quite thankfully.

Abba Libanos is set on the Hillock of Bread with a beautiful wide view of the valley below. It is different from the other churches for it is cut into the overhanging cliff and legend has it that Lalibela's wife and the angels built the church in one night. There is, indeed, an air of miracles in the high and rather shallow interior, for a faint unearthly light glows in the darkness; though perhaps it is a thin piece of marble let into the rock, similar to one I have seen in Isfahan, Iran.

We watched the shadows lengthening across the valley and made our way slowly back to where the Governor's tent had been erected in our absence; it was an elegant structure decorated with red and stood surrounded by its own low bamboo fence.

Tired and hungry, we set about cooking some food on Thedia's petrol stove. We had brought a tin of sausages and a tiny bottle of gin. Margaret and Thedia sat like potentates on their husbands' air beds while my sleeping-bag found all the bumps in the stony ground.

Suddenly, the stove began to flare and I bent down to blow it out, but it had no effect. Flames shot out and it was getting out of hand.

'Give me – give me . . .' I couldn't find the word, 'towel!' I yelled at last.

Thedia flung it at me. 'Save the sausages!' she screamed, seeing my intention, 'save the sausages!'

I slid the pan on to the ground and taking the blazing stove threw it headlong through the tent-opening where it exploded, to burn itself out in a great blaze.

One slip and the whole thing could have tipped up and the tent gone up in a bonfire. We rubbed out the tiny flame that had just started on my sleeping-bag and sat back to finish our gin. The sausages lay saved, and almost cooked, between us.

'Nice thing if we'd burnt down the Governor's tent,' said Margaret.

'Nice thing if we'd lost the sausages,' said Thedia.

Getachew put his head through the tent opening. 'You all right?' he asked.

We nodded.

'Well, tickets, please,' he said, holding out his hand. 'Forgot to collect them down in the valley.'

Young men sat outside our tent most of the night chatting, in the way of Ethiopians; and by the morning we were all a little wan. But our retinue was waiting for us and we set off before it became too hot.

The most surprising church was that of Mariam (Mary) which stands in the largest courtyard. It is unimpressive from the outside, having three porches, badly worn by erosion, and a very plain façade. However, once inside, it is enchanting with fine carving that is beautifully painted in bright colours. The friezes and carved decorations surrounding the arches give the impression of being painted on wood. Above our heads vivid round faces looked down, as well as sun and moon motives and a realistic pair of oxen locked in a fighting grip. The whole interior was covered with conventional designs that are unique to the churches of Ethiopia. A massive and beautiful cedar door had the same glow as a fine old ceremonial drum that stood on its side in one corner.

This was the people's church, for Mary plays a large part in their religious life. Boy deacons sat in the shadows of the rock walls opposite, and in these walls, cells with arches had been cut where priests sat chatting and reading. In one dark corner of the church itself I used the camera flash which revealed an old priest in a white robe sitting cradled in the very heart of the rock. Not even the crude flash could disturb his gentle expression, for it had an agelessness. But when I took another photograph he was gone. Had he ever been there? The film never revealed what I had previously seen.

We went next to the grand Medani Alem, the most majestic church in Lalibela. Alvarez, in the sixteenth century, when trying to describe it, broke off saying that he would never be believed. It is a great edifice 110 feet long and 80 feet wide, rising nearly 40 feet, and is modelled in the Greek style with graceful tapering columns that give the effect of supporting the roof. The stone, here, is a rich deep red which adds further to the startling effect. Unfortunately a corrugated iron roof has now been added which takes away something of its majesty. The interior is quite austere, with four rows of massive columns completely unadorned except for bracket capitals. The simplicity of the vast expanse, its lack of furnishings and its plain clean line is awe-inspiring and remind one of eastern Mosques.

Cut into a spur of the hill, away from the village, was the high narrow Church of St George, which is a curious monolith excavated to a great depth and carved in the shape of a giant Greek cross. The rock on this part of the hill is dull yellow and it gives the church a lichen-covered effect. The exterior is ornately carved, especially around the slim, pointed windows, and the rock has worn well, so that there is a sterile perfection about the church. Because of its great height, the interior appears small and cluttered and its vault-like ceilings are those of a mausoleum. Although it is one of the most famous of Lalibela's churches, it is more of a curiosity than a work of art and rather graceless.

Human skulls could be seen in the dim recesses of the cells cut in the surrounding walls of the court and they added to the general air of gloom. As we finally wound our way up the deep cutting towards the earth's surface, the schoolteacher pointed to some niches in the wall.

'Those,' he said, again with mock seriousness, 'were used by Lalibela's horse to take his master to safety when he was being pursued by his enemies.'

'Were they indeed!' I looked at the upturned faces all around me and they nodded vigorously.

Our final visit was to the Church of Michael where, in the vault, Saint Lalibela lies. The chapel is very holy, and it was only because of our connection with the High Priest that we were allowed in. The priest of the church showed us the carved stone on the floor below which Lalibela lay, and on the walls were several life-size carvings in high relief which were beautifully worked and the only things of their kind I had seen in the country.

This was the very heart of Lalibela, the most holy; and the resting place of the canonised king. Could it be that he was, after all, Prester John, the Priest King? Rumour has it that he lived in the mountain fastness of the country. Would it have been any easier to find Prester John than to find the Queen of Sheba? Or were they, after all, both symbols? The one, the idol men strive for and never find; and the other, the imaginary warrior-saint that women dream about? Are they embedded in the rock, as my priest in the Mariam Church had been? How easy it becomes to believe these tales, as one delves deeper into the beautiful country – and goes back over the centuries . . .

Returning to Addis Ababa I prepared for my journey south to Kenya. I had hoped to retrace my steps north to Khartoum but the rains had started and the Tessanai border was already closed.

'So you go soon – back to England,' said my clerk at the post office. 'I am sorry. I am very happy when you came to my post office,' and he moved round the corner of the counter to help me stick the stamps.

Finally, I called on Stephen Wright who is an authority on things Ethiopian and a director of the National Library. All travellers go to him for information, and he gives it with courtesy and patience whether one is a scholar or not. A rough track led through trees to a small wooden house which was hemmed in by even smaller ones occupied by Ethiopians. In the compound children played and dogs barked. Stephen Wright was a gentle, untidy bachelor with an untroubled face and the skin of a child. Books lined the walls and lay in heaps over the tables and on the chairs. Two tyrannical kittens ruled his life.

I listened enthralled to his tales of the country. 'Some day,' he said, 'I shall take a journey into the interior of the northern provinces looking at all the old church manuscripts.'

When he does he will probably unearth things that will give the answer to many questions. 'And the Queen of Sheba?' I asked, but realising the knowledge this studious hermit possessed, I feared he would be interested only in facts – not legends.

'Makeda? Oh, just a minute, the kitten wants to go out,' and he rose and held the front door open as politely as he would for the Queen we were talking about. Then he came back and sank into the broken wicker chair. 'That kitten, he'll be in by the back door in no time. They are tyrants,' but he twinkled.

'I came to look for her,' I continued, 'but it seems she is only to be found on airline posters. What do you really think?'

'There is no proof that she was here,' he said, and gave me the look of supreme knowledge of one who has passed book-learning, 'but then again, there is no proof – that she wasn't.'

I smiled. Just then the kitten bounded in through the back door.

'What did I tell you!' said Stephen Wright.

17

Wahni: The Princes' Prison Mountain

Although the last, not least.

King Lear, I. i.

I stood on the shore of Lake Tsana at Bahar Dar watching the women make endless journeys to collect water. They carried the red-brown jugs on their backs, and wound their way past the hotel entrance, democratically oblivious of any lack of right-of-way.

In the morning a helicopter was taking me to Wahni, the Princes' Prison Mountain. There was a slight chance that I would be able to land on the summit, for that was the only way the mountain could be reached. Wahni, whose existence has been referred to for centuries but upon whose summit no European has ever set foot.

The helicopter, which is hired by the Sources of the Nile Project engineers, was making a routine check on the water gauges of the rivers east of Lake Tsana, and Don Barnes telephoned me the previous evening in Addis Ababa.

'The rivers are not far from Wahni Mountain,' he said, 'we thought you might care to hire the helicopter while it's up there and have a look.'

I thanked him profusely and collected my sleeping-bag, cameras, a few tins of food and my policeman's truncheon without which I will never travel; and took a plane for Bahar Dar. This would be my last jaunt before I started on my homeward journey.

The two American engineers were camped in the hotel grounds with a young Ethiopian assistant and a cook. The pilot of the helicopter, Jean Massot, was a slight fair-haired young Frenchman who could make a plane do anything he wished. He had been a jet pilot who crashed, damaging his back, and so had switched to piloting helicopters. Among his other jobs he had piloted the film director, M. Albert Lamorisse, when he was making the enchanting film *Le Ballon Rouge*.

'I shall try to land on the mountain in the morning,' he said to me.

'And call for me the next day?' I asked.

'Well . . . yes, why not? That is, if you really want to spend the night alone up there?'

'Yes, I do.'

'But remember, I may *not* be able to land; so do not be too disappointed.'

Wahni was the last of the Princes' Prison Mountains, and for many decades its very existence had been queried, for none of the earlier travellers and writers, while referring to it, had ever seen the mountain. Its presence, however, was always felt and no prince of royal blood was ever free from the threat of being banished to its high peaks; just as from time to time a prince, reputed to have been imprisoned there, was brought down to the capital to be crowned king. Its direction lay somewhere deep in the Belesa Hills and it is doubtful if even the returning princes knew the exact location, for it was several days' journey away.

It is not known when the practice of imprisoning all the princes, except the heir, first began, but as all princes of royal blood, legitimate or otherwise, had a claim to the throne, the custom may have been in existence before recorded history. The three known prisons were all built on *ambas*, for these sheer-sided mountains made escape almost impossible. The first prison was situated on Debra Damo and in the tenth century, Judith, the Falasha queen, attacked the *amba* and massacred all the princes except one. Later, it was through this solitary survivor that the line of Sheba and Solomon was restored. After the Debra Damo massacre the custom lapsed until the fourteenth century when Amba Geshen in Lasta Province was used for this purpose, and it continued as a prison for 200 years. Finally the Moslems attacked it, murdering all the princes and once again the custom lapsed. In the seventeenth century, King Fasilidas chose Amba Wahni as a prison for his relations, and it was still in existence when James Bruce came to the country in the eighteenth century. Prior to Bruce's arrival, King John had been poisoned, and his son, Tekla Haymanot II, brought down from Wahni to be crowned king; and it was to his court that Bruce arrived, so that the traveller had opportunities of hearing many first-hand tales of the mountain; although he never set eyes on it. Johnson based his *Rasselas, Prince of Abyssinia* on the concept of Wahni although he later severely criticised Bruce's accounts of its existence, which implies that even Johnson thought that it was just another Ethiopian legend or traveller's tale.

The princes, all eligible for the throne, were, it is reputed, sent to the mountain, where many spent their whole life, leaving only if they were chosen to be king. Heavily guarded, they had little contact with the outside world, and a revenue was set aside by the king for their upkeep which was administered by the Governor of Wahni. Sometimes, if he was dishonest, he confiscated the revenue and the princes lived in great discomfort with barely enough food or clothing. During the reign of Jesus the Great, the plight of the princes was so great that rumours reached the king's ears and he went personally to the mountain to hear their complaints and to restore the revenue.

Not long after Bruce's departure from the country the custom lapsed finally, during the subsequent civil wars. The princes were released, and all of them, boys and old men who had spent their entire life on Wahni, came down for the last time. The mountain remained completely deserted and forgotten by all except those in the valley in which it stood. More recently, the mountain was located again, and Don Barnes and some of the engineers of the Sources of the Nile project had flown over it in a helicopter.

'It is a volcanic tuft,' they said, 'not much more than a pinnacle. Can't imagine how people could have lived up there. A landslide has taken the steps away so your only chance of reaching the top would be to drop on it by helicopter.'

'Is that possible?'

'It would be chancy, it's a small broken surface. And how would you get off again?'

'Do you really think it *is* Wahni, the Prison Mountain?'

'Who can tell? Only you can prove it – if you manage to land there.'

The heavens opened that evening and rain thundered down. The engineers' unit was forced to move into the hotel. They brought their dinner and invited me to join them. A sense of gloom had descended on the company, for they were having second thoughts about my proposed jaunt in the morning. The Ethiopian assistant was particularly restless, for the mountain has a bad reputation and it is not considered lucky to try and reach the summit.

'You wish to land on Wahni?' he asked me.

'Yes.'

'Alone?'

I nodded.

He shook his head. 'I would not do it,' he said seriously, 'I just would not stay alone on that mountain.'

But Jean Massot was unaffected by the atmosphere; he opened a tin of pears and offered them around. 'Early tomorrow!' he said, and gave me a large grin.

The rain had cleared by the morning, but we were not ready to set off until nine o'clock. We were taking the two engineers to the Reb River, and then Jean and I would continue alone to Wahni. Later, Jean would return and pick up the two men so that they could continue their day's work.

The helicopter was heavily overloaded. 'We shall have to see if it will get off the ground first,' said Jean. He revved the engine and the craft shuddered – if it would not rise the whole expedition would die before it started – then the aircraft left the ground heavily, hovering for a second before gliding away, rising slightly all the time. We topped the hotel roof and ran along the edge of the lake where people waved just below us. It was a glorious magic carpet feeling.

To the right the River Abai left the lake, flowing over a wide bank of rocks and around tiny green islets. Ahead of us, the east shore of the lake stretched flat and green while inland, the ground rose in ledges where small groups of *tukuls* looked incredibly picturesque at this low height. Directly ahead of us on the horizon was the now familiar canopy of mountains and high peaks which merged in a riot of purples and bronze. Somewhere in this great jagged outcrop, but out of sight, was Wahni.

The Gunmara River curled in and out below us and I could pick out the rocky stretch where I had crossed the river on my journey south. Quite soon, the Reb River also came in sight, and Jean flew lower still, following its course until he spotted the white gauge stuck in the river's bank. Then we sank slowly down on to the field beside the bank.

The two engineers climbed out; they were elderly men who viewed our exploit with increasing scepticism and watched our take-off with none of the excitement that Jean and I felt.

The helicopter rose easily now that we were lighter and gathered speed as we headed directly for the mountains. On higher ground little hills passed almost level with us and a sharp peak appeared amongst them.

'Is that Wahni?' I asked.

'No, it's just beyond, I think. You'll know when you see it.' We flew so near the peak that its shadow fell across the helicopter.

'We shall have to drop down on the plateau near the mountain,' said Jean, 'remove the doors and off-load some of the petrol.'

'Is it still too heavy?'

'There is sure to be a bad down-draught as we move over the mountain, it is not much more than a pinnacle. You won't be *too* disappointed if we can't land?'

I shook my head and tried to smile.

Now the country was opening up and ahead of us stretched a plateau. Beyond it was a beautiful deep valley with folding mountains rising each side, that stretched away to the north-west.

'There it is!' called Jean.

'Where?'

He nodded ahead. At the near end of the valley the top of Wahni the Mountain could just be seen, for it was set down in the valley and past the plateau. As we flew nearer, the whole of the mountain came into sight. It was not a mountain at all, it was, as Jean had said, just a pinnacle of rock. It rose sheer out of the valley to a height of about 1,800 feet where it faced the valley, but landslides had piled earth a third of the way up the other side. It was a volcanic tuft left from an eruption long before the valley came into being, and its top was not flat as other *ambas* were but curved and mottled like a round and shaggy head. It was certainly too sheer to be climbed without steps and it was doubtful if a helicopter would be able to land on such an uneven and small surface, which I judged at this distance to be about an acre.

As we flew nearer hundreds of vultures rose from ledges along the sides. Trees and bushes grew on the summit and the mottled top *could* be ruins for there was not a flat piece of ground anywhere.

Jean started to circle the mountain slowly. Down at its very base there was a semi-circle of wall joined to the cliff side and half-way up the cliff were the remains of a guardhouse, and above it again a strong wall had been built to protect another guardhouse on the summit. Now, no steps connected the three guardhouses. Further round, in a cluster of euphorbia bushes and juniper trees, a rectangular church gaped out from the side of the cliff, for a landslide had cut the structure in half. It was, however, by far the best preserved building on the mountain. The giant junipers that leaned at ungainly angles told of the church's great age.

Several reinforced ledges, jutting out from the side of the mountain, were white with the droppings of birds; and bushes, small stunted trees and high thistles grew over the mottled surface. Over it all was a carpet of dried grass, making it difficult to define what lay beneath.

Jean gave a wry backward glance. 'We'll drop down and make the load lighter,' he said.

'You are going to have a try?'

'Of course.'

As we cushioned down on to the plateau, people appeared over the brow of the hill; they ran forward thinking we had crashed, incredulous wonder on their faces as they inspected the helicopter; but when they realised our intention, the elders tried to dissuade us. An old man, speaking a little Italian, started to argue with Jean, who nodded but made no comment.

'Is he saying it is not safe to try and land?' I asked, as I helped Jean to remove the doors.

He shook his head and shrugged. 'Help me with the petrol tins and let us be off as soon as possible,' was all he said.

We stacked the two doors on the ground beside the petrol tins, and stepping over the landing skid I climbed into the helicopter which, with the doors off, was nothing but an open platform.

'Now hold on!' said Jean as he started the engine.

We rose dizzily because of the light load and flew in immediately over the summit of the mountain. Then, as we cushioned down towards the ground, I felt suddenly cold and sick with fear, for it was nothing more than a crumbling pinnacle of loose stones, also it was incredibly small and fell away on all sides. How could so many princes have been imprisoned here? For as many as 400 have been quoted as having lived on its summit at one time. But without a doubt, it was now possible to see beneath the overlay of grass, the definite outline of walls, passages and archways.

'Watch the tail rotor!' yelled Jean, and I leant through the gaping framework to see the rotor turning dangerously near the gnarled branches of a tree.

'Can't do it!' I called, and the helicopter rushed forward. We had no time to gain height and the down-draught caught us, sweeping the machine down the side of the cliff like a stone. Jean, working furiously to gain control and right the machine, nearly lost me and the 'little tank' for it fell on to the floor as I was taking a photograph. I made a grab to retrieve it and nearly went headlong through the opening.

'Phew!' I said to no one in particular, as I wedged the camera behind me on the seat. Suddenly all fear was gone, for I was still miraculously alive and Jean was going to make another attempt.

He brought the helicopter slowly back towards the summit and approached it from another angle. A long jagged wall ran across the very apex of the mountain and he eased the plane towards it.

'Are you going to try and land on that?' I yelled. He gave a slight nod and I could see that he was smiling.

As the machine lowered the skids began jumping up and down on the narrow line of rock, but it was too high from the surrounding ground and we swept off again. Jean tried to miss the downdraught but down we went again and this time I wedged myself in against the drop, and the rush of air.

A third time we hovered over the summit but there were always stunted trees or fallen walls in the way. I marvelled at Jean, for to crash here would be suicide as no one could reach us and we could never climb down.

Once again he flew in, this time near the gatehouse, but the ground fell away too sharply and again he flew off. I looked back at the mountain. He had warned me; and I had never expected that we would make so many attempts. So the mountain would remain as it had done for the last 200 years and no one would stand on its jagged and ruin-mottled summit.

But Jean was turning the machine again and we were flying low beneath the church. Beyond it was a reinforced ledge that looked about nine feet wide, and the mountain rose behind it, curving away slightly. The helicopter sidled up alongside.

'You'll have to jump for it,' called Jean.

'What!'

'If you want to land at all.'

My reply was lost in the roar of the engines which echoed from the rocks. Jean edged the helicopter in sideways until one skid only touched the ledge, for there was no room for the other one. Immediately the machine swung down to the right and the engines roared as he struggled to keep the helicopter level. The rotor above our heads was coming dangerously near the rocky slope of the mountain above.

'Hurry!' he yelled, as the one skid began to bump up and down on the rocky surface.

The skids of a helicopter swing out each side of the body and it is necessary to step over them to get in and out of the machine. Now, I had to hop right over the skid as it jumped up and down. At any moment, the down-draught might prove too much for the engine and Jean would be forced to fly off or be swept down. Depositing my cameras on the rocks I hopped back again for my other belongings as the skid bumped even more fiercely. After three journeys I was able to give Jean the all-clear sign.

'Clear a place for me to land tomorrow,' he shouted, and immediately he was off. The machine took a deep dip before being righted and then flew off around the side of the mountain.

Now suddenly there was stillness – and absolute quiet. The bushes which had been blown furiously by the helicopter's rotors were still again and there was nothing but the pungent smell of bird droppings.

Above me, there was the rough curve of the mountain, and the magnificent valley stretched out towards the north. I was alone on Wahni, the first European to stand on this ground, and the fact was curiously elating.

Bending down to pick up my cameras, I became frozen, for on the ground in front of me were the large droppings of a carnivorous animal! More droppings lay on the higher rocks. A large meat-eating animal had been on this ledge quite recently although, at the moment, it was keeping out of sight. I tried to think; I was here for at least twenty-four hours and could not leave except by the helicopter, which would not be returning until the morning. Having no gun it seemed wise to find somewhere to barricade myself in, should I be attacked, for this ledge was not the place to spend the night.

Slipping the thong of the policeman's truncheon on my wrist I started to climb. It was rough and difficult to judge the firm rocks under the dried grass. I dislodged a large one which rolled over the side of the ledge and crashed below, out of sight and hearing. I scrambled finally to ground that levelled out a little. Fallen masonry lay all around and the half-fallen walls formed giant ridges. On the mountain edge there was a buttress-like circular building which formed an oblong room inside; the roof had caved in but in the curve of the wall where it had joined the roof there was an inlet or tunnel cleverly devised to catch rain water. Near by was a well, filled almost to the top with stones, bird droppings and leaves. A flat stone lay across half the opening. This would be my sanctuary, if I could find another piece of stone to cover the remaining half of the opening.

Near by was an African olive tree (*Weira-olea chrysophylla*) whose branches hung low to the ground, behind it was a solid wall of granite stones and ahead the sheer side of the mountain fell away. I made three trips to fetch my belongings and put them under the olive tree. The operation left me surprisingly breathless, for although it was only 10,000 feet above sea level the air was very rare.

Taking my cameras and truncheon I climbed higher still, scrambling over the labyrinth of fallen rooms and passageways where the ground was deep in rocks and stones. Nothing remained but the ruined walls until I came to the solid stone posts of a doorway. It led into a better-planned structure that was evidently the Governor's house, for the rooms were larger and it stood on the highest point. A path led away towards the fortified guardroom that had been the only exit to the valley below. On the Governor's doorstep was a large flat stone which I managed, by turning it over and over, to place beside the other one over the top of the well.

The path coming from the guardroom or gatehouse ran past the Governor's house, across the summit, to the church on the other side. Along this narrow way, between the house and the church, were tiny rooms or cells not much more than four feet square. The number of princes imprisoned on the mountain has been quoted as anything from 50 to 400 and this amount would have varied from time to time. It was difficult to judge the actual area of the mountain for it fell away on all sides, but on such a small area even fifty princes would have made the mountain overcrowded as these tiny rooms suggested. Perhaps, after all, the princes had been confined permanently to these tiny cells, for James Bruce had remarked about one of the princes that 'he had the pale skin common to all the princes who came down from the Mountain'. The piled-up earth below the south side suggests that the mountain may have had a much larger circumference than it has today, and the fierce tropical storms and the torrential rains may one day completely destroy it.

The passageway leading to the church ended suddenly in a jumble of chaotic fallen masonry. The shock of the landslide had levelled out the buildings completely and taken away half of the church, which stood on a lower level. The curved half roof was plastered with yellow limestone which gleamed in the sunlight and was the only splash of colour on the high monument of stone. The old junipers at the rear had been dislodged also and lay in a tangled mass struggling to keep alive.

The church had two sections with an outer passageway that had been roofed with wood, for some of the cross-beams were still in place. The gabled roof of the church itself was reinforced with five inner buttresses and between them were thin tiles made of tufa similar to those used in Fasilidas' castle at Gondar, which proved without a doubt the connection between Wahni and the capital. On the outside of the wall which was nearly three feet thick, finely carved maskals, also of tufa, were let into the plaster. Nooks were set in the wall of the outer passageway and were surmounted with wooden cross-beams. The arched outer doorway had an old cedar door that was silver-grey with age and worn into deep ridges by the wind and rain. At one end of the building, at the apex of the roof, a rounded mount for a maskal stood, and at the other end a similar one lay fallen in the passageway, though the maskal had long since gone.

The main section of the church was finely plastered and the dividing wall into the sanctuary had two arches, one of which had been crudely filled in with bricks and rough stones. On the left a mock arch was painted on the plaster to correspond with the bricked-in one. Except for the inlaid tufa maskals and the square tufa tiles everything had been removed or lay buried beneath the debris on the floor.

Beyond the church at the rear was a thick mass of fallen juniper trees, and as I climbed under them it was quite dark. On the ground were several red-brown wine jugs similar to those the women had been using at Bahar Dar, although these were smaller with two slots instead of three around the neck for the carrying cord. Nearer the precipice edge there were the remains of a thick wall and two solid pillars three feet in diameter that were also plastered with yellow limestone, which showed that another building as well as part of the church had fallen in the landslide. In the dim light under the junipers and with the wine jugs just as they had been left, I could visualise the mountain as it had been and the princes sitting here and sipping wine – one of them perhaps for the last time before leaving for the capital. I wondered whether John, son of Jesus the Great, had sat here when he had been summoned to be king, only to meet his death by poison a few months later.

I selected a wine jug to take with me and was moving out of the shaded gloom when suddenly I heard the sound of a voice. It had a quick clear tone of authority. I crouched where I was, listening, but there was no further sound except the fluttering of the vultures on the ledges around me.

I made my way along the side of the mountain, clockwise towards the guardhouse, and came to a promontory where another group of junipers grew. Growing junipers mean churches and I wondered if perhaps a smaller *tukul*-type of church had originally stood here.

Across a deep crevice was the guardhouse and its doorway led directly on to the gaping void, for another landslide had made the deep ravine and taken the steps to the valley below with it. I edged my way with great difficulty around the crevice where the whole side of the mountain seemed insecure and finally reached the path leading to the guardhouse. Only the shell remained, but the large wooden door which opened to the valley below still hung dramatically on its hinges. It was worn and corroded where it had received the full force of the wind and rain. Down the path behind me, to the guardhouse and through that door, the princes had finally passed one by one, leaving the door hanging as it is today. The mountain, deserted, began to disintegrate as, bit by bit, it fell into the valley. I looked through the doorway at the sheer drop and wondered what kept the guardhouse from crashing down also.

I turned and made my way up the path that led to the Governor's house. The way was not as easy as it must have been for the princes whose every arrival was along this path; hundreds of them who never turned to retrace their steps. Along here also had come the three small sons of Jesus the Great who were sent to Wahni after their father was murdered. They were the children of his much-loved mistress Ozoro Kedeste, and two of them were later to become kings.

The path took a wide curve, and near the north face a ledge, similar to the one I had landed on, gave a magnificent view of the valley and plain beyond. Here, miraculously, there were still the remains of a garden, and aloes grew from the reinforced wall. It was bright and gay, and even the vultures had not fouled it. These precipice drops were no doubt protected by wooden balustrades and the princes must have gathered here to watch the occasional procession, heralded by the beat of drums, as it came from Gondar and made its way up the beautiful valley. What news would it bring? Of recent wars, victories or defeats; or had they come to claim another king?

The sun was moving towards the broken line of hills to the west and the valley below was deepening to purple in the fading light when finally I came to the olive tree where I had left my possessions. There were no villages in sight in the valley and a tiny stream, determining the valley's base, zig-zagged into the distance, paltry and futile in comparison with the splendid slopes each side. With the dusk I felt a sudden chill for the whole black night lay ahead. Already the vultures were settling on the rocks and ledges around me.

There was a sound of engines and the helicopter came into view, flying in from the direction of Gondar. Jean, returning to Bahar Dar with the two engineers, had come to take a last look at me. I climbed to the summit as they circled. Now, if I wanted to, was my chance to leave the mountain before nightfall, but I grinned back when Jean waved an enquiry, and the machine, with a last dip towards me, flew off towards the peak to the south-west.

The scores of vultures, disturbed by the helicopter, began to circle above me just as the plane had done. Hundreds of them moved in a steady anti-clockwise stream, and each bird had its eye on me as the circle became smaller and smaller. It was a great swirling umbrella of vultures with thousands of eyes turned towards me. Now the whole sky above was dark with the revolving, repulsive birds. I stood undecided, then turned and fled to the shelter of the branches; but had I fallen they would have pounced, for I was their target and the only living thing in sight. Deprived of their prey they broke up in disorder and finally settled back on the ledges below.

I built a fire close to the rocky edge and away from the dry grass. Wahni was a great stage for the valley and the mountains surrounding it; and legends would build up about the high ribbon of smoke that came from my fire and was seen for the first time in living memory.

Beyond the mountains to the west were glimpses of a vast plain, and as the sun set a sharp wind sprang up bringing black clouds tumbling across it. The wind, reaching the mountain, swept round it and set up a curious moan amongst the walls of the Governor's house behind me. I thought of the ghost-like church which would be quite dark now and of the gloomy courtyard under the juniper trees. The light faded as I cleared the remains of the meal, and far beyond the plain there were the first flickers of lightning. I threw the canvas wrapping of my sleeping-bag over a low branch and stacked my belongings beneath it. Finally, when the last vestige of light had left the valley, a great black space yawned ahead, and in its depths a drum began to beat. It was the sound that links all Africa, Christian, Moslem and pagan; was it telling of a birth, death, a marriage or of the thin line of smoke that had risen from the mountain? Lightning came nearer and illuminated the plain where the heavy clouds had broken and were falling with the complete gusto of a tropical storm.

Animals, I thought, would not attack in a storm, but I really knew nothing of the habits of wild carnivorous ones. I crouched in my sleeping-bag beneath the canvas, watching the storm racing across the plain, and as it came nearer the thunder followed fast on each flash.

Suddenly the storm cascaded down. The rain hit the ground with a heavy drumming and the lightning and thunder crashed simultaneously. The mountain shuddered under the impact, and I lay, part of it, on the exposed surface. With each flash the whole magnificent valley came vividly into sight in a kind of stark daylight, only to fall back into a dim grey outline again. All around me the dry earth was soaking up the rain. It was in a storm such as this, that the landslides must have happened, for it pounded the mountain on all sides. Gradually the great storm was moving past the mountain and once again the thunder began to follow up each brilliant lightning flash.

Then I must have fallen asleep for I woke with a start. The storm had passed and the moon was so brilliant that the dried grass looked like snow. I lay listening, for something had woken me. But there was complete stillness; was the creature still there – or had it moved stealthily away? Finally, I climbed out of the damp sleeping-bag and moved into the open. Foolish perhaps, for it was as bright as day; but there was no sound except for the far drum that kept up its steady beating.

Wahni stood refreshed and clean after the downpour and the leaves on the bushes glistened. The thing that had woken me was not unfriendly. Some wild animals sense fear and this is the reason they attack; but one person alone, inarticulate, is more likely to be accepted by them; and there was nothing round me but a great stillness – and the smell of the refreshed earth.

I stumbled over the flat stones lying across the well-face, comforting perhaps, but unnecessary; and then went back to the shelter of the overhanging branch. Many times during the night I woke with a start, with the same strange contact, but there was always silence, except for the drum, and I would fall asleep again.

Dawn was coming into the valley when I finally woke; and as I coaxed a fire with the damp twigs, the colours heightened all around me. The valley was more beautiful than ever. It was understandable that when Johannas was taken from the mountain he pleaded to be allowed to return. I had been here less than twenty-four hours, seeing only one sunset and one dawn, but each change of light completely transformed the surrounding valley.

I was still trying to clear a space for Jean to land when the helicopter appeared; it had arrived much too early, but Jean's face broke into a relieved smile when he saw me, for he had obviously been worrying. He flew off to the plateau to remove the doors again.

Gathering my possessions together I tried to stifle my disappointment at not having had time to make another trip round the mountain, and when Jean returned I had not cleared sufficient space. Now, the situation was desperate for there was a strong wind and I ran to several places and watched Jean bring the helicopter down, but each time the space was not large enough. Finally, he signalled me to go back to the ledge where I had landed.

Despite the strong wind, there was no other way back. The sleeping-bag, slipping from my grasp, rolled to the mountain ledge where it balanced for a second before settling back again. Jean, hovering in the helicopter near by, grinned at me across the void.

He brought the helicopter slowly in towards the ledge. I watched the top rotor arm come perilously near the mountain above me as I crouched on the rocks. The engine was racing furiously as Jean tried to counteract the wind, and the nearside skid moved in over the ledge and began bouncing up and down. I grabbed the wine jug, my cameras and the spoor to identify the animals, and jumping over the skid placed them on the seat. I had to make three trips before I was able to climb in finally; and immediately we were off. I sighed with relief; it had been much more difficult to board the helicopter than to leave it, for by now I realised what the whole operation really entailed and how hazardous it was.

We circled the mountain again. It looked so different to me now. I knew it all – the half shell of the church with the crosses of tufa, the fallen junipers and the olive tree where I had slept, the aloes growing from the wall and finally the great door of the guardhouse swinging open over the precipice to the valley below.

Suddenly, as we turned towards the plateau, I wished, desperately, that I had not come away, that I had been able to stay. As I gave Wahni a last glance, the vultures were settling back again but of the animals there was no sign.

The villagers of the plateau crowded around asking questions and shaking my hand. They smiled broadly. Was I not tired? Surely I had not slept? What had I found up there?

'Just this jug' – I held it up – 'and yes, I did sleep.'

Jean studied my face. 'You look fine,' he said, almost accusingly.

Everyone but me, it seemed, had had a restless night.

'Sorry,' I said to Jean, 'in my excitement I forgot to hold up a handkerchief for you to test the wind.'

'That's all right,' he said, 'we made it.'

When the doors were replaced we set course for Bahar Dar once more. The adventure was over. For Jean it was just another flight.

'Thanks,' I yelled above the roar of the engine.

He turned and smiled. 'All right?' he asked.

I nodded. It was certainly something to have flown with such a man.

Epilogue

I sat waiting in the Curator's office of the University College Museum in Addis Ababa feeling fine, for danger is the best tonic. I had come thousands of miles to find the Queen of Sheba, but instead I had found an adventure far more exciting. On my lap was the wine jug from Wahni, and in my pocket, the spoor. The Curator, a dedicated and busy man, came quickly into the room.

'What can I do for you?' he asked.

'I have been up on Wahni Mountain and . . .' I began.

'You have what!'

'I was dropped by helicopter,' I explained.

'Well, that is *most* interesting!'

I held up the jug. 'I brought this down from the church and as you have a museum, I thought you might like to have it . . .'

'Yes,' he broke in, taking it from me, 'we would indeed.' He examined it carefully. 'You don't want it yourself?'

I shook my head. 'It belongs here.' And diving into my pocket I pulled out and unwrapped the spoor. 'And could you tell me what sort of animal this would be?' I held it up on the piece of paper.

He took it from me. 'Did you find it up there?'

I nodded.

'It's a carnivorous animal and I'm pretty certain it is a leopard. You didn't see it?'

'No. Could they live up there?'

'They are great climbers, it is possible.'

'So,' I said, getting up, 'leopards. Well, I'm off tomorrow. Good-bye.'

He came with me to the door, the jug in his hand. 'Are you sure you would not like to keep it – as a memento?'

I looked at the jug, it was my last link with the mountain but I shook my head and walked down to the Land Rover. I needed no memento of Wahni, for the silent, deserted mountain was there now, for ever, in my consciousness.

Acknowledgements

I am deeply grateful to Colonel le Blanc and his party who saved my Sahara journey from disaster, and to the American personnel, Jean Massot and the Ethiopian Airlines for making my Wahni adventure possible.

Once again I must thank Mr Sydney Bridges for managing to send welcome mail to the most remote places and to my many friends for their encouragement, especially during the writing of the first part of this book.

I cannot mention individually the many other people of all nationalities who so spontaneously gave me help, but it was through them that the journey there and back was made possible.

JOURNEYS

Other books in the series:

The Valleys of the Assassins by Freya Stark
Introduced by Monisha Rajesh

A Vagabond for Beauty by Everett Ruess
Introduced by Paul Kingsnorth

A Time of Gifts by Patrick Leigh Fermor
Introduced by Jan Morris

The Cruel Way by Ella K. Maillart
Introduced by Fiona Mozley

Mississippi Solo by Eddy L. Harris
Introduced by Adam Weymouth

Through Khiva to Golden Samarkand by Ella Christie
Introduced by Caroline Eden

In a Land Far from Home by Syed Mutjaba Ali
Introduced by Taran N. Khan

Desert Soul by Isabelle Eberhardt
Introduced by William Atkins

Gone Away by Dom Moraes
Introduced by Jeet Thayil